FRONTIER OFFICERS IN COLONIAL NORTHEAST INDIA

FRONTIER OFFICERS IN COLONIAL NORTHEAST INDIA

Suhas Chatterjee

AKANSHA PUBLISHING HOUSE
NEW DELHI-110002 (INDIA)

AKANSHA PUBLISHING HOUSE
4649-B/21, Ansari Road
Darya Ganj, New Delhi - 110 002
Ph.: 23263193 / 9811582579 / 09435116718
Fax: 011-23263193
Email: ektabooks@yahoo.com
www.akanshapublishinghouse.com

Frontier Officers in Colonial Northeast India

First Published 2009
ISBN 978-81-8370-168-6

PRINTED IN INDIA

Published by Akansha Publishing House, New Delhi and Printed at Aryan Enterprises, Delhi.

To

Sukumar Chatterjee
My Elder Brother (1917-1980)
&
Kalyani Chatterjee (1926-1999)
My Elder Sister-in-Law

Contents

Preface

I have compiled the treatise with the simple aim to give the scholars a glimpse of the renowned frontier personalities shaping the British frontier policy acting in different capacities as civil and military officers under trying circumstances in a hostile climate to open up the North-east to the world.

They studied carefully the topography of the hills and plains, made survey of the forbidden land, mixed with the unknown people at the risk of their lives to know their customs and usages, gave a shape to their languages and made them conscious of their rights. In short, today's North-east what we know now, is the product of their hard labour, sacrifice (a large number of them were killed or died of disease) and farsight. To get a clear picture of the evolution of the region from its unknown, dark existence, and to get an idea about the policies and plan of action of those officers it is necessary to read their memos, notes and letters. There had been, however, a large number of such officers but I had selected only four; Lieutenant Colonel F.J. Lister, Lieutenant Colonel T.H. Lewin, Sir John Edgar and R.B. McCabe. Those Goliaths came to India in the 19th century to transform the North-eastern hills into a prosperous province full of life and expectation. Their role had been exceedingly vital in the most critical juncture of history in making the North-east.

The work is principally based on records and thus, I have quoted them exhaustively. Herodotus once commented on the topic of objective history, "I am under obligation to tell what is reported but I am not obliged to believe it". I have followed this motto. The reports are reports or the records are records and one officer is connected with the other officer and one place is related to other place, one tribe is the relative of the other and one policy is complementary to the other.

All ideologies in history are notorious. Nationalism, Marxism or Objectivism are also ideologies. A historian may love his country as citizen but as a practitioner of a discipline which has fairly rigorous standards of objectivity, his fidelity is to his discpline.' I have endeavoured hard to remain faithful to my discipline and it is for the reader to judge it.

I am grateful to ICHR, New Delhi for the financial assistance I received and to N.A.I., New Delhi, West Bengal State Archives, Calcutta; National Library, Calcutta for the collection of materials, to Prof. Rita Kalita and Nandita Mazumdar, the two Research Assistants of Project. Miss Rupali Dutta, Silchar helped me in typing the manuscript, Ambujaksha Mukherjee, Calcutta, Mahitosh Purkayastha M.P., Silchar and Amal Prabha Das, Gauhati helped me in collecting the materials. I extend my gratitude to all of them including the publisher of the book.

Suhas Chatterjee

Abbreviations

A.L.I.	Assam Light Infantry
A.R.	Assam Rifles
As.R.	Asiatic Researches.
A.H.T.	Arakan Hill Tracts
B.A.S.J.	Bengal, Asiatic Society Journal
B.J.P.	Bengal Judicial Proceedings, (Cal, W.B. Archives)
B.L.I.	Burma Light Infantry.
B.P.P.	Bengal, Political Proceedings, (Cal, W.B. Archives)
B.R.P.	Bengal, Revenue Proceedings. (Cal, W.B. Archives)
Capt.	Captain
C.H.T.	Chittagong Hill Tracts.
Col.	Colonel
C.S.	Civil Surgeon
D.C.	Deputy Commissioner
E.A.C.	Extra Assistant Commissioner
I.C.S.	Indian Civil Service
I.F.Extl(A)	India, Foreign Department (National Archives, New Delhi.)
External (A)	Proceedings. (National Archives, New Delhi)

I.H.P.	India, Home Dept, Proceedings (National Archives, New Delhi).
I.P.P.	India, Political Proceedings (National Archives, New Delhi)
I.R.P.	India, Revenue Proceedings (National Archives, New Delhi)
J.A.S.B.	Journal, Asiatic Society of Bengal.
Lt. Col.	Lieutenant Colonel.
M.P.	Military Police/Member of Parliament.
NEHU	North Eastern Hill University.
NEIHA	North East India History Association.
NHMP	Naga Hills Military Police.
P.O.	Political Officer (North and South Lushai Hills)
S.L.I.	Sylhet Light Infantry.

The old spelling of the place names and the names of the persons have been retained in the work.

R.Buridihing	R. Bhagdai
Majuli	Golachat Nagoora
Jorhat	LHOTAS
Rangpur	EASTERN NAGAS
Dimaspore	Nine duars
ANGAMIS	Jerung
Kohima	Moteleon
Meenah	Garos
SIBSAGAR	Ramray
Godgoon	Mariau
Abiors	Nurtung
Mishmis	Moeyong
Khamtis	Simlee

Sadiya	Nangkrem
Dihong	Nungklow
Saikhawa	Myrong
Tezoo	R. Digaru
Dibang R.	(Territory of Burmanlk)
Lattoro	nungtong
Singphos	Moprem
Beesa	Molem (mylliem)
Ols Beesa	(Territory of Singmanlk)
Hukwang Valley	Nuspung
Patkai Hills	Moflung
Burma	Panchpunji
R. Dihang	Cherra
Kuju	chella
Rangagora	Pandua
Dibrugarh	Chattok
Jaypur	Sylhet
Bahat	R. Surma
Nigroo	Jaintiapur
R. Sisang	Nortung
R. Chindwing	Jowai
Lower Assam	Cherrapunji
R. Brahmaputra	Sylhet
Jayantia	
R. Kallang	Osimlee
Rahachokey	Gobha
R. Kapil	Syung
Gauhati	
Raneegaon	
Sonapur	

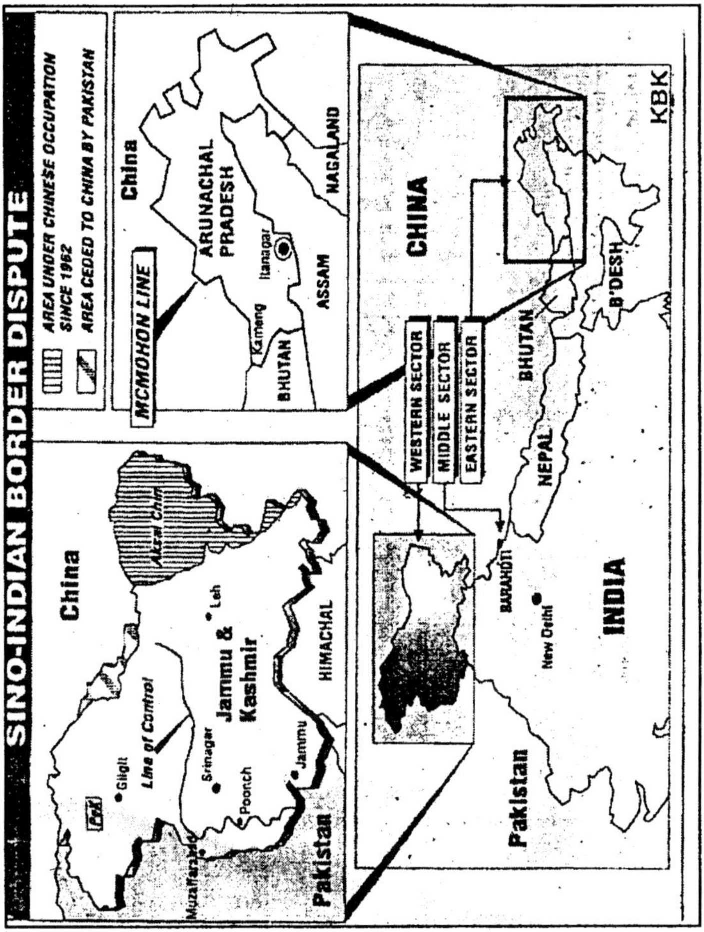
SINO-INDIAN BORDER DISPUTE
AREA UNDER CHINESE OCCUPATION SINCE 1962
AREA CEDED TO CHINA BY PAKISTAN
China
Aksai Chin
Leh
Jammu & Kashmir
Line of Control
Gilgit
PoK
Srinagar
Poonch
Jammu
Muzaffarabad
Pakistan
HIMACHAL
China
ARUNACHAL PRADESH
MCMOHON LINE
Itanagar
Kameng
BHUTAN
ASSAM
NAGALAND
CHINA
WESTERN SECTOR
MIDDLE SECTOR
EASTERN SECTOR
BHUTAN
NEPAL
B'DESH
BARAHOTI
New Delhi
INDIA
Pakistan
KBK

Harvesting of Supar Cane

Mithun Fighting

Men's hair style : Hair knot positioned:
Masho at the side of the head
Pawi on top of the head
Paite and Lusei at the back of the head

Hair style of the different Zo Tribe, from Vumson

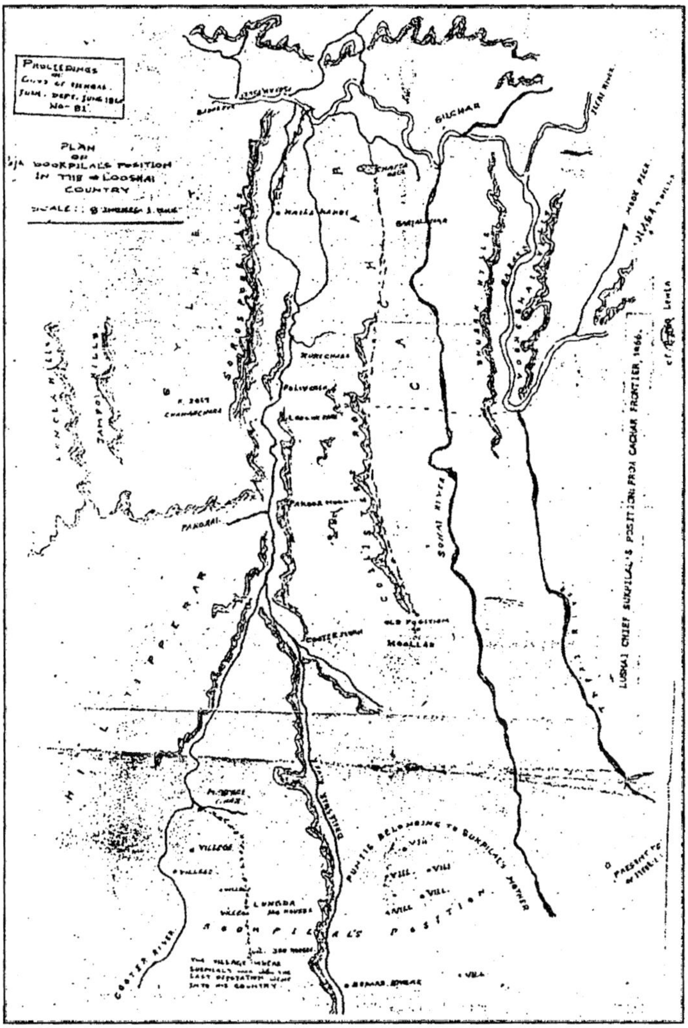

Lushai Chief Sukpilalis Position: from Cachar Frontier, 1866

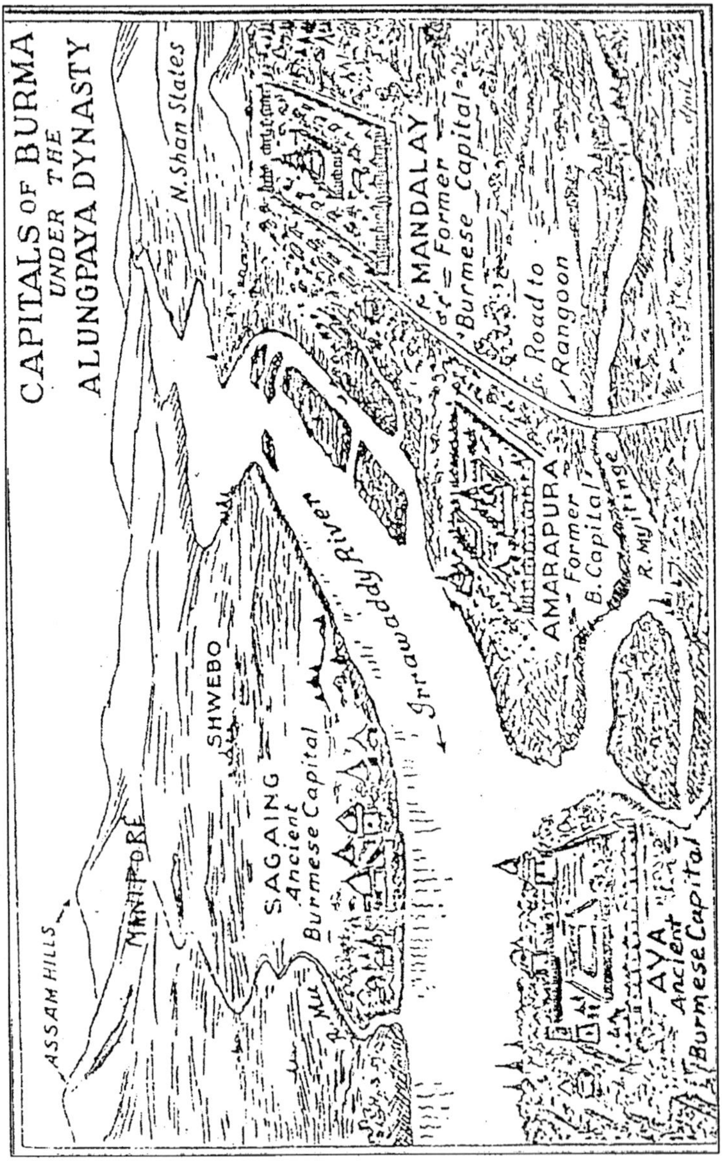
CAPITALS OF BURMA UNDER THE ALUNGPAYA DYNASTY
N. Shan States
MANDALAY
Former Burmese Capital
Road to Rangoon
AMARAPURA
Former B. Capital
R. Myittinge
Irrawaddy River
SHWEBO
SAGAING
Ancient Burmese Capital
MANIPORE
ASSAM HILLS
R. Mu
AYA
Ancient Burmese Capital

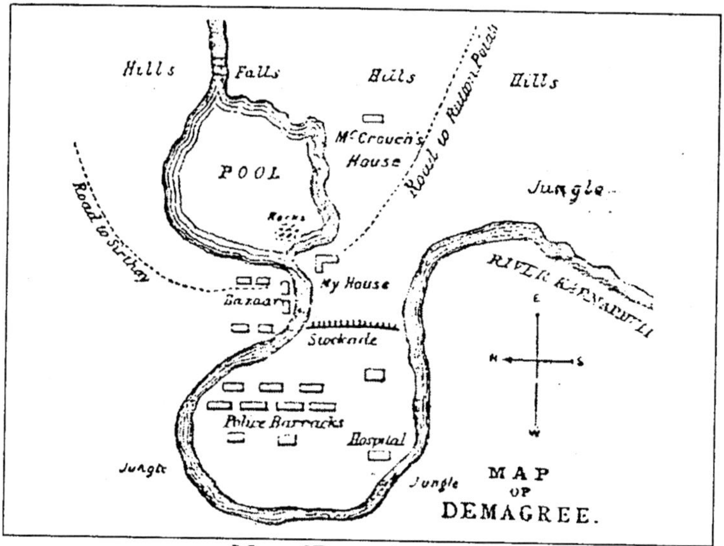

Map of Demagiri, 1871

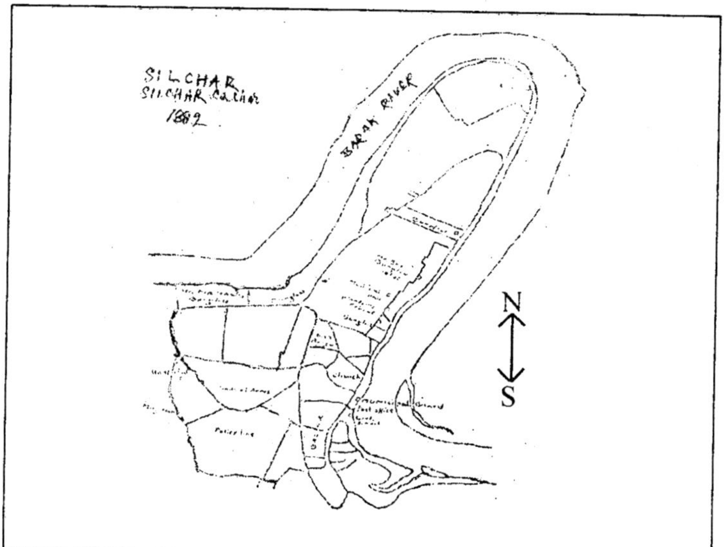

Map of Silchar Town, 1882

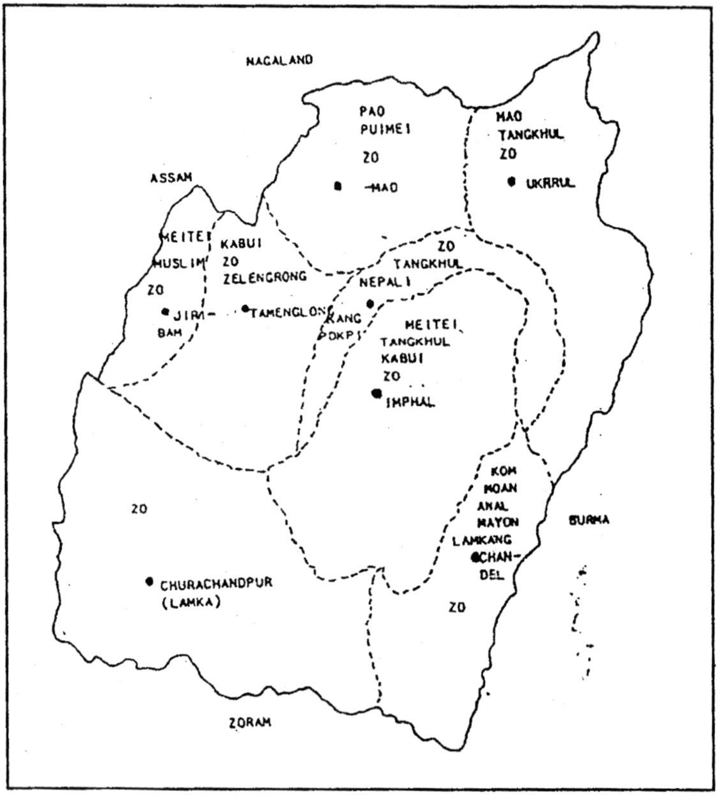

Map of Manipur

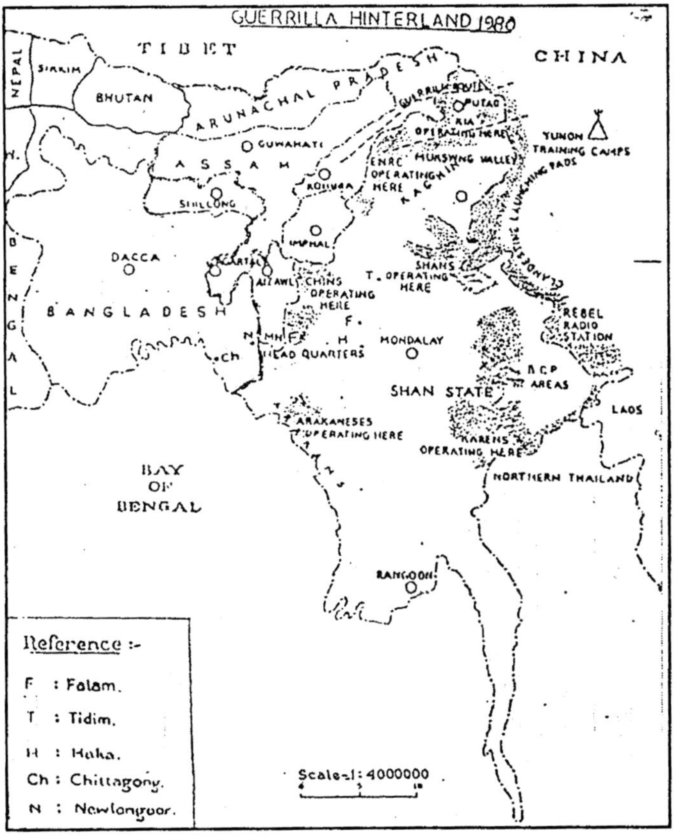

Guerrilla Hinterland, 1980

1

Lieutenant Colonel F.J. Lister

The celebrated British Political Agent, Khasi (Cossia) Hills had been a fine soldier and a wise Frontier Officer. He joined the East India Company's armed forces as a cadet and was admitted in the Assam Light Infantry but soon got transferred to Sylhet Light Infantry. He took direct part in the First Anglo-Burmese War (1824-26) where he displayed his military abilities. He was rewarded for his courage and valour and was elevated to Officer Commanding, SLI in 1829. His exploits have been highly extolled by historians A C Chowdhury (*Srihatter Itibritta*) and Sir Edward Gait. Lister's punitive expeditions against the head hunting Nagas and Garos brought them under control. Lister was successful in penetrating into the inaccessible areas of Naga Hills and Garo Hills where from the British influence gradually extended to the hilly terrains.

At the close of the First Anglo-Burmese War, David Scott was appointed by the Governor General as the Political Agent for Assam, with Cherrapunji as the headquarters. Cherrapunji was in Khasi Hills (now Meghalaya). The difficulties faced by the enterprising soldiers in the North-east had been the unhealthy, hostile climate and the poor communication. Roads were of utmost necessity for the movement of the armed forces. Edward Gait writes in *History of Assam* "as soon as the Brahmaputra valley had passed under British rule, the shrewd mind of David Scott had been impressed by the expediency of opening direct communication between it and the valley of the Surma; and in 1827 he had in interview at Nungklow with Tirat Sìngh, the *Syiem* of that place, and other Khasi chiefs, at which they unanimously gave their consent to the construction of a road from Rani, via Nungklow, to the Surma Valley. The project was at once put in hand; a track was cleared, and bungalows were erected at Nungklow. The officers employed on the work mixed freely with the tribesmen and for eighteen months the greatest apparent cordiality prevailed. But, in April 1829, the Khasis, alarmed by the foolish boast of a Bengali peon, who in a quarrel, taunted them with the prospect of subjugation and taxation as soon as the road should be completed, made a sudden attack on the small party. Lieutenant Bedingfield, one of the two officers at Nungklow, was enticed to a conference and massacred; the other Lieutenant Burlton, defended himself all day against greatly superior numbers, and at night fled some way towards Gauhati. He was overtaken and put to death with most of his followers, of whom only a small remnant escaped to British territory. David Scott himself had a very narrow escape, having left Nungklow for Cherrapunji only a short time before the rising."

Troops were immediately called up from Sylhet and Kamrup and vigorous reprisals were undertaken. Lister was the Officer Commanding SLI Battalion. Lister advanced with his artillery (1829) from Sylhet, in his forward march he avoided rest despite the heavy strain but his contingent had to face difficulties because of the peculiar character of Khasi Hills. Moreover, the Khasis dodged the British forces to make several surprise night attacks and before the English could take position they left and got faded into the forests. But Lister was commander of indomitable energy and carried his mission to a success. In the punitive expedition against the Khasis other than the SLI there were 23rd Bengal Infantry and a strong detachment of armed police. All under the command of Lister assisted by Lieuts Townshend, Vetch and Brodic.

Lister proposed to David Scott "the Khasi chief of Cherapunji be given a land grant at Bholagunj (Sylhet) and in exchange the government should acquire the land for the office complex of the Political Agent at Cherrapunji", to which the authorities of Fort William readily agreed (1830). Thus, the inmical chief of Cherrapunji was won over. The task of Lister, thus became little easier, however, the loss inflicted on the government contingent by the freedom loving Khasis has been massive. The troops became restive; Lister proposed an increment of allowances to the government employees which the Government of India agreed.

"I am directed to desire that you will communicate to Captain Lister and the officers of corps the acknowledgements of the Governor General in Council for their active and zealous exertions in the hills. As a reward to the men of corps for their good conduct, His Lordship in Council has been pleased to grant them Batta of Re 1 per mensum during the time they were actually employed in the Hills, and to resolve that in future, they shall be entitled to the some indulgence whenever they may be engaged in service in the Cossiya hills thus placing them on a footing during such service, with the local corps in Assam."[1]

The increased hill allowance was an incentive to the soldiers fighting in an alien territory under trying circumstances. But the Khasis made occassional counter raids into the British territory shaking the confidence of the residents of the border. Lister was however, resolute and his courage and endurance proved effective. "Suffering frequent defeats, one chief after another made his submission. On 9th

January, 1833 the ringleader Tirat Singh, surrendered himself, and a general pacification followed almost immediately. The chiefs were allowed to retain a large measure of independence, but they had to submit to the general control of a Political Agent, who was thenceforth stationed in the hills and dealt with all serious cases of a criminal nature. They had also to agree to the construction of such roads, bridges and roadside bungalows as might be considered necessary. The first Political Agent was Captain Lister of the Sylhet Light Infantry who held the post for more than twenty years (1835-54)".[2]

It is pertinent to point out in this connection that after the death of David Scott (1833) T.C. Robertson and Colonel F. Jenkins officiated his post. But they did not reside at Cherrapunji. The geographical remoteness from the seat of governance accounted for the failure of the authorities to look properly at the problems in their right perspective and this led growing restlessness among different conflicting Khasi chiefs. The two years (1833-34) absentee rule of Khasi Hills led the administration to realize the defects and they created a separate dignified post Political Agent, Cossya Hills; Lister immediately after his appointment moved to Cherrapunji from his military residence in the plains of Sylhet. Despite the damp and inimical climate of the rainfed hills of Cherrapunji he never grumbled and lived there for more than thirty years.

Lieutenant Inglish was the son-in-law of Lister. He was also the Assistant Political Agent. Both of them were in the SLI. Robertson, the Political Agent withheld the title of Raja from Rajendra Singh of Jaintia and even returned the letter of the Supreme Government which addressed Rajendra Singh as Raja (letter dated 28 Feb 1834). The action of Robertson was not only a violation of norms but also the principle for which the administration stands. He was angry as two British subjects were sacrificed before the goddess *Kali* in Jaintiapur. He planned annexation to Jaintia kingdom and instructed Lister and Inglish to make an economic assessment for the Jaintia *Raj*. Lister informed Robertson that cash revenues to Jaintia amounted to Rs.30,000/- annually in addition to what was paid in kind and that "a treasure amounting to nearly 20 *lacs* of rupees had accumulated in the royal vault."[3] On the basis of that information Robertson imposed a heavy tribute on the Raja and finally recommended his deposition. During the regime of Jenkins in March 1835 the British government informed the young Raja Rajendra Singh the confiscation of his properties in the plains.

On 15 March 1835, Captain Lister took formal possession of Jaintiapur and issued a proclamation announcing the annexation of the Jaintia Pargana to the British Dominion. The dependency of Gobha met the same fate a few weeks later. Deprived of his valuable possessions in the plains, Rajendra Singh gave up in disgust his unremunerative terrritory in hills which passed into the hands of the British. The hill tribes of Jaintia, however, did not submit to the new regime so easily. They broke in to open rebellion which was easily suppressed and very liberal terms were given to the insurgents by Captain Lister to weaken their opposition. The hillmen were interfered with as little as possible; no revenue was demanded from them and the hill chiefs or Dolois were left in the administration of petty cases.[4]

So far the Khasi states were concerned the British Government followed a uniform policy. The *Syiems* of the semi-independent Khasi states were permitted to exercise, with the aid of the durbars and elders, sole-criminal, civil jurisdiction in their respective states over their own subjects on matters pertaining exclusively to them. The dependent chiefs were permitted to investigate and decide all civil and criminal cases in which the parties were own people with the exception to cases of murder, homicide and accidental death which were reported to the Cherra authorities for their decision. Both categories of states were bound to take to the Cherra court cases in which British subjects and the inhabitants of more than one state were concerned. These Khasi states came within the jurisdiction of the Political agency at Cherrapunji when it was instituted on 11 February 1835 under Captain Lister, the Political Agent and his Assistant and son-in-law, Henry Inglish. British Paramountcy was further extended over the Khasi states by formalizing succession of chieftainship.[5]

Lister, The Political Agent

Thus, began the diplomatic career of Lieutenant Colonel Lister in March 1835. He conducted tribal negotiations with sagacity and courage but did not hesitate to resort to punitive measures whenever necessary. He earned immense popularity among the different Khasi chiefs and helped consolidation of British rule in Khasi Hills. The Supreme Government was impressed by the outstanding services rendered by Lt Col. Lister. He was termed as the worthy successor of David Scott. Lister was, however, basically a solider and displayed his unique capabilities in military operations. So the Honourable Company often requested him to take to arms to save the administration from the political imbroglio in Naga Hills, Lushai Hills and Garo Hills. He responded to those calls, hooked his pen a while, put on his uniform and saddled his horse to the field to charge the brigade. His military adventures were all crowned with success. In his chequered military career Lister surpassed any one in the history of modern Assam who played the vital role in subjugating the wild races. Not only the top brasses of the army but the successive Governor Generals also had a very high esteem about his power of handling most difficult situations.

Lister and the Lushais (Mizos) of Tripura

The British district Sylhet had its border in southeast touching the state of Hill Tripura and also the Lushai Hills (unadministered). The Paite (Pytoo) Kukis of Lachukla's clan swooped upon the Kachubari village in Sylhet committing large scale massacre (1843). The punitive expedition, 1844 by Captain Blackwood suppressed the Lalchukla's clan but the Sylhet border remained defenceless as before because the Kukis again raided the British territory in the cold season in 1847. The District Magistrate of Sylhet sent the SLI to the affected frontier to restore confidence among the demoralized villagers. The Sylhet authorities accused the Raja of Tripura of dereliction of duty and the Raja's office retorted promptly. Thus ensued a wordy duel between the District Magistrate of Sylhet and the Political Agent Tripura involving the Foreign Department of the Government of India. When both the central and local authorities were seriously thinking over the problem of the security of the eastern border of Sylhet, there came the news of Kuki attack upon the SLI on January 1848. Cooper, the Magistrate of Sylhet, entrusted with the law and order of the district was indolent and he neglected to conduct a proper enquiry of the incident and simply accused the Raja of Tripura as a source of the trouble. The negligence of Cooper annoyed the Government of Bengal relating to the enquiry of the incident was not complied with. The authorities in Calcutta took a very serious note of it. Lord Dalhousie, the Governor General, issued a minute empowering Lieutenant Colonel Lister to institute an enquiry of the matter.[6]

The Minute of Lord Dalhousie, The Governor General

"I have no confidence in Mr. Cooper's willingness or ability to do what is necessary especially under the new circumstances which have arisen to embarrass this case. "I propose therefore, to request to Col Lister to proceed in person to the spot where the outrage is reported to have taken place, taking with him, or at all events putting in motion, such a force as he may judge necessary for any subsequent operations. I would propose also that full power be given to Col Lister to conduct the enquiry and to conduct any subsequent proceedings which may be judged necessary "I would propose further to instruct Col Lister that if upon enquiry he shall find that the attack on the guard made on 12th January was made by an armed force to any extent, or if he shall be satisfied that the massacre committed in April was upon the bodies of person settled in the British territories, he shall proceed to take effective measures with the troops under his command to inflict such punishment on the Kukies as they may most sensibly been and as is usual in similar raids on the frontier.

(On the margin... I should consider this infliction of punishment necessary under all circumstances but especially when the Raja is manifestly either unable or unwilling to punish himself.

Lord Dalhousie)

"If on the contrary he should decide that the occurrence of 12 January was only a squabble which may be reached and punished sufficiently by the civil power. He shall direct that proceedings may be taken by it. And if his enquiry should clearly satisfy him that the massacre of the 13 April was committed within the hill territories of Raja as has been alleged he should then abstain from any further proceedings. I am given to understand that the decision of this alternative may be safely left to Col Lister's judgement and experience. "I would gladly wait until we could hear the result of the enquiry. Mr Cooper has been directed to make supposing him to have commenced it before issuing any instructions at all. But time passes urgently and it appears to me to be before anything indispensable that those who live under our rule should see that we are willing and able to protect them, and that the barbarous tribes in the vicinity should be made to feel that we are not powerless for that purpose and that they cannot injure us with impunity.

"I am unwilling to act in any matter of this kind without consulting with my colleagues in the Govt. of India. I have therefore sent this statement of the case in hopes that they may consider my views correct so that we may act at once, and they save the present season.

Sd. Dalhousie 24-1-48
1 concur
Sd. F. Millett 24-1-48"[7]

As per instruction contained in the Minute the Secretary to the Government of Bengal, F.J. Halliday wrote to Col. Lister, the Political Agent, Khasi Hills on 25 January 1848 asking him to take the charge of the matter.

> "Under these circumstances and considering the new circumstances which are now reported to have taken place with your detachment on the Rajah's frontier and which are not improbably connected with the events of last April, the Governor has determined to place the matter entirely in your hands; being convinced that he may rely with confidence on your judgement and experience to bring it to an early and satisfactory conclusion.

"With this view the Governor has resolved to appoint you, and you are hereby appointed and invested with the full powers of a Magistrate in the district of Sylhet, for the purposes of this investigation you are requested to proceed to the scene of these outrages with all possible expedition."[8]

He was assured that Cooper had been instructed to assist him whenever necesssary and the Tipperah Rajah was also informed in the usual manner through the local authorities, to cooperate with him. He was also empowered to take the number of armed force men as he thought necessary. And if he found in his investigation that the outrage was committed within the British territory, "You will proceed forthwith with the troops under your command and without any further instructions from Government, to beat up the quarters of the offending tribes living beyond our frontiers and to inflict upon them such military punishment as in your judgement they may most sensibly feel and as usual in cases of similar outrages by barbarous frontier tribes.

> "It will be the duty of the Rajah of Tipperah to assist and cooperate with you in any incursion you may requiring to make within his territory for these purpose but it will not be necessary that you should await his assent to your crossing his frontier, and you will not fail to note and report to government if he should make any underhand opposition to your progress should he make any open resistance you will treat him, as a possible enemy."[9]

Abstract of the letter was also sent to the Raja of Tripura, Raja Kissen Kisore Manikya.

The Secretary, Government of Bengal informed Cooper the Sylhet District Magistrate, and Dampier, the Superintendent of Police, Lower Provinces, were also formally instructed to cooperate Lister and informed them, 'Colonel Lister has been directed to make his reports direct to the Government."[10]

The Military Board requested Lord Dalhousie, to make the military survey of the disputed spot of the occurrence of the raid by Captain Maxwell as that would define the boundary line as well as the actual place of occurrence. Accordingly, the Secretary Bengal government further informed Lister that Captain Maxwell was willing to serve under him, "you are accordingly requested to call upon Captain Maxwell if you should consider it necessary.[10a] "However, Captain Maxwell because of his heavy engagement in the road construction work at the Chittagong could not join Lister's party and J.H. Maxwell substituted him. Returning from the spot of enquiry Lister wrote to the Secretary, Bengal Government on 19 February 1848.

> "I have the honour to acquaint you for the information ofthe Right Hon'ble the Governor of Bengal that I have returned from the Eastern frontier were agreeable to instructions - conveyed in your letter No.11 dated 25th January 1848. I visited Lall Mee Sing's Baree. The post of the detachments of Sylhet Light Infantry Battalion Sing See Raja, the scene of the third massacre and am of opinion that the localities of these late translations are entirely within the Tipperah Raja's independent territory."

The deserted state of the whole country within the confines of the hills precluded the possibility for procuring evidence respecting either the boundaries or the occurrence which have given rise to the immigration. This however is of no moment as Lt. Fisher's Report in connexion with his map as sufficient to prove the matter of territory.

"The hill of Chattachoora is noted in the report of which I append an extract as being situated in Badarpur or Sidessor Range in latitude 24^0 19^0. All territory north of this line assigned to the British Government with the exception of Dharmanagar, which with all land south of the above mentioned line is placed in the dominions of the Tipperah chief. A place therefore from Kailasshar in a direction any way south east must necessarily be entirely within that person's jurisdiction, we marched from Kailashar at 8 A.M. on the 11th instant attended by a small escort and arrived at Lal Mee Sing's village at 6 P.M. The estimated distance being twenty miles and the direction south-east as per accompanying sketch.

> "On the 12th we proceeded towards Sing Shee Raja at 10 A.M. reaching the ruined village at 4 P.M. The distance about 12 miles and the direction south-east.

> The other two scenes of massacres lying still further, so I did not visit them as from the aforementioned reason, I was satisfied of their position within the Tipperah frontier and every additional step in their direction would take us farther from that of the British Government. "Lall Mee Singh's village and the other localities are situated between the Surajog and Jampoe ranges, both of which run north and south and extended southward some fifteen or twenty miles from the former place at about the distance between these two ranges is another small range of hills running east and west, apparently joining on to the Savajog only as mere is an opening between it and the Jampoes.[11]

Lt. Col. Lister further stated "there is a conflicting evidence as to the owner of this small hill. But the sketch map of Fisher proves that this hill comes under the territory of Tipperah and that it can in no way affect the question of boundary."[12]

He also stated that he had withdrawn the advanced armed guards for not only this was objectionable but also put strain upon the supply position.

With respect to the attack upon the guard considering the extent which the English in the first instance became aggressors, in occupying the village whereby the inhabitants were compelled to fly to the jungles, Lister could not think himself justified in carrying into effect the orders contained in the paragraphs 10 especially as it authorised such only in the event of sufferers residing within the British territories. He had however demanded Lall Mee Singh to be given up, to account for his share in this transaction. The local authorities of the Raja at Kailashar were under an engagement to produce him within fifteen days, and in case of this agreement being fulfilled Lister had the honour to request instructions how the case to be disposed of.

He further stated that he had returned to Sylhet posting a company at Hingajee, pending the final adjustment of the case.

He also complained of the ill defined southern boundary. "In conclusion permit me to state that the southern boundary seems ill defined and little known a matter to which I would direct the attention of Government suggesting the construction of permanent pillars on conspicuous hills in the absence of a natural boundary, without which the imaginary boundary a line of latitude must continually afford, grounds for dispute."[13]

Extract of a report on the boundary between the Sylhet and the Independent Hill territory of Tipperah addressed by Lt Thomas Fisher, 24th Regiment H T to the magistrate of Sylhet without date para 19th. By a decision of Mr Ewing, Magistrate of Sylhet in 1820/21 the whole of the villages watered by the Simla and Lungaee nullahs together with the ranges called the Siddheswar and Sevallia Hills were declared to be within the Company's territory and it was determined that the boundary commenced at Chattachora, vide Plan Latitude 24'17" north Longitude 92'10" E and extended in an irregular line to Kasinagar in *pargana* Patharia."[14]

He also pointed out that a letter of an Amin addressed to the Magistrate, Mr. Roberts of Sylhet in 1801 stated that the place between Patharia (Sylhet) and Dharmanagar (Tipperah Ind. Territory) was within the Tipperah Raja's territory and the stream in qustion had been claimed by the Political Agent of Raja. "The place Kasinagar is called by the people of Sylhet as Surma chera and they claim it within the Company's territory but a careful examination of all the evidences prove that the idea of the Sylhet people is not correct and the stream regarded as the boundary."

Lt. Col Lister.[15]

Lister in his report to the Bengal Government informed that his investigation was similar to that of Lieutenant Maxwell of Bengal Engineers who met him personally and supplied him with Banner role and chainmen. The Nazir of Sylhet obstructed Maxwell in his work. "There being nothing further for Lieutenant Maxwell to do at this season of the year I have permitted him to return to the Presidency reporting his arrival to you (Secretary)".

The report of the Maxwell is important as it related to the boundary between Sylhet and Tripura. It is quoted here, "I have the honour to compliance with your instructions to forward a sketch of the ground showing the relative position of Lall Mee Sing's Baree, the stockade and place of the late massacre in the neighbourhood with the boundary line between the Hon'ble Company's territory and the Raja of Tipperah and at the same time make the following report. "Lall Mee Sing's Baree and stockade are situated about half a mile from the banks of the Deogung river on the east side Oonkattar Sarajung range of hill about 24 miles to the south east of Hungjuah or 8 miles south east of Kailashar and according to the Boundary Line laid down by the Late Captain Fisher within the territory of Raja of Tipperah.

"Referring to Captain Fisher's own words in pointing out this position of the boundary, vide report para 19th latter part, he states, it was determined that the boundary commenced, at Chattachora, vide place Lat 24'17 N Longitude 99'10E and extended in an irregular line to Kasinagar."

"Latitude 24'17 is therefore it will be observed the most southern point of the British territory at this spot and it is evident if for no other reason should this be considered as the true boundary and it is admitted by Government, I believe as a boundary which should be respected by both parties till government decided otherwise. All to the south side of it must be beyond the Company's territory and amongst other places

Lall Mee Singh's Baree, are as shown in the plan which is upwards of eight miles to the south of this.

"This places of massacre Singhshepuja, Dokompore Baree and Lampore Lall's Baree are as seen in the plan much further south than even this and consequently still further within the Rajah of Tipperah's dominions."

Laying aside, however, Captain Fisher's boundary and even following that as laid down and shown to me by the Nazir as his desired line, it will from the following errors he has made in his sides of the frontier, be impossible. I conceive in any way to bring these points within our territory. In the Nazir's imperfect knowledge of the country as it really is and which has misled I believe the authorities at Sylhet had been forwarded to Govternment three points have erroneously been taken for granted.

1st. The Jooree river rises in the Sarajoy range of Hills.

2nd. That the Jampoe range of hills i.e., those marked in the sketch as such and that in the continuation of which Satoo is situated runs into the Sarajoy range a little below the latitude of Kailashar and the Lall Mee Singh's Baree is on the east side of this.

3rd. That the Chattachoora Teela or peak the boundary line should run from is not correctly laid down by Captain Fisher but should be as pointed out by the Nazir about miles further south at a point in the Langbear and Singture ranges.

Now could the hill and rivers be so disposed of a glance at the sketch will show it would have the desired object or bringing the places under dispute within the British territory but as the two first of these suppositions are totally incorrect even allowing the third which at best is more than doubtful this arrangement is upset.

The Sarajoy and Jampoye ranges do not approach one another but run in a parallel direction north and south nearly and at the distance of about eight miles. The Goori river rises close under the latter and to the eastward of Lall Mee Singh's Baree.

Capt. Fisher's plan and boundary compared with the country as it really stands, and we observed it is tolerably correctly laid down and there can be no doubt as to what he intended as the line Chattachoora Tila being admitted by all parties as a point in the Badapore range, there are however not marks upon the peaks, by which the country people can be guided and without a campus and Captain Fisher's plan to refer to a mistake to be made.

Where boundary line strikes as at a,b,c,d, pillars might be built to advantage, but is likely a road to these points would have to be cut through a dense jungle and the materials conveyed there either by coolies, mules or elephants the expense of each pillar would be considerable.

The nature of the ground of Lall Mee Sing's Baree to *Jal nadi* also extending to the south is one mass of dense bamboo jungle and forest and can only be valuable to the owner from the numerous herds of wild elephants it shelters with the exception of a few patches round Lall Mee Singh's Baree, little or no longer or no land it cultivated.

Sd. Harley Maxwell.[16]

In recognition of the Lister's service Halliday, the Secretary Bengal Government (later on Governor) wrote to Lister on 26 April 1848:

> "I am directed by the Right Hon'ble the Governor of Bengal to acknowledge the receipt of your dispatch of 19th Feb and 29 March last respectively. In the first of these your report, your first visit to the scene of the massacres committed by the Kookie tribes in April last and your observations upon the boundary question between the territories of the British Government and those of the Raja of Tipperah and declaring yourself

stasified that the place of massacres is far within the Raja's boundary.

"In the second dispatch you report your second visit to the same spot in company with Mr. Cooper and Lt. Maxwell and you transmit a copy of Lt. Maxwell's report upon the boundary dated 25th March and his sketch of the frontiers to illustrate his observations.

"Governor approves of your report and thinks that as the massacres took place within the Raja's territory therefore no necessity for taking any other steps regarding those occur-rence; Governor also approves of the military withdrawal from the advance posts. He also thinks undesirable to call Lall Mee Singh for his any share in the massacres."[17]

The Governor also regretted that the civil authorities of the Government were wrong in determining the question of the boundary as it misled the Government at Fort William. He also informed that the magistrate of Sylhet had been directed to dismiss the nazir immediately who obstructed the survey work. The expenses he applied for sanction were sanctioned and Governor also stated that the Military Board would be consulted the demarcation of the boundary permanently which would be economical and useful, as suggested by Lister and Maxwell.[18]

Halliday praised Lister for his service and requested the Military Board to submit a plan and estimate for drawing the boundary between the territory of the East India Company and the Raja of Tripura. The Board was further requested to consult Lt. Maxwell who was in Calcutta.

Thus, because of Lister the boundary between Sylhet (now Karimganj in Barak Valley, Assam) and Tripura was clearly defined to avoid future political complications. The investigation, of Lister is characterized by his qualities of leadership. He was capable of harnessing the talents of his subordinates and boosted the morale of the workers to effect a team work. Lister was the Political Agent of Khasi Hills but the Honourable East India Company retained his service as the Officer Commanding in the Sylhet Light Infantry. And that was necessary, so it was he who was the sole authority to decide the number of Companies and the quantity of ammunition to be despatched in a particular expedition. During the Blackwood's Expedition 1844 he sanctioned four Companies to capture the Paite (Pytoo) Kuki chief Lalchukla. But in the present expedition which was personally led by him had five Companies of soldiers. Lister originally belonged to the Engineering Division of the army, so, in road construction work or survey work he had expert's knowledge. In fact, as an officer of the armed forces he was possibly the most versatile one in the North-east and the Government of India valued his suggestions and sought his advice frequently.

In the military history of India Lieutenant Colonel Lister left an indelible mark as a dynamic officer of significant military acumen. His contrubutions as a diplomatic officer was well-known. During his twenty years of service as the Political Agent of Khasi Hills he made impossible possible. He brought the whole of the Khasi Hills under the strict administrative control of the East India Company and considerably tamed the wild tribes. The tribes also gradually got accustomed to the principle of inviolability of the British boundary. The experience made them wise to realize that a price was to be paid for stepping over the line.

Lister and the Lushais (Luchays) of Cachar Frontiers

John Edgar, the Civil Officer, Left Column of the Lushai Expeditionary force 1871-72, in his famous report (1872) describing the past historical connexion with the Lushais wrote that Lister's operation had been a great success and there had been no raids since the expedition for a long time.

Let there be an analysis of the event necessitated the armed intervention of Lister. Captain Verner, the Superintendent, Cachar in his letter dated 21 November 1849 to Lister informed that he had collected evidence from the two Kukis of the affected village, according to them the attackers, principal chief Lalingbhoo remained at home in the distant hills but under his instructions his two sons Barnerlal and Lalpooe with some 200 followers advanced towards Cachar. Verner also pointed out that Salpooe Raja had been friendly chief receiving subsistence from the Government and also had promised to supply Kukie coolies to help the road construction in the border region. Salopooe's *mantry* met personally recently the Superintendent in his court.[18a]

On the basis of the letter from the Superintendent Cachar, Lister, the Political Agent, Khasi Hills, informed the Secretary, Bengal Government, J.P. Grant on 31 December from Cachar that he (Lister) visited the scene of massacre at Roopa Chera with a view to determine whether the place was within the British territory or not.[18b]

"The village on the Roopa Chera in which the murders were perpetrated is beyond dispute is within our present boundary. It is situated eight miles south by east of Chargola on the fork of Roopa chera and *Simlah nuddi* and is full three days march directly from Chuttar Choora, the boundary laid down in the map of Capt Fisher. As to the perpetrators of crime he states that according to the Superintendent, Cachar the crime was committed by Lushai Kookies an independent and powerful tribe, occupying a tract north east of Chittagong and some nine or ten days march south of Cachar. Raja of Tipperah also in a recent statement had stated that the Lushais do not come under his authority. Lister also informed that the country south of Cachar was dense jungle and very difficult to get the supplies so he proposed to take only the essentials there.

Accordingly, Lister advanced to the Mollah or Mora's punji on the hills far south of Cachar at the head of the SLI troops. He conducted the operation from 1 January 1850 to 23 January 1850 and communicated immediately on his return to Cachar to the Secretary, Bengal governemnt of the safe arrival at Silchar and informing him that he would send his detail report from Cherrapunji. Further, stating only for the present that his expedition had been a success. He had destroyed the village of Mulla, the *sardar* in the Roopa Chera raid. He had destroyed the grains and also killed 40 men or Mollah. "Because of the small number in the force I considered it safe of come back to safety and I think a large number of force is needed to create an impression on the mind of this powefrul and wild tribe, and I hope that the Government will also form the same opinion."[18c]

Report on the Expedition Mulla

Lieutenant Colonel Lister sent his detail repo t on the Expedition to the Secretary, Bengal Government on 2 February 1850 (vide B.J.P. 27 February 1850 No.36 *Lister's Report).*

Lister submitted his report of the expedition to the Secretary Government of Bengal from Cherrapunji on February 2, 1850. He stated that the expedition started from Silchar on 4-1-50. The detachment was consisted of 200 men. The road was dangerous because of small rivulets and dense jungles and absence of thoroughfare. The elephants and other caravans found it extremely difficult to penetrate in to those dense jungly hills. Lalpoe Raja, of course, helped him with Kooki coolies. On January 1850 the contingent reached the Mullah's village. Mullah took a very strategic position in his cantonment on the top of a high mountain. Considering the small number of force in the contingent Lister considered it risky and improper to follow Mullah further up so he retreated after destroying the village of Mullah. The return journey took from 17th to 23rd January. He explained that the expedition was made to cut short else severe damage should have caused to expeditionary force in case of delay.

The Lushai Socio-Military Pantheon

"The Lushais are very powerful tribe under the government of six *sardars*, of whom one is the acknowledged chief. They have their separated cantonments with a number of dependent villages attached. In these cantonments the fighting men reside. In the dependent villages are located their *ryots*, who merely used as coolies and for tilling the soil. They consist in many instances of the captives they have brought away in their different expeditions, or great part of them probably taken as mere children and generally reconciled to their captivity."

"The fighting part of the Lushai population is composed to Lushais who appear to be cross between the Kookies and Burmese; secondly a certain number of true Burmese entertained for the purposes of warfare and thirdly of refugees and outlaws from Manipur and our own frontier."

He sayd that the chief of the head of the tribe is known as Barmooielin (Barmoolin) who has 300 hundred Burmese in his service. His headquarters is a village south west of Mullah's village which Lister saw from his telescope. This is a very big village of 3,000 houses. The sardars subordinate to him can raise a fighting force 5-7 thousand men. The Burmese has the muskets and the others are armed with *daos* and spears. That is why Lister did not take the risk of further advance.

"I have before remarked that the Lushais are a cross between the Kookies and Burmese, and this opinion is strengthened by the belief universally prevailed, that a part of the Burmese army which occupied Telyne and its neighbourhood in 1824 never returned to Ava but settled in the jungles south of Cachar. Almost all the Kookie tribes are migrating in their habits, changing their residence every two or three years, but in the substantial way in which the Lushai villages are built I am convinced that they are a stationary tribe and this stamps them from as different from the other Kookies who one and all entertain a great dread of this."[19]

Lushai Defence

He informed the Lt. Governor, how he had overcome such a powerful tribe. He state that during his expeditions the fighting men were absent from their cantonment and were in their maurading excursion. Besides, the expedition was a sort of surprise to them who thought that their cantonments were only known to themselves. He had many spies with him. The spies, when he reached the villages of Mullah, desisted him from further advance.

The Lushai country consisted of several hills run from south to north Cachar and Chittagong were the two terminal points of these hills. The Chittagong side faces the steep mountain ranges, many uneven ranges and swamps face the Sylhet and Comilla side. Whereas, from Cachar a chain of hills runs down unbroken into the Lushai country and, according to Lister, along this a good practicable road might be constructed.

Recommendations of Lister

Lister did not finish his duties simply submitting an official report of the expedition but he also recommended certain measures for the security of the Eastern frontier.

He suggested the formation of a border security force consisting of three thousand men. From five hundred to one thousand of these would be required for keeping open the road from Cachar, and protecting the various depots. A portion of this force must consist of Europeans. The Europeans having the experience of the character of the

Burmese stockade should be taken in to the border security force.

The occasional poweful demonstration of force would yield no result. Small and sporadic British expeditions would excite the spirit of revenge of the tribes. The only remedy lay in breaking the spirit of Independence of the Lushais.

Handling of the delicate problem of the Lushais was closely connected with the affairs of Manipur and Tripura. For an effective settlement of this cooperation of the Rajas of Manipur and Tripura was necessary.

For the maintenance of peace in the southern border of Cachar the help of the settled Kukis in the British frontier was essential. Those Kukis would collect necessary intelligence and in case of emergency they would render their service as frontier guards. For this purpose Lister proposed a few hundred Kukis of Cachar frontier should be armed with muskets; and they should guard the paths and bypaths under a young and enterprising European officer.

Results of the Expedition

The Government of Bengal readily agreed to the last mentioned suggestion of Lister and appointed him as the Frontier Officer to ward off the Lushai raids. The unnecessary interference of the local officers of Sylhet into the frontier affairs came to an end. The burden of vigilance on the frontier fell upon an officer of considerable rank under the direct control of the Fort William. Thus, new chapter was introduced in the Lushai policy of the government. The company moved from its old base of Sylhet to a new base Cachar for the exploration of the Lushai frontier.

Importance of Lister's Expedition

British connexion with the Lushais, in the true sense of the term, owes its origin to Lister's expedition. Formerly, the

British Government suffered from a sense of megalomania entirely alien to its traditional political spirit. Neither the local authorities nor the authorities of the Fort William endeavoured to collect valuable information regarding the topography, political organizations of the country and people of the Lushai Hills. The local authorities considered the unique military prestige of the Company was sufficient to draw the admiration of the wild children of the hills. Besides, the local officers failed to study the Lushai problem in the proper perspective when they were busy in quarrelling with the Raja of Tripura, a great political change took place in the Lushai Hills. Laulul dynasty of the Lushai clan firmly established its hold over the whole of the hilly country south of Cachar and east of Chittagong. All these did not come to the notice of the local officers. Lalingbhoo, of whom we came to know of at the time of Roopacherra raid, was the son of the chief Lalul, the founder of the Lushai dynasty. The danger lay in the southern frontier of Cachar and Lushais of the Lalul's family were the authors of all the massacres committed on the frontier. After the expedition of Lister, the English gradually came in direct contact with the ruling Lushai clans and ultimately annexed the Lushai Hills from them.

Inglish Company and Lister

Lindsey Company was pioneer lime and saltpetre company in Sylhet with a huge annual turnover. Lindsey left Sylhet in 1789. Robert Reid and George Inglish set up the Reid and Inglish Company in 1794 which subsequently became the Inglish Company (1819). Harry, the eldest son of George Inglish, the enterprising lime merchant, became the sole proprietor of the Inglish Company as his brother John sold out his shares to him and enjoyed an easy and carefree life in London. The company was the largest industrial concern in the low countries of the Bengal presidency with a very good liason with the government. The East India Company appointed Harry Inglish as the Assistant

Political Agent, Khasi Hills (1835) under Lt. Col Lister. Harry Inglish worked as Assistant Political Agent from 1835 to 1850. When Lister led his famous expedition against Mollah, Harry officiated the post of Political Agent. Harry married the daughter of Lister. The necessities of commerce compelled Harry to give up his government job. In the Inglish Company there were large number of Khasi and Jaintia workers and many influential Khasis were engaged in lime business as *gomostas* (agent) and lessees of the lime mines. Lister took advantage of this by distributing monetary favour and spread the network of spies in the Khasi and Jaintia Hills.

Lister was not merely the Political Agent of Khasi Hills but also the civil judge. Lister for the first time made revenue settlement in Khasi Hills and his settlement formed the basis for future settlement. In 1854 Lister relinquished his high post and the Commissioner of Assam created a new post Principal Assistant Commissioner of Assam with Cherrapunji as the headquarters. The post of Political Agent, Khasi Hills was abolished.

Lister had been a versatile genius. He was a brave soldier of proven calibre, skilled diplomat, tactful administrator and shrewd but competent civil judge. Lister was an Engineer by profession and when made revenue settlements in Khasi Hills he made intensive survey of the land, came to know of the coal mines and lime-stone mines of Khasi Hills. He was indirectly connected with the lime business through his daughter. He was aware of the mining potential of the area and informed the authorities of Fort William about it. R.G. Hadden of Messrs Goldstone Wyllic and Company was sent to the Khasi Hills and Sylhet to conduct the survey as to the possibilities of drilling pertroleum by the government.[20] Lister for a while engaged himself in orange plantation and exported them to Calcutta market in association with his son-in-law Harry Inglish. Thus, Lister opened up the Khasi Hills and Sylhet for commercial activities and in a sense he laid the real foundation of modern commerce in Meghalaya. Lister was a rich man invested his money in shares of different companies and has close connexion with the Managing Houses in Calcutta. He returned to England as an wealthy person living the life of a Nawab in London.

Lister and Sylhet Infantry

With the advance of Burmese up to Manipur and finally to Cachar, the security of the British district, Sylhet was threatened. The authorities of Fort William became aware of the situation, Gobinda Chandra the deposed ruler of Cachar and Gambhir Singh took refuge in Sylhet. Edward Gait writes:

> "The defence the Surma valley was entrusted to a force called the Sylhet Local Battalion, afterwards the Sylhet Light Infantry, with headquarters at Sylhet. It was raised in 1824, and was recruited chiefly from Manipuris who had left their own country and settled in Sylhet and Cachar during the internal troubles and frequent Burmese invasions of the first quarters of the last century. Two companies of this regiment were stationed at Silchar, and at a later date it also occupied Cherrapunji."[21]

SLI played a vital role in the First Anglo-Burmese war (1824-26). The prolonged war in the unknown hostile hilly terrain compelled the authorities of Fort William to organize a force, proficient in hill operations. Thus SLI was revamped and reconstituted under the able leadership of Major F.J. Lister who upgraded the force and beefed up its intelligence network involving the non-combatants. The force was fully equipped with up to date ammunition.The men of the force were recruited from the Gorkhas and the Punjabis replacing the older recruitment norms. The headquarters of the force was shifted from Sylhet to Cherrapunji when Lister moved to Cherrapunji as the Political Agent Khasi Hills. Though decentralised in action SLI in its approach became a personalized one, Lister remained in charge of SLI in addition to his political post. The SLI defended the Sylhet and Cachar borders from the Lushai Kuki incursions and tackled the larger problem of law and order in the district of Sylhet. SLI conducted several punitive expeditions in to Khasi, Lushai and Naga Hills. Lister led several expeditions personally. The operation at Khonoma in Naga Hills (1849) at the outskirt of North Cachar Hills was conducted by the SLI. Cachar Levy was a battalion of SLI and its head Mr Grange, considered as the father of Frontier Police and he led several successful expeditions in to the Naga Hills. Lieutenant Colonel Lister, the main pillar of SLI, was the guiding spirit and leader of the force. The SLI developed a new military culture unknown in the frontier history under Lister's leadership. Vincent, Blackwood, Campbell, Butler, Johnstone, Grange etc the giant military officers who played crucial role in the trans-Indo Burma border in the 19th century, all had a stint of service in the SLI and had the opportunity to receive training from Lister. Lt. Col. Lister was a source of perennial inspiration to them. Almost all the military historians have showered unalloyed praise on Lister. The SLI later on got changed to Lushai Hills Military Police Battalions and 8th Gorkha Battalions. Finally they got merged into Assam Rifles.

Assessment of Lister

During the early part of Queen Victoria's reign only the daring younger generation of England seeking fortune came to India to join East India Company's service and the more daring amongst them opted for the military service, and Lieutenant Colonel F.J. Lister belonged to the latter category. He was indeed, a brave soldier having romantic liaison with the vicissitudes of a soldier's life. Lister had been a down to earth military activist who moved in the inaccessible, dense forests and insurmountable hills with rifles and bullets slung across his back. When charged the artillery he seemed to be absolutely fearless. His operations were mostly crowned with success. His had been an eventful military career and awards and medals had come a plenty. But Lister was not merely an officer of the armed forces he was also an important Frontier Officer of caliber and as such played a very vital role in formulating and handling the British frontier policy. His well written numerous reports were the basis of many important decisions of the Supreme Government in Fort William. As a diplomat he had been shrewd and often resorted to bribing the opponent to win a price. He broke the persistent Khasi resistance by liberally distributing cash to the Khasi chiefs. Similar tactics were contrived to deal with the Lushai-Kukis and Jaintias. Lalmir Sing was heavily bribed to assist the English to capture Lalchukla. A large section of the servants of East India Company were corrupt and they had no qualms of conscience wither to accept or distribute graft. Lister was no exception to the general run of the Honourable Company's personnel.

Lister's dealing with Rajendra Singh, the young *raja* of Jaintia had been very harsh. Rajendra Singh was a victim of a carefully laid plot of political fraud. T.C. Robertson was the chief person to hatch the conspiracy to confiscate Rajendra Singh's property and possessions in the prosperous plains. Lister's exaggerated report strengthened the well laid game plan of Robertson. The plea of justification of Lister's conduct that he had been acting under the instructions of the superior officer is a weak defence and contrived because he was working at tandem. Biased Robertson even did not carry out the Supreme Government's instructions. Triumphant Lister entered in to Jaintia capital, Jaintiapore at the head of a garrison to take possession of the deposed *raja* whose faith in British sense of justice was completely shaken. Here also Lister acted under the instruction of his superior officer Colonel F. Jenkins but the entry of Lister into the defenceless Jaintia capital had been like a medieval Taimur's aggressive about performed in a miniature scale. Raja Ram Singh, the grand father of Rajendra Singh had been comrade-in-arms, only a few years ago of Lister and Robertson in Anglo-Burmese war (1824-26) but the camaraderie soon gave into the greed of looting the treasure of the hapless native. How much of the confiscated treasury reached Fort William is at anybody's guess. The share of Lister and Harry Inglish had not been insignificant. The revolt of 1857 was engineered by greedy officers like Lister and his ilk. As Political Agent of Khasi Hills Lister had to maintain the law and order and his motto being *pro rege, lege et grege* and anybody found breaking the Company's law were sternly brought to book. Whatever may be his motives Colonel Lister did draw attention to a potentially explosive problem- ethnic uprising that had been left unresolved since the incorporation of small but ticklish principalities in to Company's dominion in the low countries of the Bengal Presidency a few years ago.

However, his administration of justice was not always free from all the hassle, despite the drum beating of the Company officials about its efficacy. So far the natives were concerned Lister's law enforcing machine was as punctual as the rising sun. He had to dither, however, when he had an axe to grind and in that connexion he could hardly be distinguished from a muslim Kaji of his preceding age. The Inglish Company carried on the monopoly trade in limestone. But the monopoly was not the result of market economy but an enforced one. The lure of profit often invited the Calcutta merchants, and all of them Europeans, to the lower provinces to start the lime business but George Inglish, the father-in-law of his daughter and the Managing Director of the company restored to flagrancy to harass such entrepreneurs after abducting and not infrequently murdering their agents or representatives. And all these were made to restrict competition. But Lister persistently refused to take cognizance of the crimes and did not initiate action against the culprits. All such digressions of Lister were known to his subordinate

European officers and though they disapproved of Lister's malafide acts privately or disliked the Harry Inglish, Lister's son-in-law, they could not bring it to the notice of the Supreme Government for fear of reprisal. Lister, thus ruled like a dignified despot, almost independent of the Supreme Government situated long six hundred miles away. Edward Gait *(History of Assam)* writes:

> "That the Sylhet district, which had previously been administered entirely from the headquarters station was clearly impossible, in a way to deal adequately with the requirements of a tract containing a population of two millions, and possessing a most difficult and complicated system of land tenures, and in which the communications were almost inaccessible at certain seasons of the year. To remedy this state of affairs, four outlying sub-divisions were formed, viz. Sunamganj, Habiganj, Maulavi Bazar and Karimganj and a separate officer at headquarters was told off to deal with *Jaintia parganas.*"

It is no wonder that Colonel Pollack went to Assam shortly before the formation of the Chief Commissionership (1874) had a very poor opinion of the manner in which the province was governed. But discharging the duties of a civil officer with occasional bouts of digressions or his unsavoury personal behaviour should be given much prominence and for that Lister ought not be slighted nor his action be construed as *mala fide;* taking the stock of the turbulent political condition prevalent in Assam and Lower provinces of Eastern Bengal and the awful transport condition in his territorial jurisdictions Lister had to act according to the exigencies of a particular situation. He did not consider it negative to reap the whirlwind. Everything was necessary if that suited the administrative needs. Moreover, he worked in a system which was by itself a corrupt one. The system improved sufficiently with the creation of the Chief Commissionership in Assam and by the change in legal machinery of Assam including

Sylhet. Under a vastly transformed scenario the new national perception is bent on pointing out that the Officer Commanding, SLI had much fighting but little glory. But it is Lister who gave the government a credible defence policy to fight the disruptive forces. Without Lister at that critical juncture the much needed peace would have remained illusive to the distrubed 'Lower Country' gasping under the impact of Burmese aggression - for many more years. His long twenty years of colourful and formidable administration - which had been the logical fulfilment of David Scott's dream - witnessed Lister's concern for the solidarity with the stability and peace of Honourable Company in the *terra incognita* of the Northeast of the Empire. His conviction to restore order at any cost isolated and marginalized the disturbing element along with their fissiparous tendencies who had thrived on erroneous passive proposals of bureaucratic inaction. His stable administration ultimately unshered in a new era of tremendous financial and economic spin offs for the Lower provinces. The flourishing tea industry in the next decade was the direct outcome of the strong rule of the Officer Commanding SLI. The bright side of Lister's character had been unlike many of his imperialist compatriots of upper India, he never allowed himself to be a prisoner of the politics of hate and for that reason he was never out of tune with the needs of the time.

In criticizing the officials like Lister we often forget that Lister was an officer of the East India Company and not of the British Crown, besides, he had been primarily a military officer with strong mould, naturally, his civilian image lacked the refinement of administrative candour. He was never shy of his military image and this paramount military concern often compelled his civilian task to play the second fiddle of the military amplitude.

NOTES AND REFERENCES

1. From Chief Secy, Govt. of India to David Scott, dated 26 June 1829, I.H.P. Aug. 1820.
2. Edward Gait, *History of Assam* pp 354-55.
   Also Barpujari, *Problem of the Hill Tribes North-east India,* Vol 1, p. 81 - H.K.
3. *Annexation of Assam* (1st Edition 1944) p. 151 - R.M. Lahiri.
4. *Ibid.,* p. 157.
5. *British Policy Towards the Khasi States-* David R. Syiemlish, *Studies in the History of North East India. Essays in honour of H. Barpujari,* ed. J.. Bhattacharjee NEHU, Shillong, pp. 186-193.
6. B.J.P. 17 May, 1848. No. 86 Minute by the Governor General dated 24 January 1848. Also, Suhas Chatterjee, *Mizoram Under the British Rule,* (1st Edition 1984), pp. 29-30.
7. *Ibid.*
8. *Ibid,* pp. 28-29.
9. *Ibid.*
10. B.J.P. 17 May 1848 No. 89.
11. B.J.P. 17 May 1848 No. 117 Lister to Halliday.
12. *Ibid.*
13. *Ibid.*
14. *Ibid.*
15. *Mizoram Under British Rule,* p. 31 - op. cit; vide also Lister's letter to the Bengal Government of the same proceedings ante.
16. B.J.P. May 1848 No. 117.
17. B.J.P. 27 Feb. 1850 No. 37, Grant to Lister.
18. *Ibid.*

18a. B.J.P. 27 February 1850 No.37 Supra.

18b. B.J.P. 27 February 1850 No. 30

18c. *Ibid.*

19. *Ibid.*
20. *Mizoram Under British Rule,* pp. 31-32, *op cit.*

20a. Achyuta Charan Tattvanidhi, *Srihatter Itibritta* Vol.2, Canto 5, Chapter 4, p. 69 (1st Edn). About Jayntia rebellion see also H.K. Barpujari, *Problem of the Hill Tribes North-East Frontier,* Vol. II, pp. 74-83.

21. *Assam Rifles,* p. 7 *op. cit.*

2

Thomas Herbert Lewin

Thomas Herbert Lewin, the legendary Frontier Officer earned commendable esteem and respect of the people for whom he had worked. He explored the unknown territory Chittagong Hill Tracts in Lower Burma. He had the rare capacity to mix with the hill tribes of different denominations in the inaccessible terrains with courage, endowed with presence of mind very often, he turned the tortuous course of events to is own advantage. Being a man with large heart he had the means to influence the simple hillmen who came ungrudgingly to the fold of the British administration.

Although Lewin's entire itinerant career had not been spent in the eastern hills of India yet North-eastern region especially the Lucia Hills (Misogamy) had been his principal place of interest. He is also probably the first among the Europeans to make an indepth study of the different hillmen living the Chittagong Hill Tracts and Arcane. In his student life he studied Geography and Classics. He had a very good command over the language and his reports and memoirs bear the stamp of this. He gives the detail geographical account of the Chittagong Hill Tracts in a beautifully ornate language. He wrote his account in 1868. But what he wrote one and half a century ago is still regarded as the most authentic geographical account of Chittagong Hill Tracts.

He made his visits to those dense forests and unfriendly regions on foot or by boats and shafts for collecting materials. Rarely, in the history of Northeast frontier of India we come across such a daring and inquisitive officer who opened up vast tracts of land before the modern world. His enterprise is so exciting that even the Christian missionaries whose contributions in taming the savage hillmen is second to none, lose colour when we compare with Thomas Lewin's. He kept his diaries and updated his notes frequently and published some of them.

Regarding the geography of Chittagong Hill Tracts he writes:

The area of the Chittagong Hill Tracts is estimated to be 6796 sq. miles. The most noticeable feature of the country is that it is divided into four river valleys, marked out more or less distinctly by well defined chains of hills running parallel from the south in a northwesterly direction. The Sunglow and Matamore river, until they enter the plains, run parallel to the hill ranges, forming two of the fever valleys alluded to. The Kurnafoolee and Fenny river, however, run transversely across the line of the hills. The river valleys here are formed by large tributary streams entering the Kurnafoolee at right angles to its course.

The soil of the district is composed for the most part of a rich loam, but in many parts the hills are found to consist of a schistone clay, much resembling sand stone in appearance, which falls to pieces very easily on force being applied. In the alluvial valleys and water courses large pieces of dicotyledonous wood are frequently found lying in a horizontal position: They are usually more or less petrified.

The climate of the Hill Tracts is distinguished by two characteristics; its coolness, and its unhealthiness as regards foreigners. There are not hot winds in the hills, and the hottest part of the year is tempered by cool sea breezes. It is the custom of the people to remain in their villages until the cultivation season commences in May, and then the whole countryside moves up, every man to his patch of cultivation, on some lofty hill. It is to this custom, I consider that their comparative immunity form sickness may be traced for hill men on abandoning their usual mode of life, and taking to other occupations not involving the periodical move to the hill tops, are nearly as much subject to fewer as the people of the plains.

During the months of November, December, January and February, dense fogs settle over the hills during the night, seldom clearing away until the middle of the following day. Those fogs, however, do not seem, to have an unhealthy effect, as the four months in which they prevail are the healthiest throughout the year. During the month of February some rain generally falls being about 120 inches. During the rainy season, it is well nigh impossible to move about the country on account of the rising of the hill streams. Before the setting in of the rains, the hill people lay in a stock of provision as at that season of the year bazaars are abandoned by the men of the plains, and trade almost entirely ceases.

It is at his season of the year that the large floats of timber come down with the rising of the waters from the hills.

The most unhealthy month of the year is September, the close of the rains. Fever of a bad type is then very prevalent. In the months of April and May the epidemics of small pox and cholera make their appearance, ceasing at the commencement of the rains. The prevalent wind during the rains and hot seasons is from the south west. An easterly wind, if of long continuance, is said to be unhealthy. In the cold season the wind generally comes form the north. At the commencement and breaking up of the rains, violent storms of thunder and lightening occur.

Where the hills rise to any considerable height, they become rocky and precipitour, the lower ranges being composed generally of sand or a rich loam. The dark brown rocks, of which the higher ranges are composed, are undoubtedly of igneous origin; indeed subterranean volcanic force must at some remote period have caused the strange billowy upheaval of the face of the country, which gives it its present distinctive character. On the 2nd April, 1762 Chittagong was violently shaken by an earthquake, the earthquake, the earth opening in many places, and throwing up water and mud of a sulphurous smell. At a place called Bardavun a large river dried up; and at Bakur Chunak, near the sea, a tract of ground sand down, and 200 people, with all their cattle, were lost. Unfathomable chasms are described as remaining open in many places after the shocks, and villages, some of which subsided several cubit, were overflown with water, among other, Deeepgoung, which was submerged to the depth of 7 cubits. Two volcanoes are said to have opened in the Seeta Cunda Hills. The shock was also felt at Calcutta. There are at present in the Seetakoond Range, in the Chittagong District, several hot springs, from one of which an inflammable gal rises in such quantity, that it is kept constantly burning over the spring. I Have heard also of hot springs existing in the Loonghem Range in the district, but I have not visited them. Salt licks are found at many places in the hills; the best known are those at Bang-a- mora, in the north, the Mawdang Tlang, in the eastern part of the district.

Lignite is found at two or three places in the hills, but no coal has as yet been discovered. An inferior species of limestone is found in the places; on being burnt, however, it has not given a return sufficient to render its manufacturer profitable.

In many parts of the district are found large and richly alluvial plains, covered for the most part with forest trees. These plains, if cleared of timber, would be found admirably adapted for plough cultivation. Far in the jungles on the banks of the Myannee, an affluent of the Kassalong River, are found tanks, and the remains of masonry buildings, evidence that, at some by some period, the land here was cultivated and inhabited by men of the plains. Tradition attributes these ruins of aormer Rajah of Hill Tipperah, who it is said, was driven from that part of the country by hordes of hill men coming from the south. At one place only in the hills, at Rangamuttee, on the Kurnafoolee River, has the usual method of cultivation by the plough been introduced; and there are about 120 families of Bengalees who till the land. The settlement, although established some six years ago, does not appear to have increased either in numbers or in the area of land brought under cultivation, along the whole border of the district adjacent to enter the hills. They are, I believe, principally deterred from settling there by the insalubrity of the climate, which seems, to be deadly to their race, although innocuous to the hill-men.

There are at present no roads in the district, the nature of the country, indeed, with its transverse ranges of hills, offers very great engineering obstacles to the construction of roads or the employment of wheel carriage. Paths there are, of course, in every direction; but, with the exception, country can make use of .the favourite path throughout the district is the sandly bend of a stream as it offers coolness for the feet a hill range, however, this sort of path necessarily becomes of a precipitous, not to say break neck, description.

Bazars or Markets

During the last few years a line of paths has been cut through the jungle, connecting the Government frontier guard posts and the three principal stations in the Hill Tracts: these paths, however, are cut chiefly with a view to military defensive operations, and are not much used as yet by the country people. There are four bazaars or markets in the hills to which the hill people resort to barter their produce for such articles of daily consumption as salt, spices, dried fish and the like which are only procureable from the plains. These bazaars are situated at Kassalong. Rangamutee and Chandragoona, on the Kurnafoolee, and the Bundravun, on the River Sungoo. The bazaars at Chandragoona derives a fictitious importance form that place being at present the head quarters of the district; but should the central station be at any time removed, the bazaar would collapse, the position occupied not being a true mercantile centre, ant the bazaars, moreover, being brought into a competition which it is unable to sustain with the adjacent market of Rangonea, which is an old established place for barter, much resorted to by the hill population.

The population of the hills also resort to such of the markets of the plains as may be within a day's journey form their homes, along the border of the Chittagong District.

The hill men bring down for sale cotton and timber, either in the rough the oil hewn into boats; and if much pressed for money, they collect for sale the oil bearing seeds of a tree in the in jungle (*chalmongree*) or cut and flat down a raft of bamboo they also occasionally bring in for sale ivory and wax in small quantities. The principal articles disposed of the hill people in the bazaars are salt, tobacco (in small quantities), piece goods, metal goods, trinkets, dried fish, pigs and cattle. About 50,000 cubic feet of timber per annum, it is calculated, is brought down yearly to the plains form the hill tract forests; and 55,854 maunds of cotton are estimated to be yearly exported by the hill people, this in addition to the not inconsiderable quantity reserved by them for home consumption. The hill tracts, indeed, seen peculiarly well fitted, both in soil and climate, for the production of cotton. The quantity produced, however, depends, almost entirely upon the amount of rain fall..Too heavy a fall of rain spoils the cotton crop; there is especial sanger of this at the commencement of the rains, when the plants are young. Measures have been taken to introduce improved varieties of the cotton plant among the hill tribes. The flora of the Hill Tracts is of the Malayan type; The forests being principally of brilliant, glossy evergreen trees.

Throughout the whole district are found large tracts of valuable forests trees. Teak is not indigenous, but thrives if planted, it grows, however, plentifully in the forest on the other side of the hill range separating this district from Arraccan. A large trade in railway sleepers has lately sprung up from the port of Chittagong; the port conservator estimate that upwards of 30,000 sleepers have been exported during he last two years.

As yet no organized inquiry into the vegetable products of this part of the country has ever been instituted, and but little consequently, is known on the subject. The tea plant is believed to be indigenous in the district, but it has not hither to been found in abundance. The fir tree and the caouchouc tree are found in the lofty hills in the east of the district; but the hitherto unsatisfactory relation existing between us and the more remote hill tribes have prevented any use being made of there other wise valuable forest products.

In the wilder parts of the district the forest trees are festooned with numerous ligneous creepers (*Phytocrene*) hanging in a labyrinth of coils from every tree; some are as thick as man's arm. On cutting one of these, Water is obtained, and as thwte grow on the loftiest hill where water is often not obtainable, this property of theirs is most useful. The must curious thing is, that should the coil be cut in one place only, so as to leave two pendent ends, no water issues. It is necessary to cut a piece clean out of the creeper with quick, consecutive stroke, before water is obtained. If with an unskilled hand three or four hacks are made before serving it, the creeper trickles out about half a tumler full of clear, cool water. The Hill men explain this by saying that when the stem is cut the water tries to run away upwards.

There is also a tree in the jungles called "chowr" by the Bengalees, and "samul" in the Tipperah tongue. The young shoots of this are delicious eating, being white and tender, with a filbert flavour. Between the other husk and the trunk of this tree is a soft layer of substance that makes an excellent timber.

"In shady spots is also found another edible plant something like asparagus; the Bengalees call it " tera". It is cultivated as vegetable by the Bangalees, But the wild variety growing the virgin soil of undisturbed forests is far superior.

The young shoots of the cane and bamboo, just as the young plant emerges from the earth, are very good eating. On the hills also, the wild yam is found plentifully, so that no man able to search for food in the jungles could starve ion these hills.

The hill people have many plants and simples which they use medicinally. They make tow or three halos form the roots and leaves of plants, they also use a certain creeper in catching fish; this plant, when steeped in a stream,. And the water confined by a dam, has the property of intoxicating and stupefying the fish, which come floating, belly, upwards, to the surface of the water, and are then easily caught.

There are eleven varieties of the bamboo found thoughtout the hills, and canes grow in profusion. The cane is the hill man's rope; with it he weaves baskets, binds his house together, and throws bridges over the otherwise impassable hill toreents.[3]

Bamboo and bamboo products

The bamboo is literally his staff of life. He builds his house of the bamboo; he fertilizes his fields with its ashes; of its stem he makes vessels in which to carry water, with tow bits of bamboo he can produce fire; its young and succulent shoots provide a dainty dinner dish; and he weaves his sleeping mat of fine slips thereof. The instruments with which his women weaves their cotton are of bamboo. He mares drinking cups of it, and his head at high rests on a bamboo pillow; his forts are built of it; he atches fish, makes baskets and stools, and thatches his house with the help of the bamboo. He smokes form a pipe of bamboo; and form bamboo ashes he obtains potash. Finally, his funeral pile is lighted with bamboo The hill man would die without the bamboo, and the thing he finds hardest of credence is that in other countries the bamboo does not grow, and that, man live in ignorance of it. Throughout the whole of India, indeed, the bamboo occupies a forward place in the domestic economy of the inhabitants. It remained only that it should be defied; and this, it seems, has been done. In Dr. Balfour's account of the migratory tribes of central India (*J.A.S.*, No. 61 of 1844) he tells of a ribe called the Bhatos, a tribe who follow the profession of athlete, and perform most of their feats with the aid of a bamboo.

"Their patron goddess is Korewa, an incarnation of Mahadeva. Her shrine is situated at the village of Thekoor, near Kittor, around which temple consecrate it It is now called 'gunnichars' or chief, and receives their worship annually. To marriage, of disputer requiring arbitration , or the occurrence of knotty points demanding counselors or arbiter, and all prostrate themselves to it before commencing the discussion of the subject before them. "This is certainly the best kind of chief I ever heard of."

In like manner, one of the clans in the Hill Tracts (the Riang Tipperahs) offer worship to the bamboo.They do not, however, go the length of the Bhator, in considering it as a chief, for it is to them merely an imperson ation or representative of the deity of the forest.

Cultivation

The mode of cultivation pursued in the hills is common to

all the tribes; indeed, wherever hill tribes; are found throughout India. This special mode of cultivating the earth seems to prevail. It is known as " toung-ya" in Baurmah and Arracan, as " dhai-ya" in the central provinces, while here the method is usually called "joom" and the hill men pursuing it "joomiahs".

The modus operandi is as follows: In the month of April, a convenient piece of forest land is fixed upon, generally on a hillside, the luxuriant under- growth of shrubs and creepers has to be cleared away, and the smaller trees felled: the trees of larger growth are usually denuded of their lower branches, and left standing. If possible, however, the *joome* fixes upon a slope thicklyu covered with a bamboo jungle of the species called "dolloo" this, compared with a dense tree jungle, is easy to cut, and its ashes, after burning, are of greater fertilizing power. Although the clearing of a patch of dense jungle is no doubt very severe labour, yet the surroundings of the labourer render his work pleasurable in comparison with the toilsome and dirty task of the cultivators of the plains. On the one hand, the hill man works in the shade of the jungle that he is cutting; the is on a lofty eminerce, where every breeze reaches and refreshes him; his sprits are enlivened and his labour lightened by the beautiful prospect stretching out before him: while the rich and varied scenery of the forest stirs his mind above a monotone. He is surrounded by his comrades; the scent of the wild thyme and buzzing of the forest bee are about him; the young men and maidens sing to their work, and the laugh and joke go round as they sit down to their mid day meal under the shade of some great mossy forest tree.

Harvesting of Sugarcane

On the other hand, consider the moiling toil of the cultivator or the plains. He maunders along with pokes and anathemas at the tail of a pair of buffaloes, working mid leg in mud; around him stretches an uninterrupted vista of muddy rice land; there is not bough or a leaf to give him shelter from the blazing noon day sun. His women are shut up in some cabin, jealously surrounded by jungle; and if he is able to afford a meager meal during the day, he will munch it souls, sitting besides his muddy plough; add to this, that by his comparatively pleasurable toil, the hill man can gain two rupees for one which the wretched ryot of the plains can painfully earn, and it is not to be wondered at that the hill people have a passion for their mode of life, and regard with absolute contempt any proposal to settle down to the tame and monotonous cultivation of the dwellers in the low lands.

The *joom* land once cleared, the fallen jungle is left to dry in the sun, and in the month of May it is fired; this completes the clearing. The firing of the *jooms* is sometime a source of danger, as at that season of the year the whole of the surrounding jungle is as dry as tinder, and easily catches fire. In this way sometimes whole villages are destroyed and people have lost their lives. I have myself seen a whole mountain side on fire for four days and four nights, having been ignited by *joom* firing. It was a magnify- cent sight, but such a fire must cause incalculable injury to the forest; young trees especially would be utterly destroyed. Generally, however, by choosing a calm day, and keeping down the fire at the edges of the joom by beating with boughs, the hill people manager to keep the firing within certain prescribed limits. A general conflagration, such as I have mentioned, is of quite exceptional occurrence.[4]

If the felled jungle has been thoroughly dried, and no rain has fallen since the *joom* was cut, this firing will reduce all, save the larger forest trees, to ashes, and burn the soil to the depth of an inch or tow. The charred tees and logs previously cut down remain lying about the ground; these have to be dragged off the *joom,* the piled up all if round;

and with the addition of some brush wood form a fence to keep out wild animals.

Work is now at a stand still, till the gathering of heavy clouds and the grumbling of thunder denote the approach of the rains. These signs at once bring a village into a state of activity, men and women, boys and girls, each bind on the left hip a small basket filled with mixed seeds of cotton, rice, melons, pumpkins, yams and a little Indian corn; each takes a "dao" in hand, and in a short time every hillside will echo to the "hoiya". Or hill call, (a cry like the Swiss jodel), as party answers party from the paths winding up each hill side to their respective patches of cultivation. Arrived at the *joom*, the family will form a line, and steadily work their way across the field. A dig with the blunt square end of the dao makes a narrow hole about three inches deep; into this is put a small handful of the mixed seeds, and the sowing is completed. If shortly afterwards the rain falls they are fortunate and have judged the time well; or (unparalled luck) if they get wet through with the rain as they are sowing, great will be the jollification on the return home, this being an omen that a bumper season may be expected.

The village now is abandoned by everyone, and the men set to work to build a house, each in his own *joom* for the crop must be carefully watched to preserve it from the wild pig and deer, which would otherwise play havoc among the young shoots of the rice. The *jooms* of the whole village are generally situated in propinquity; a solitary *joom* is very rare. During the rains mutual help in his neighbour's joom. No hoeing is done; the crop has merely to be kept clear form weeds by hand labour, and an ample return is obtained. If the rain be excssive however, the cotton crop is liable to be spoilt, as the young plants die from too much water.

The first thing to ripen is Indian corn; that is about the end of July. Next come the melons, of which there are tow or three sorts grown in the jooms; afterwards vegetables of all sorts become fit for gathering. And finally, in September, the rice and other grain ripen. At this time the monkeys and jungle fowl are the chief enemies of the crop. In the month of October the cotton crop is gathered last of all, and this concludes the harvest. The rice having been cut, is beaten from the ear in the joom: it is afterwards rolled up in the village.

The country suffers sometimes severely from the visitations of rats. They arrive in swarms. And seep every thing before them: they eat up standing corn and empty the granaries of the hill people- nothing stops them. They are said to come from the south, and strange to say, disappear as suddenly as they make their appearance. The hill folk gravely assured me that during the last visitation, which occurred in 1864, the rats were transformed into jungle fowl; in proof of this, they point out a peculiar draggling feather in the tails of the jungle fowl, which they assert to be rat's tail.

Besides grain and cotton, the hill tribes grow tobacco. This is planted principally in small valleys on the banks of the hill streams.

The best tobacco is grown in the country near the Mathamoree river.

Throughout the whole of the Hill Tracts I know no single instance of a hill man cultivating with the plough: indeed it is rare to find a man earning his livelihood in any other way save by joom culture. Near the villages of some of the chiefs a few acres of plough cultivated land may sometimes be seen; this, however, is invariably tended by Bengallee servants engaged for the purpose. The forest conservancy restriction lately introduced will, however, that it is thought, induce many of hill population to settle down as plough cultivators.

In the country adjacent to the Fenny, where in consequences of constant *jooming*, jungle had wholly disappeared. And grass taken its place, the attempt was once before made with every prospect of success: owing to their fear of the independent tribes, the people of that part of the country were unable to move to fresh *joom* land further eastward, and their own country was thoroughly exhausted from over-cultivation; but they steadfastly held all of form, the plough, preferring to earn a precarious subsistence by the cutting and selling of bamboo and the hewing out the boats. Some few of them, who had or could borrow a small amount of capital, took up the profession of itinerant traders; while others earned or added to their means of livelihood by rearing and herding cattle, for which the country afforded ample pasturage.

The independent tribes have now, however, become quiet, and the people of the Fenny have since then steadily moved to the eastward, and occupied fresh *joom* land.

The Villages

The villages of the hill people are formed chiefly by communities composed of persons connected either by blood or marriage. The site of the village is changed as often as the spots fit for cultivation in the vicinity are exhausted. Land once *joomed* cannot be recultivated for a period of eight to ten years, as in less than that time a sufficient growth of the jungle does not spring up to give the necessary coating of fertilizing ashes, without which the *joom* crops would yield but a poor return. They do not seem to be acquainted with the method of terrace cultivation pursued in the Himalayas; indeed the slope of the hills in most parts is so steep, that it is doubtful whether this mode of cultivation would be practicable.

I have sometimes met a hill community as they were changing their residence: long files of men, women, and children, every soul of the village, in fact, proceed to their new place of abode, each one with a long circular basket slung at the back and supported by a broad strip of soft bark passing over the forehead: each family accompanied by a numerous tribe of the very curly tailed blackhilll dog. In some of the baskets are their household goods; in others, a child and a young pig sleep contendely together. In the old village they have left behind, perhaps, half their property, and this without fear, as there are no thieves in the hills. One of these deserted villages presents a curious spectacle; there are all the evidences. Of occupation and recent life, but every living creature has disappeared. Granaries may be seen half full of grain: large wooden mortars of pounding the grain, the weaving implement of the women, and some half finished clothers,[6] all left behind for them to take away at their leisure. They have gone probably a long distance (two days's journey) to the new site of the village; and on arriving there, every family has to build its own house.

Each tribe in the hills has a different way of building; and of this I shall speak further, when referring to the distinctive peculiarities of each tribe. Our own tributary hill tribes all build their houses of bamboo, raised form the ground about ten feet, on bamboo supports with numerous smaller bamboo props supporting the floor the roof, and the walls, in every conceivable direction. The floor and walls are made of bamboo split and flattened out; the numerous crevices give free access to every breeze, and render a hill house one of the coolest and most pleasant of habitations. The roof is also of bamboo crosspieces, thatched with palmyra, of "atop" leaves, called by the Bengallees "krook pata." This forms an impervious and lasting roof, which need only be renewed once in three years, whereas the ordinary grass thatched roof has to be repaired every year. A hill house perched in an exposed position on the ridge or spur of a lofty eminence looks the frailest structure in the world; its strength, however, is surprising, and in spite of the fearful tempests that sometimes sweep over the hills, I never heard of a house having fallen or being injured by the wind.

The Animals

The domesticated animals of the hill people are the "guyal", the cow, buffalo, goat, dog, cat, pig and the common fowl.

The four last named animals are common to the whole district. Long haired varieties of the cat, dog, and goat and are found among the independent tribes. The guyal, also are rarely found with any tribe save those that are independent of our authority. The cow and buffalo are principally found among the people inhabiting the Fenny River country, as that part of the district offers the greatest advantages for pasturage.

One of the most marked peculiarities of the Hill Tract forest is their silence. There would seem to be but few wild animals in the hills, numerically speaking. I have traveled for miles in the wildest part of the district without seeing fur of feather; almost every species of white animals, however, is found in the hills; and to be good and successful hunter is a great merit in the eyes of the tribes.

The gibbon monkey it is found throughout the hills, and towards the south on the coast the fisher monkey (*Simian synomolgus)* is met with. The lemur is also not unfrequently met with. There are also the small common monkey, which , in large flocks does dire mischief to the standing crops of the hill men, and a long tailed white whiskered variety, the lungoor. The flying fox (*Pteropus edulis*) the horse shoe bat, the small houses bat or flitter mouse, are all found in the hill; also the musk rat the badger, the malay black bear, several species of wild cats. Tigers are not uncommon, but they do not do much harm. The wild dog is said to be met with, but I have not seen it. The mongoose, the large dark- brown squirrel, the red squirrel, the yellow bellied variety, the field rats, the bamboo rat, and the prorcupine (*Histrix leeucorus)*, are all more or less frequently met with. The elephant and the Assam rhinoceros are common. The former roam in large herds of 100 to 150 all over the district. The double horned Sumatran species of rhinoceros was formerly thought not to be a native of this part of the country, but a specimen has recently been captured alive, and brought to Chittagong by Captain Hood, of the Elephant Khedda Department. It was smooth-skinned and unmistakably two horned. A small, black species of hog is found throughout the district, as also the barking deer, the munntjak, and samber; guyal and wild buffalo are not uncommon. Of birds we have the following varieties: the beemra *(Edolius remifer)*, shrikes, the bulbul, warblers, the water wagtail, hoopoe koel, the carrion crow (this bird is found largely along the western frontier, but ceases entirely on going far east), minah hornbill (*buceros cavaturs*), small green parrots, a large blue king fisher with a red neck, a small variety of the same species, the night-jar, the anvil bird, the peacock, argus pheasant, the matoora or Arracan pheasant, the buton quail, jungle fowl, green pigeon, the large wood pigeon, ling dove, kites, fish eagles, and a few wild ducks and snips. I have seen one partidge, but they are very rarely found in the district. The boaconstrictor is common, and is found of enormous size. Several kinds of poisonous snakes are also met with.

British Relations with the Hills Tribes

The earliest record of our dealings with the hill tribes is a letter from the chief of Chittagong to the Governor General, the Honourable Warren Hastings, Esq, dated 10th April, 1777, in which he reports that, mountaineear named Ramoo Cawn, who pays the Company small revenue on their cotton farm, has since May being here, either through ill usage from the revenue farmer, or from a disposition to revolt, for some months past committed great violence on the Company's landholders, by exacting various taxes and imposing several claims on them with no grounds of authority or legal demand." The letter goes on to state that writer "was flattered with hopes of securing the person of this said Ramoo Cawn; but this scheme proved abortive, as the men fled from his usual place of residence.

"He has now assembled men in yet larger bodies," and has called to his aid large bodices of Kookie men, who live far in the interior parts of the hills, who have not the use of firearms; and whose bodies go unclothed. This conturmacy on the part of Ramoo Cawn was subsequently met by stopping all supplies, and not allowing the hill people to have access to our bazaars; and these measures appear to have been successful, as we hear no more this person. Tradition in the hills tells us of such a rising of the Chukma tribe; and the reference to this Ramoo Cawn, or Khan, I am more disposed to ascribe the disturbance in question to the Chukma tribe, as the along, of all the hill people, employ a quasi Mohammedan nomencalture. The Kokie men, however, referred to, do not appear to have quieted down so quickly, for in November, 1777, we find the chief of Chittagong addressing Captain Edward Elleske, commanding the 22nd Battalion of sepoys, and ordering some men to be sent " for the protection of the inhabitants against some kookies", and " to assist in making a Kheddah. From the above letters and other sources, I gather that we at that time collected revenue from the hills in the shape of a tax on cotton brought down from the hills, which tax was formed out to some second party. It is also curious to note that as early as 1777 the Government had established Kheddahs, and drew their supply of elephants partly from this district.

Administrative Measures

The records having reference to our relations with the hill tribes, obtainable in the Government offices at Chittagong, are but scanty and intermittent. The attention of the executive seems to have been principally directed of the administration of the District of Chatagong proper, and it was only when some lawless outrage or default of tribute payment forced them into notice that mention is made of our frontier tribes. There are, can only conclude that the tribes were quiet, and the authorities content to let them remain so.

On the 6th May, 1784, Government wrote to Mr. Irwin, the chief of Chittagong, desiring to have his opinion fully, whether, by lenient measures, the inhabitants of the hills might not be induced to become peaceable subjects and cultivators of the low lands. No practical result, however, ensued, and the tribes do not crop up again until the 21st April, 1829, when Mr. Halhed, Commissioner, writes that he finds that the hill tribes are not subject, but merely tributaries. "I do not recognize any right on our part to interfere with their internal arrangements. We have no authority in stance is guaranteed by a third party, resident in our own territory, and who is alone responsible. He derives his own profit from the agreement with us. He is merely an agent, or mooktear, or medium of communication between his constituents and the authorities. He is not the ruler of the clan he represents, and possesses no control over the member of it.

Up to 1829, therefore, we seem to have exercised no direct influence or rule over the hill tribes in the near neighbourhood. However, of a powerful and stable Government naturally brought the chiefs by degrees under our influence, and by the end of the 18th century every leading chief paid to the Chittagong Collector a certain tribute or yearly gift made to purchase the privilege of free trade between the inhabitants of the hills and the men of the plains. These sums were at first fluctuating in amount, but gradually were brought to specified and fixed limits, eventually taking the shape, not of tribute, but of revenue paid to the state.

Until the year 1860 it appears we did not interfere directly with the internal economy of the hills. In that year, however, the independent tribes, known by the generic name of Kookies, committed some murderous outrages on British subjects in the adjacent District of Tippearh. These raids were of so organized a description, and on such large scale, as to cause well founded anxiety to Government; and in July, 1860, a Superintendent of Hill Tribes was appointed to the charge of the hills, which were henceforth known by the name of the Hill Tracts of Chittagong. The committal of the raids was clearly brought home to the tribes residing in the northeastern part of Hill Tracts, and, accordingly, on the 27th January, 1861, an expedition, under the command of Major Raban, entered the hills, and inflicted punishment on the tribe principally concerned.

The primary object of the appointment of a Hill Superintendent was the supervision of the independent tribes; and for the next few years attention was principally directed to the preservation of the peace of the frontier. In 1867 the official designation of the officer in charge of the district was changed from Superintendent of Hill Tribes to Deputy Commissioner of Hill Tracts, and he was vested with full control of all matters and at the same time the district was apportioned into subdivisions, and subordinate officers placed in charge thereof.

General Instructions

The general instructions of Government for the guidance of the Hill Tract authorities (Government of Bengal, letter no. 3300, dated 20th June, 1860) are comprehensive, and so indicative of the wise and beneficent course of policy which has been pursued towards the hill people, that I venture to give here an abstract there of, as follows:-

Ist.-To allow no middle men between the hill men and "hakim", mooktears or attorneys being prohibited from employment in matters between hill man and hill man.

2nd.- Simplification of procedure and freedom from expense were attained by directing that equity, guided by the spirit of the law, should be observed, no stamps required, and no costs further than actual and necessary expense. Justice, in fact, to be administered in the simplest and most expeditious manner possible.

3rd - The customs and prejudices of the people to be observed and respected. We are to interfere as little as possible between the chief and their tribes.

4th- The deputy commissioner was vested with the full powers of a magistrate, his orders being appealable to the Commissioner of the Division, who also has the final decision on all heinous cases.

Crafty Bangallee Litigants

Such were the principles of administration as at first set on foot, but subsequently, by degrees, and until within the last two years, there was a perceptible tendency to revert to Regulation procedure; attorneys had imperceptibly crept into practice, and an appeal to Calcutta in even now. Every efforts, however, is used to check and discourage litigation; and whenever practicable, cases are referred to the arbitration of village juries, the parties seldom any appeal or dissatisfaction.

The introduction, indeed of mookteārs among a people simple and unused to law, is at all times highly inexpedient. Their employment tends to crowd the courts with petty, vexatious, and disgraceful suits. Nothing is so productive of evil passions as facilities for their gratification. The mookteārs tamper with the simplicity and ignorance of the people, and draw them into litigations, in which the sole persons benefited are the mookterars themselves. They thrive by quibbles, quirks, and chicanery, and like vermin swarm where there is most corruption. They are to the law what quack doctors are to physic exciting the malady for the purpose of profiting by the cure, and retarding the case in order to pocket the fees; as also in medicine, when a man has once dabbled in patent medicines and infallible specifics, he is always poisoning himself and others by quack drugs, so in the law an ignorant person who has once been tricked into a dispute and embroilment. During the last two years the employment of mooktears has been discouraged in cases between hill men, and in hill matters which requires special and local knowledge of customs and the like; but in appeals before the Commissioner, mooktears are allowed to appear, as the hill men are often ignorant of the language spoken in the plains of Chittagong where the Commissioner's court is held.

In these hills, also as in Sonthalia, the crafty Bengallee mahajuns of the plains have wrested the law from its original intent, and turned it into an engine where with to reduce the people to a condition of slavery. In an ill fated hour the hill man borrows a few rupees from some mahajun; he wants the money, either because his crops have failed, or his son is to be married, or for some other reason. He can neither read nor write. Consequently the bond in which the transaction is recorded usually binds him to repay some enormous amount of interest, of which he is totally ignorant. Time goes on, the money becomes due, and is generally paid. In the latter case the mahajun say, "Go, my son, I destroy the bond, the debt is cancelled," here he will tear up some paper before the hill man, but most certainly not the bond. The debtor goes away satisfied to his home, leaving the *mahajun* chucking in his sleeve at his successful villainy. After a short interval the *mahajun* repairs to the Civil Court, and, with an injured aspect, lays a suit for the recovery of the original debt, interest, and costs of suits, according to his bond. Formerly, when the summons to the hill man to appear in the suit was issued through a Bengallee peon, the *mahajun* would simply bribe the summons bearer, who would report the summons as duly served, without going near the pseudo debtor's house. Should the mahajun not be successful in this, he will lie in wait at the river side, and when his man comes down of the day fixed for the hearing of the case, he will seize upon him, " Ai *bapre* great is my misfortune, you have been summoned, my friend, quite my mistake; I have no case against you; you know, we made all square between us when last we met. I am afflicted for your trouble, but come with me, you must eat and drink at my expenses some small return for all this needless bother." So off goes the befooled hill man, and never appears in his case, when, according to laws, a decree in default is given against him. In another case, supposing the hill man to have paid part of his debt, and to owe the remainder, the mahajun will then met him outside the Court, make a compromise with him, and agree to withdraw the case. The man goes away, while the mahajun, on his part, does not withdraw the case, but takes decree in full exparte, in default of the debtor's attendance. These are not imaginary cases, but have come actually under my own observation. Numberless are the tricks to which the crafty Bengallee resorts, and gradually he accumulates over his victim's head an amount of legally authorized debts, which the wretched creature can never hope to pay off. He then becomes the bond slave of the *mahajun;* for him he toils, for his profit he clean a joom, raises cotton, or hews out a boat, and even death does not release him, for the load descends upon the shoulders of his son.[12]

Latterly so many cases came before the courts, of a nature such that a permanently state of ill feeling between the hill population and the mahajuns was to be apprehended, that it was found necessary to limit both the amount of interest on a debt recoverable by law, and the time during which a decree might be allowed to remain unexecuted. Twelve percent per annum is now granted by the Courts and on a decree being obtained, the creditor is compelled to enforce at once.

The appointment of an officer for the exclusive supervision of this district has greatly ameliorated the condition of the hill people in this as in other respects, and the Special Registration Rules which have been lately introduced have now entirely put a stop to the nefarious practices above referred to.

It would be a mistake, in my opinion, to introduce into this district the Regulations, Legal Codes, and Procedures, as followed in other parts of India. Such a measure could not fail to be most unpopular and distasteful to the people at large.

Man, in his earliest condition, in a state of quasi barbarism. Law is, or ought to be, the expression of the popular voice; the measure prescribed and agreed to by the people in general, from time to time, for the safeguard and protection of their lives, liberties, and property: law is the concretion or aggregate of hundred of years of trial and experiment. We should not, I think do well to put aside custom and rules which have existed among the hill people from time immemorial, and supply their place by Codes utterly dissonant to their whole mode of life and thinking. This would not be law, but the tyranny of a strong minority over a simple and ignorant majority. Such a tyranny was that which in ancient times among the Hindoos prescribed mutilation as penalty for spitting on the robe of a Brahmin. See in Bengal, a wealthy Zamindar is put is jail for bribery, or here in these hills a chief is punished for keeping slaves or levying what we call an illegal cess on his people. When that Chief or that Zamindar leaves jail, his people will flock round him to do him honour as an injured person. I do not attempt to defend slavery or to infer that bribery should not be put a stop to; I only say that there is no law the fraction of which carries with it no social penalty.

Revenue of the Hill Tracts

The revenue of the Hill Tracts consists chiefly of the tribute which is paid to Government by the chiefs of the tribes. A considerable sum money is also obtained yearly from the tolls levied on behalf of Government on all spontaneous forest produce brought down by water or river routes to the plains. The rear of the inroads and attacks of the independent tribes on the frontier has hitherto prevented the large level tracts existing all over the district from being occupied and cultivated by Bengallee settler, but a movement is now commencing, and during the last year or two, much land along the Chittagong border of the district has been leased to men of the plains, and there is but little doubt that under more favourable conditions of territoriality the greater portion of the district will be brought under cultivation, and that the main source of revenue, as in other parts of India, will arise from the land tax.

Hill Tribes of Chittagong

T.H. Lewin had been a keen observer of mankind. He had an intense passion to study the socio-economic aspects of the different hill tribes living in Chittagong Hill Tracts. It is said that Lewin discovered Lushai country (Mizoram) and he is an authority on the early history of the Lushais (Mizos). But we must not forget that Lewin also gave us an authoritative account of the other hill men too including the Chukmas and Arakanese. His training in classical languages in England as a student gave him the requisite insight into his investigations. His investigations bear the stamp of a versatile scholar with deep insight into the real problem. His language is simple but penetrative. He goes on depicting, in his *Wild Races,* on the Hill Tribes of Chittagong.

1. The KHYOUNGTHA, or Children of the River, who are of pure Arracanese origin, speaking the ancient Arracan dialect, and conforming in every way to Buddhist customs under this head may also be made the Chuckma tribe, for reasons which I shall state hereafter.

2. THE TOUNGATA, or Children of the Hills, who are of mixed origin, if indeed they are not the aboriginal inhabitants of country. They speak numerous and diversified dialects, and are more purely savage than the Khyoungtha. Under this head are included the Tipperah and the Lhoosai, or Kookie tribes, with their offshoots.

The word Khyoungtha and Toungtha are both Arracanese "Khyoung" , a river; "toung", a hill; and " tha" or "tsa", a son. They are used as generic terms, to denote the hill tribes, by only such of our tribes as speak by Arracan dialect. The other tribes have each their own way of specifying themselves and their neighbours. Which will be alluded to when speaking of each tribe in particular; but none of them appear to have any general term for all hill dwellers.

The Bengallees distinguish hill men into two classes. The friendly tribes living close along the Chittagong District border they call *Joomias*; and all other hill men, more especially if unable to speak the vernacular of Bengal, are distinguished as Kookies.

The greater portion of the hill tribes at present living in the Chittagong Hills undoubtedly came two generations ago from Arracan. This is asserted both by their own traditions and by records in the Chittagong Collectorate. It was in some measure due to the exodus of our hill tribes from Arracan that the Burmese War of 1824 took place, which ended in the annexation to British territory of the fertile province of Arracan. As this is a point interesting, not only from its local bearing on the hill tribes, but also in a larger and more important historical sense I shall trace here the way in which the dissensions between the English authorities and the Burmese, which eventually culminate in war, hinged in a great measure upon refugees from the hill tribes, who, fleeing foom Arracan into our territory, were pursued and demanded at our hands by the Burmese.

The Earliest Record of Two Letters

Among the earliest records that we have our dealings

with the Burmese are two letters, written, one by the King of Burmah, the other by the Rajah of Arracan to the Chief of Chittagong, and received about the 24th June, 1787, couched as follows:-

"From the Rajah of Arracan of the chief to Chittagong. Our territories are composed of five hundred and sixty countries, and we have ever been on terms of friendship, and the inhabitants of other countries willingly and freely trade with the countries belonging to each of us. A person named Keoty, having absconded from our country, took refuge in yours. I did not however pursue him with a force, but sent a letter of friendship on the subject, desiring the Keoty might be given up to me. You, considering your own power and the extent of your possessions, refused to send him to me. I, also, am possessed of an extensive country: and Keoty, in conesquence of his disobedient conduct and the strength and influence of my King's good fortune, was destroyed.

"Domcan Chukma, and Kiecopa lies, Marring and other inhabitants of Arracan, have now absconded and taken refuge near the mountains within your border, and exercise depredations on the people belonging to both countries, and they, murdered an Englishman at the mouth of the naf, and stole away everything he had with him. Hearing of this, I have come to your boundaries with an army, in order to seize them, because they have deserted their own country, and disobedient to my kind rule, exercise the profession of robbers. It is not proper that you should give asylum to them or the other Mughs who have absconded from Arracan, and you will do right to drive them from your country, that our friendship may remain perfect, and that the road of travelers and merchants may be secured. If you do not drive them from your country and give them up, I shall be under the necessity of seeking them out with an army in whatever part of your territories they may be. I send this letter to Mehomed Wassene. Upon the receipt of it either drive the Mughs from your country, or, if you mean to give them an asylum, return me an answer immediately.[13]

This letter is explicit enough. The fugitives referred to are evidently men of the Chuckma and mrung hill tribes, who to this day preserve the recollection of their ancestor's flight from Arracan. The persons in question were probably the Chiefs of the clans, and the driving of them from British territory would have been equivalent of the expulsion of the whole clan.

The other letter from the King of Burmah is evidently a covering epistle, from beneath the shelter of which his representative of Arracan should fire his sharp little pop-gun of defiance. His magistery of the Golden Foot and the White Elephant writes in a broad umbrageous manner, that even to the present day carries with it a sense of comfort to the reader. The missive is most curious and characteristic. I shall therefore give it *in ex-tenso.* It marches in broad epic periods, with a roll as of deep toned gongs a barbaric clash of cymbals.

Letter from Turboomah, Principal of the Burmese, forwarded by his orders through the head person in charge of the Arracan country.

"I am lord of a whole people and of one hundred and one countries, and my titles are Rajah Chatterdary (sitting under a canopy) and Rajah Suraj Bunshee (descendant of the sun, and sitting under splendid canopy of gold). I hold in subjection to my authority many Rajahs. Gold, silver, and jewels, are the produce of my country; and in my hand is the instrument of war, that as the lighting of heaven, humbles and subdues my adversaries. My troops require neither injunctions nor commands and my elephants and horses are without number. In my service are ten *pundits,* learned in the Shaster, and one hundred and four priests, whose wisdom is not be equated, agreeably to whose learning and intelligence

I execute and distribute justice among my people, so that my mandates, like the lightning suffer no resistance or control. My subject are endowed with virtue and the principal of justice and refrain from all immoral practices; and am as the sun, blessed with the light of wisdom to discover the secret designs of men".

"Whoever is worthy of being called a Rajah is merciful and just to wards his people. Thieves, robbers and disturbers of the peace, have at length received the punishment due for their crimes, and now the word of my mouth is dreaded as the lighting from heaven".

"I am as a great sea among two thousand rivers and many nullah: and I am as the Mountain Shuncroo, surrounded by forty thousand hills, and like upto these is my authority extending over one hundred and one Rajahs. Further, ten thousand Rajah pay daily attendance at my durbar, and my country excels every country in the world. My palace, as the heavens, studded with gold and precious stones, is revered more than any other place in the universe. My occupations resemble the business of the chief angels, and I have written into all the provinces of Arracan with order to forward this letter in safety to Chittagong, formerly subject to the Mogul Rajah, by whom the country was cultivated and populated, and who erected twenty-four hundred places of public worship, and made four and twenty tanks (here follows a long list of the names and palaces and forts said to have been erected by the above Rajah). and by Umbung Dumah, Rajah of Omerpoor. Previous to his accession to the Rajagyee, the country was subject to other Rajahs, whose title was Chatterdary (sitting under a canopy) who erected places of worship and appointed priests to administer the rites of religion to people of every denomination (observe the tolerance of the Buddhist); but at the period the country was ill governed, previous to the government of the countries Rutanpoor, Doowady, Arracan, Dooraputty, Ramputty,

Chaydog, Mahodyne Manang, in whose time the country was governed with justice and ability, and his wisdom was a shining light, and the people were happy under his administration. He was also favoured with the friendship of the religious men of the age, one of whom, by name Budha, resorted to his place of residence, and was solicited by the Rajah to appoint some one for the purpose of instructing him in religious rites; and Thawhmarey was accordingly appointed agreeably to the Rajah's requisition.

"At this time it rained from heaven gold, and silver, and precious stones, which were buried under ground in charge of the above priest, whose house also was of gold and silver workmanship, to which the above priest, whose and worship the deities; and the Rajah kept a large establishment of servants and of slaves at the temple for the service of travelers and passengers, and his time was engaged in the studying of the five books. He always refrained from immoral practices and deeds interdicted by his religion, and his priests abstained from the flesh of geese, pigeons, goats, hogs, falsehood and drinking were unknown in the age".

"I likewise preserve a line of conduct and religion similar to the above; but conduct to my conquest of Arracan, the people were as sankes wounding men a prey to enmity and disorder, and in Magadha, Mayenwong, Darawody, Chagadag Rahmawady there were eaters of the flesh of man, and wickedness prevailed amongst them, so that no man relied upon his neighbours. At this time, one Buddha Dutta, otherwise Seeryboat Ghakoor, came down in the country of Arracan and instructed the people and the beasts of the field in the principles of religion and rectitude; and agreeably to his word, the country was governed for a period a five thousand years, so that peace and good will subsisted among them".

"Agreeably, hereto is the tenour of my conduct and government of my people, and as there is an oil, the produce of a certain spot of the earth, of exquisite flavour, so is my dignity and power above that of all consulted with others of that class, represented to me, on the 15th of the month Praso 1148, saying, do you enforce the laws and customs of Seeryboat Thakoor, which I accourdingly did, and moreover, erected places of divine worship, and have conformed myself strictly the laws and customs of Sery Tumah Cuckah, governing my people with lenity and justice".

"As the country of Arrakhan lies contiguous to Chittagong, if a treaty of commerce were established between me and the English, perfect unity and alliance would ensue from such engagements. I therefore have submitted it to you that the merchants of your country should resort hither for the purpose of purchasing pearls, ivory, wax and that in return my people should be permitted to resort to Chittagong for the purpose of trafficking in such commodities as the country may afford; but as the Mughs residing at Chittagong have deviated from the principles of religion and morality, they ought to be corrected for their errors and irregularities according to the witten laws, in so much as those invested with power will suffer eternal punishment in case of any deviation from their religion will hereafter be translated to heaven. I have accordingly sent four elephants teeth under the charge of thirty persons who will return with your answer to the above proposals and offers of alliance".

These letters were received during the administration of Lord Conrnwallis. They were followed up almost immediately by the entrance into our territory of a force of armed Burmese under the Sirdar of Arracan. The Chief of Chittagong, in the same month of June, writes to the Governor General in Council reporting this incursion, and stating that he has declined to respond to the overtures of alliance until his armed force was withdrawn. At the same time he states that in his opinion the refugees should be driven out British territory. He adds also that these fugitives were persons of some consequence in Arracan, and reports, further, that Chukma Sirdar, who had fled from Arracan, had been arrested and confined by him. He concludes by stating his opinion that this Sirdar and his tribe have no intention of cultivating the low lands in a peaceable manner, but have taken up their abode in the hills and jungles, for the convenience of plundering. Ten years before this, in the year 1777, it appears from a letter dated 31st May, from the Chief of Chittagong to the Honourable Warren Hastings, Governor General that some thousands of hill men had come from Arracan in to the Chittagong limit, having been offered encouragement to settle by one Mr Bateman, who was the chief governing officer there at that time. These migrations were evidently for a long time a rankling sore to the Burmese authorities, and Macfarlane's *History of British India,* page 355, records that in 1795 a Burmese army of 5000 men again pursued some rebellious Chiefs, or, as they called them, robbers, right into the English District of Chittagong. These Chiefs, who had taken refuge in the three were put to death for atrocious tortures."[4a]

In 1804 Macfarlane records that disputes continued to occur in the frontiers of Chittagong and Tipperah, but the organized forays into our territory hardly assumed any definite form until when a rupture ensued, disturbances rendering the Burmese apt to provoke and take offence, was undoubtedly the emigration to our hills of tribes hither to subject to their authority.

Origin of the Tribes

The origin of the tribes is a doubtful point. Pemberton ascribes them a Malay descent. Colonel Sir A. Phayre considers two of the principal tribes of Arracan, who are also found in these hills, to be of Myamma or Burmese extraction. Among the tribes themselves no record exists, save that of oral tradition, as to their origin. The Khyoungtha alone are possessed of a written language; they have among them several copies of the Raja Wong, or *History of Kings of Arracan,* but I have been able to discover no records whatever as to there sojourn and doings in the hills. The jounght, on the other hand, possess no written character, and the langauges spoken by them are simple to a degree, expressing merely the wants and sensations of uncivilized life. The information obtainable as to their origin and past history is therefore merge and unreliable.[14c]

The general physique of the hill tribes is strongly Mongolian. They are, as a rule, short in status, about 5 feet 6 inches in height. Their faces are broad; the nose flat, with perceptible bridge; the eyes narrow and set obliquely in the head, high cheek bones, and no beard or moustache. They have an honest, bright look, with a frank and merry smile; and their look does not belie them, but is a faithful index of their mental characteristics.

The complexion of the Khyoungtha tribes is clear yellow or wheatish colour, much resembling the skin colour of the Chinese. The Toungtha however are dark and swarthy in complexion.

Before noticing in detail the peculiarities and distinctive signs of each separate tribe, I shall describe certain habits and customs which are common to all of them:- The first and perhaps the most marked distinction is their mode of cultivation, which has already been described by me; next in importance is the relation of master and servant, or as we should call it, slavery, throughout the hills. Servants, as we understand the term, that is persons doing menial service for a certain wage, there are none, but the universal custom prevailed in the hills, until within the last five years of having debtor slaves, persons borrowed money from their chief or some other well-to-do individual, and gave on of their children or a female to serve as menial servant until the debt should be paid or cancelled. This service took the place of interest on the money lent, no interest being payable; but the creditor was bound to release the slave on the repayment or tender of the original sum borrowed. The condition of these so-called slaves was very little different indeed from that of free people. They were treated as members of the creditor's family and were never exposed to harsh usage. They could not be sold or transferred to another owner. Their position in all cases was far preferable to the falling bondage in which hill men were subsequently often legally held by the Bengallee mahajuns, as already described in part I. Since we have taken in hand the direct management of the hills, this system has been put down with the strong hand; upwards of three hundred debtor slaves have been released; some of these latter returned afterwards to their debtors to fulfil their engagements. The Chiefs and principal men, however, being immediately under the eye of authority, were unable to retain in their houses a single menial, and the ordinary daily work of their housed suddenly fell upon their wives and daughters. As a consequence of this measure, confidence between debtor and creditor was shaken. The hill men no longer sought assistance from their chiefs, or sought it uselessly. They could neither read nor write. Bangallee, which was the language of our courts; and even the ability to speak this alien language was uncommon among them. How they can draw up the bond by which only debt could be legalized? How become acquainted with or comply with the procedure of Act VIII of 1859. According to which all suits for debt must be laid?[15]

The consequences of our action being such the old system under which hill people borrowed from each other in time of need having been possible, being substituted they fell easy victims to the mahajuns, who expounded the law very much to their own advantage. The fault of our measures lay in their suddenness; there was no intermediate though previously in the abolition of slavery in our West Indian colonies, the measure was there introduced with great caution and by progressive stages.

Slavery in the Hills

The slavery in these hills, if indeed, it can be called slavery, was of the mildest description and was the deliberately adopted custom of the majority of the people, not a bondage imposed by force. We are I think, too apt to connect the idea of slavery with the whip, chains, and cruelty; but it should be remembered that in the lower ranks of progress slavery does good work; without it, indeed, civilization would have been well nigh possible. Slaves exempt man from the otherwise all powerful necessity of working for his life, from earning bread by the sweat of his brow, and gives leisure for thought and culture. It is not so many centuries ago since even in our own England modified description of slavery existed; and in the early growth of a people there always has been and must be, slavery, if they are to rise in the scale of races. Among the hill tribes labour cannot be hired; the people work each one or himself. In 1865, in this district, a road had to be cut; but although fabulous wages were offered, the hill population steadily refused to work, and labourers had to be imported at a great expense from Chittagong District.[16]

It would, I think, have been wise had we recognized and modified this all, this hill institution, not as slavery, but as a labour, or so much cash; but above all, measure should have been taken to make the language of the Courts identical with the vernacular of the people.

There is another, a detestable and actual slavery in these hills, which formerly existed among our own tributary tribes, but is now only carried on by the independent tribes beyond our jurisdiction. This is the captivity to the bow and spear:- men and women taken prisoners by force in war, and sold like cattle from master to master. The origin of this custom, if not indeed the origin of the chronic state of warfare in which all hill people seem to live, was the want of women.

Among the hill people the women is the hardest worker, the chief toiler; and naturally enough their constant and incessant labour in all weathers kills the women of a tribe, or renders them more liable to the insidious attacks of disease. Hence, among some tribes, as the Todas of the Neilgherries for instance, was the strange custom of polyandry prevailing; but among the tribes here a simpler course was adopted – the law of the strongest:

The good old rule, the simple plan
That he shall keep who has the power,
And he shall keep who can.

Those who had few women went with arms in their hands, and took what they wanted from a weaker community. Another custom, which too often served as a cloak for obtaining of slaves, was that of demanding 'goung hpo" a usage answering to the wehrgeld" of compensation for the homicide of a relative, which occupies so large a place in the ancient jurisprudence of the Germans. This is the cause of pretext of almost every raid that is committed. It is the enforcement of demands, either of claims made by a strong village on a weak one for "ata" (black mail), or the price of the head (Arracanese "goung", and "hop", price) of some diseased member of the stronger community. It is practice among them, on the death of any member of village, to saddle it upon some village which he may lately have visited and to demand a certain price for his life.[17]

The Khyoungtha

The Khyoungtha are subdivided into clans, mostly taking their names from the different streams on which they live.

They all dwell in village communities having a Roaja, or village head, through whom they pay revenue. The villages to the south of the Kurnafoolees River are subject to a chief, called the Bohmong (from the Arracanese " boh", a head, and "mong", leader), whose residence is at Bundrabun, on the Sungoo river, while those to the north of the Kurnafoolee acknowledge the supremacy of the Mong Rajah. The tribute paid to these Chiefs is from four to eight rupees yearly for each family. Unmarried men, priests, widows, widowers, and men who do not cultivate but live by the chase of wild beasts, are exempted from paying tribute. In addition to the money payment, each adult is liable to work for three days in each year, without pay, at the Chief's bidding. An offering of the first fruits of rice and cotton of every man's field is also made to the Chief. The position of Roaja, or village head, is more an honourable than a profitable one: he is chosen by the villagers, and appointed by the Chiefs, to whom he must present a "nuzzer" on his nomination being ratified. The office, generally speaking, descends from father to son. The Roaja decides all petty cases and disputes that may occur in the village, and for so doing he receives certain fees from both parties, according to custom and the importance of the case. In some instances he receives from the Chief a percentage on the yearly revenue collections.

Colonel Sir A. Phayre, in his *Account of Arracan (Journal of Asiatic Society of Bengal,* No. 177 of 1841) says that the Khyoungtha and Rakhoingtha, or Arracanese, are of the same race. Like the Burmese, their Rakhoingtha signifies an inhabitant of the Rakhoingtha country while Khyoungtha means those who inhabit the banks of mountain streams, and support themselves by hill cultivation.

Hill Mughs

To the Bengalis of the plains the Khyoungtha is known by the name of Hill Mugh, but this is entirely a misnomer. Colonel Sir A. Phayre rightly states that this name exclusively belongs to a class of people residing in the Chittagong District, called Rajbunsees, or Mughs, who are the offspring of Bengali women by Burmese when the latter possessed Chittagong. They are well known in Calcutta as Mugh cooks, and are doubtless worthy people in their way, but are far removed in regard to manliness, uprightness, and all that we think noble, from the Khyoungtha of hills. The Khyoungtha, like the Burmese are Buddhists, and believe in the doctrine of meteapsychosis, or the transmigration of souls. Each successive life is as it were a furnace by which the soul is refined, and so rises, step by step, to perfection, until eventually the state of "Nirban" is attained. I have heard stores of men who, is dying, thought they were sure of attaining this culminating point of perfection, and who are said to have expired with a very similar phrase in their mouths to that recorded of one of the Caesars on his head- *"Ut puto Deus for"*. This state of existence has in general been represented to mean merely annihilation, but this is not in the case; such at least is not the idea that Buddhists attach to it. Crawford in his *"Ava"*, Vol. II, Appendix, No.II., page 140 says that this misconception has thrown an unmerited share of obloquy on the worship of Buddha. Dr. Buchanan remarks that the term has been incorrectly translated *(Asia Research,* Vol. VI., p. 189); and Coleridge defined it correctly in his "Essay on the Philosophy of Indian Secraties" (*R.A.S.* Trans., Vol I, p.556). We say that God is Heaven. And the Buddhists also believe that "Nirban" they are incorporated with God, absorbed in, and partaking of, the perfection and ecstatic calm surrounding and emanating from the great power of the universe.

Religious Rites

Before their conversion to Buddhism, they probably performed the same simple natural religious rites which we see to this day among the wilder hill tribes, that is, offerings of rice, fruit and flowers, to the spirits of hill and river. This custom, indeed, although very unorthodox, is followed by most of the Khyoungtha at the present time. There is no such thing as caste among them; all are equal. It is in the poser of any one who feels a vocation for it, to devote himself to the service of God, and become a "Raheyn". He will then leave father, mother, wife, and children; and dependent for clothes and daily bread upon his fellow countrymen he will pass his time in parayer, the education of the young, and the ministration of such ceremonies as funerals, fasts,&c., in which his fellow-men require the sanction and assistance of a minister of religion. Neither is it "once a priest, always a priest". For should he find out that he has mistaken his vocation, he can leave it, and again become a member of the laity, living, loving and marrying as they do.

The ceremonies of Buddhistic worship are simple and few; the presence of a priest is not indispensably necessary; prayers are made of offerings of flowers, food, &c. are placed before the shrine of their great apostle Gaudama by the people themselves. In many villages, indeed, there is no priest; and as the priesthood are a peripatetic fraternity, this does not much matter. The priest in fact is not so much a minister of religion, as a recipient of alms, holy man who has given up this world and its pleasure, and devoted himself to God. Hence it is I think that the priesthood in Burmah have never been the gasping an ambitious body that they have been at one time or another in all other counties in the world; hence, also, that in the struggle between Buddhism and Brahmanism. The former, the pure and self denying fell before popularity seeking religion of the Hindoo priest. Buddhism is a leveling faith. In matters relating to man and his soul it admits of no distinctions; there is no royal road to Paradise, the only superiority of man over man is gained by virtue and good deeds. No one can go among a people professing the Buddhist faith with seeing their superiority in manliness, truth, self-denial, and all the sterner, nobler class of moral excellences. These characteristics have naturally operated strongly in raising the social status of the weaker sex; and honourable position. Among our hill Buddhists, women are respected, and occupy an honourable position. They enjoy great freedom of action, and are unmistakably a power among the people. They as well as the other sex, can work out their own salvation and attain 'Nirban'. In many parts of the hills may be seen aged women, whop in the close of their life have devoted themselves to God's service; they occupy separate houses, however, and do into live in the "khiongs", or temples.

The Khiong

In each village is seen the "khiong", or house or religion. It is bamboo structure raised some six feet from the ground, generally built under the shade of some trees, with a clear space in front, where the young men disport themselves in the evening. Inside, on a small raised platform of bamboo stands an image of Gaudama, the last Boodh, made either of wood pagoda shaped head-dress indicative of supreme power. Before it are placed offerings of flowers and rich, which are brought fresh every morning by the girls of the village, who at the same time, bring, in covered trays, the daily food of any priest or wayfarer who may be resting there. Around the youngsters learn to read and write. By the side of the image of Boodh generally hangs a small stand of bells, and in morning and evening the villagers in twos and threes will ascend the small log of wood, cut into steps, by which the "khiong" is approached, remove their turbans, and no hands and knees reverently salute the semblance of their revered teacher, first ringing the bells to let him know that they are there. Each on prays for himself, save that now and again a father may be seen leading his young son by the hand and teaching him how to pray. The "khiong" is the great resort of all the bachelors of the village; it is there that all the talk and gossip goes on. At evening time, when the sun westers, and it grow cool, they assemble at the "khiong", the lads and lasses play sit above and the game derives its name, is the seed of a creeper, in colour and smooth- ness like our English horse chestnut; it is about an inch and a half in diameter; and half an inch thick, in shape circular and flattish, with a small level spot at the base of the seed on which it is placed edgewise for the players to pitch at. Each player has his won "konyon" the great art is to nick your opponent and knock his seed over. The knoyon" is propelled by the middle finger of the right hand, which serves as a sort of spring pulled back by the left. The side gaining most nicks and wins.[20]

Shiang Pruhdo

Every year at the "khiong" just before the commencement of the jooming season, the ceremony of "shiang pruhdo" occurs. This is a religious rite, approaching closely in significance to our "confirmation". The young boys of the village, on attaining the age of eight or nine years, are clothed in the yellow garments of the priesthood, have their heads shaved, and at the "khiong" go though a ceremony which seems to be on their part and at the "khiong" go though a ceremony which seems to be on their par a kind of assumption of religious duties. They sit all in a circle before the priest; before each one is an offering according to the means of his par-ebts, of rice, of cloth, and before each burns a little lamp, which is kept trimmed land bright during the ceremony by the sponsor, or nearest male relative of each, who sits behind; each of the acolytes reverently joins his hands, bows his head, and makes the responses after the presiding priest-After the ceremony they remain in the "khiong" dressing and living as priests for seven days, during which time they must eat simply, and in- dulge in no sports or vain pastimes. Women do not participate in this rite, but it is common for a man to perform it tow or three times during his life. Is any one dear to him sick, or has he escaped form any danger, he performs the "shiang" as a kind of acknowledge of God's mercy, or a supplica- tion for bearance. In the Hill Tracts, besides the small "khiongs" (temporary structures built of bamboo), which are found in every village, there are two temples sacred to

Budha, to which the hill people resort in large numbers at the time of their festival in May. One temple is situated at Bundrabun, the residence of the Bohmongm, and the other in the Chittagong District, Thannah Raojan, close to the border of the Hill Tracts. This latter temple is known by the name of Mahamunnee. This would appear to be a name brought form Aracan, for Colonel Phayre, in his *Account of Arracan*[21], says that "King Tasandsa-thoo- veeya built of Mahamunnee temple Arracan in honour of a visit Boodh Gaudarma. I have frequently been present at these religious gatherings, and the scene is a strange one.

An account of a visit paid by me last year to religious festival at the Mahamunnee temple may not perhaps be out of place here. On arriving at the spot, the first thing that attracted my attention was the temple. It was square in shape, standing in the centre of small bricked court, the outer wall of which, however, was not more than five feet high, so that one could look over it. I ascertained that there was no objection to may entering the temple, and then proceeded to view the interior. The center was occupied by an enormous setting figure of gaudama, the last Boodh, of about 50 feet in height, prainted and gilt. This was the inner shrine, ad round it ran a square vaulted corridor, on all four sides, about 12 feet broad and perhaps 150 feet square. On entering this outer corridor which being but scantily furnished with windows, was in comparative darkness, I saw before me a shavenheaded yellow robed priest, sitting the ground, surrounded by a crouching circle of devotees. The bowed had of the postulants were shaven, the through their hands, form man to man, ran, a white thread, the tow ends of which were held by the priest, who with an unmoved aspect, undisturebed by my entrance, was monotonously reciting a prayer or invocation, which was repeated in a broken jumble by the persons before and around him. At his feet was a small heap of money, doubtless the offerings of the neophytes; and before each man was a vessel of water containing fresh green leaves.

Dress and Habits

The devotees were males of all ages: some boys of eight to ten, some adult, and one old man. I found that this ceremony was a dedication of themselves to the service of Gaudams, involving a course of fasting and abstinence form all secular amusements and thoughts for a short period, generally of nine days, answering, I fancy, to the French 'neuaine'. After theyhad been duly consecrated, they assumed the yellow garments of the priesthood, to be doffed, however, at the expiration of their period of retirement. The ceremony is, believe, by no means penitential one; but it is supposed that an occasional exercise of self-discipline is pleasing to the diety, and likely to bring good forturne, specially, when, as at present, it is performed at the commencement of the year. The place of the gathering lay just at the junction of the planes and hill; and form both directions, as the day drew on and the shadows began to lengthen, characteristics groups began to make their appearance. From the plains came the well known greasy bunniah in his chronic condition of perspiration; the plausible cloth merchant (when native can adjust a turban like him?); the black and sinewy coppersmith; and the general store keeper: this latter being generally a Musulman of middle of age and debauched appearance. These all began to establish themselves in temporary bamboo sheds or shanties, which my atleast were the different bands of hill people, who might be seen coming in, party after party, form the direction where in the distance rose the wooded hills blue against the horizon.

Their parties were always village communities, numbering form eight to ten up to thirty individuals, first would be seen the drummer, who advance with the proud consciousness of leadership to a spirted accompaniment to the tom tom. Next came the village head man, or Roaja, dressed in clean, white, home spun garments, with his scarlet bordered cloth wound round his shoulders, toga fashion. After him would his wife, middle aged but still to the comely presence. She would generally have a flower in her hair, and carry in one hand an earthern- bowled pipe with silver stem. Following lowing her, one by one, would troop in the maidens, dressed very becomingly, with a white turban loosely bound round their heads, their faces (very pretty ones in some cases) exposed, bearing a merry, frank expression while form their luxuriant black hair would peep a flower, a lemon-coloured or child, or some bright jungle creepers blossom. They wore a dark blue skirt of home spun cloth with a scarlet border. Round their bosoms was wound a soft, white cloth barred with chaocolate colored stripes; and in case the girls were of wealthy family they would have a silver chain round their necks, or wear perhaps a skirt of purple silk instead of dark blue home spun. Sometimes a young lady would be seen saucily puffing a roll of tobacoo, cigar fashion, while she turn to talk, over her shoulders, to some tall, strapping young villager, betrothed perhaps, who would walk quietly in the rear, carrying on his back, slug over his forehead, in hill fashion, the long basket, or 'tooroong', containing the supplies of his party. There were generally more women than men in the parties, and some of them had even brought with them their little ones to share in the good luck which was to accrue to the pilgrim. Night closed in, and still party after party thronged to the place in close succession. As each village company arrived they defiled before the temple, not entering however, but each one making a salute with both hands joined as thy passed, and then proceed-ing to take up their quarters under the trees around. There they lit fires; the women began to cook; and the social pipe was passed form hand to hand. As I went to sleep that night wind, mingled with the melody of the hill 'basuli', or clarioned, and interspersed with the wild hill cry, which is like a quadruplicated Australian 'Cooey'. The sound of the basuli strangely reminded me of the Swiss Ranz des Vaches.

Festivals

The next morning the fest a was in full wing. The temple was surrounded by a fringe of saffron robed, shaven headed priests, or 'Shiang Phras', as they are called, sitting in dulleyed abstraction each one under shade of his own enormous red umbrella. Some of them were telling their heads: others, spectascles on nose, were gravely mumbling forth sacred readings form bundles of strange Pali covered palm leaves; here and there noticed a repletion of the searing in ceremony of the night before. The temple was crammed with devotees, male and female hill people, everyone, not a Bengali among them. Their devotion, which was energetic, consisted apparently in walking round and round the other corridor surrounding the image, in pairs of man and maid, or occasionally in male fours were organized squalls were imminent, for the young bachelors, each with a flower behind his left ear, a basuli in his hand and roll or tobacco in his mouth, would jauntily parade round the sacred building, stretching forth a lawless arm towards any female thy might pass, now disarranging the turban of some buxom matron again snatching a kiss from some little maiden shrinking under the wind of her father or brother and naturally these little familiarities would occasionally produce a row. Immediately, however, any such disagreement seemed impending, both parties would be seized and promptly bundled out of the temple, while the women would be surrounded and carried round and round the corridor, in the midst of a knot of laughing, teasing lads. The majority of the people at the fair were young; hardly a single old man of woman, a single old man or woman, indeed, could be seen.

Outside, in the bazaar, the throng was equally close. Here were shops whose whole stock-in-trade consisted of long strings of small, yellow candles and heaps of crackers; there was a vendor, who dealt, to all ape-pearance, exclusively in red threads, strings of colored beads, and cheap fiddles. The sweetmeat shops came out in magnificent style, and here one would often see some well looking lad treating his sweetheart to cakes, or loitering, hand in hand with her, to the next stall where in rich and dazzling profusion were displayed bright yellow silk handkerchiefs, with a flaring red pattern, a define, white muslins such as could not be made at home in the villages. One enterprising speculator had brought higher peep show, evidently the first thing of the sort that had ever been seem in the country in one might judge by the crowds of men and women round it, all eager to see, at one pice peep, the marvels of Delhi, Calcutta etc contained with the magic box. The shops of the coppersmiths glistened with all sorts of shining and quaintly shaped vessels, while above all the din and glamour was heard the never cessing, wailing melody of the hill basuli. The music has a strange and characteristics effect on the hill people. I have seen women weep at the sound, and no hill man would dream of entering upon a courtship without the aid of this basuli. At night the scene was rendered, if possible, more picturesque by the lighting up of innumerable small candles, of which every one carried one, and some enthusiastic worshippers as many as four. Crackers also added to the life of the scene, and to fasten one to a woman's dress seemed to be thought as great fun here as it would have been at an English fair.

Round and round went the stream of pilgrims in the outer corridor, singing as they went in strophe and anti-strophe of male and female voices. Not for a single hour, day or night, was there as far as I could ascertain, any intermission to this constant circling; as some became tired, their places were supplied by others, and this lasted for three days. On the day on which the fair terminated, some six or eight long bamboos, with pendant white flags of coarse cotton cloth, ornamented with a fringe of split bamboo, were erected with great ceremony in front of the temple. I saw one village community also of about thirty souls, who, before leaving underwent a blessing from one of the priests. The ceremony was in this wise:- A small hole was dug in the ground and in it some silver and copper coins were place, and water poured over this was erected a small tripod of split bamboo, which was crowned with fresh, green leaves, and round this again was wound the mystic white thread, chich extending thence, passed through the hands of all the circle, who received it kneeling, passing finally into the hands of the Shiang Phara. In the centre knelt the village headman and his wife both elderly and honest looking. Mumble mumble went the venerable priest, dragging his beads slowly throuth his fingers, and' make haste, father, cried a pretty, coquettish looking little wench it was soundly rated by the house mother at the conclusion of the ceremony. An hour after the whole grove was empty, and all the gay crowd of honest, simple people had disappeared as quickly as they had come; nothing was to be seen but a stray shopkeepers here and there, packing his gods, of reckoning his profits.[23]

Dress of the Khyoungtha

The dress of the Khyoungtha is simple. The men wear a "dhoyak", or cloth of soft, home-spun cotton, round the middle, reaching from the hips to blow the knee. In persons of rank the "dhoyak" is longer, reaching almost to the around, and generally made of silk or fine muslin; to this added a "ranjee," or short jacket with sleeves, tying or buttoning at the throat. All males wear the "goungboung", or turban, which however, is wound round the head in the manner different to that of the natives of Hindoostan. As a rule, no shoes are worn. The women generally do not wear a turban, but on feast or festival days they bind a bright colored keredef loosely round the hair. Around the bosom is wound a cloth about a span wide, the arms the neck being exposed. They wear also a "tabween" (called " tanuin" in Burmese), or petticoat of cotton or silk. It has no tie or fastening, but is brought round the waist with the edges twisted in the depth on by the swell of the hips. It open front, and singles, so that in walking the ritht leg and part of the thigh are exposed. The men often tattoo their arms and legs with blue figures of dragons and other arebesques; it is usual slow the tattoo the name of God on the shoulder. This custom of tattooing originated, they say, in ancient times among the people of Sandoway in Arracan, an well as thesome what free dress of the women. A certain queen noticed with regret that the men of the nation were looking their love and abominable practices, from which the worst possible result might be expected. She therefore prevailed upon her husband to promulgate a rigorous order, prescribing the reform of petticoat to be worn by all women in future, and directing that the males should be tattooed in order that, by thus disflguirng the males, and adding piquancy to the beauty of the women, the former might once more return to the feet of their wives.

This custom, however, as regards women's dress is probabley of very ancient origin, for it is recorded in Plutarch's *Lives*, in this comparison between Numa and Lycurgus, with reference to the Spartan women, that "the skrits of the babit which the virgins wore were not sewed to the bottoms, but opened at the sides as they walked, and discovered the thigh.[24]

Flowers

Men and women both among the Khyoungtha are passionately fond of flowers; it is the offering of women to the gods, of men to their mistress. The young maidens wear constantly in their hair the graceful white or orange colored blossom of the numerous orchids with which the forest abounds; and a young man will rise long before dawn and climb the loftiest hills and trees to win his sweet heart's smile, by bringing her a flower that others do not possess. The males generally stick a bunch of flowers of sweet smelling herbs into the turban, or through the lobe of the ear, which is generally perched with a large hole, which serves also as a receptacle for a spare cheroot.

Of ornaments, both sexes alike wear pendant, earrings and bracelets of silver or gold. The women in addition large truncated hollow cones of silver stuck thought the lobe of the ear; these are used as flower holders. Bead of cored for the neck are also much prized as a female ornament. Their mode of kissing is strange: instead of pressing lip to lip, they apply the mouth and nose to the cheek, and give a strong inhalation. In their language they do not say, " give me a kiss" ; "Smell me."[25]

Goung or Bachelors Dormitory

In the village communities, ever as the adults have a recognized village head, so also is there a head boy appointed to control the boys of the village. This custom seems to prevail among all hills people. Mr. Hunter, in his *Annals of Rural Bengal* (page 217), records that a similar arrangement prevails among the Sonthals. This head of the juvenile community is called the "goung" . I shall give here, an illustration of their village customs, a recital which I heard told at the camp fire one night in the jungles, by one of our placement of the Palingtsa clan. He said, "I will formerly goung over the unmarried lads of Hrraphroo village; this was when I was about 17 years old. At night, all who were unmarried, and weaned from their mother, use to sleep in the 'khiong'. One night Oygiyn, and Reyphew, and Chaindra, came to me and got leave to go and sleep with their sweet hearts. The girls were named Aduhbyn, Hiapyn, and Adushsheay. I remember their names quite well; they are married now, and two of them have children. Our lads went by stealth, of course: if the parents had known it there would have been a row. Next day a little girl told me that Pyrha, another of our lads, who had not got leave to sleep out, had passed the night with her sister. This was quite contrary to rule, and it was therefore determined to punish him. Next day we all went to the Roaja's joom to help to build his house, and it the evening, when we returned, we made a big fire on the bank of the stream that runs through the village; and I sent and called Pynhal, but he was afraid, and would not come; he stayed in his father's house and said he had fever. I knew that was only an excuse, so I sent three lads to bring him forcibly, and they went brought him, although his mother abused him much; but the father and mother could not hurt them, as they were acting by the "goung's order. When he came, I called upon him to say why he had slept away form the 'khiong' without leave. At first he denied all about it, and then I brought forward the little girl, and he asked her, 'how did he know it was I; it was dark'; and she said, 'The moon shone of your face in the early morning when you opened the door to go away'. When he heard this he saw there was no escape, and he fell at my feet and asked forgiveness; but I fined him three rupees on the spot for the sake of discipline. In Colonel Dalton's paper on the 'Coles of Chota Nagpore', he speaks of their being in each village of the Oraoon tribe a bachelor's hall where all the young unmarried men sleep at night. He mentions also the elder lads are placed in authority over the younger in front of the bachelor's hall a cleared space is kept for games and dancing It is curious to observe how similar are the customs among the tribes here.

According to the European ideas, the standard of molarity among the Khyoungtha is low. It is not thought a crying sin for a maiden to yield to the solicitations of her lover before marriage; indeed, a girl generally has two or three sweet hearts before settling down to a wedded life. The intercourse between the sexes before marriage is almost entirely unrestricted, although the Khyoungtha in this respect are rather stricter than the other and wilder tribes. After marriage, however, a chastity is the rule, and one seldom hears of such an unfaithful wife; and this is not improbable, as marriages in the hills are unions of inclination, and not of interest. Some girls there are who marry their first love, but the proverbial inconstancy of men extends even to these hills, and the lover too often only gathers the flower in order to throw it away. Girls marry at the age of about sixteen and a youngman generally begins to think of taking a wife before he reaches the age of nineteen. The women sometimes do not think it beneath them to make advances in a modest way. One of our police constables came to me one day to ask for leave of absence for a week. I asked him why he said, "a young maiden of a village has sent me flowers and brine rice twice as a token, and if I wait any longer, they will say I am no man."[26]

Love Songs

"Pawn" and betel are universally eaten by Khyoungthas, and they are not unfrequently used as a means where with to make amatory propositions. Thus a leaf of pawn with betel and sweet spices inside, accompanied by a certain flower, means, "I love you" . If much spice is put inside that leaf, and one corner turned in a peculiar way, it signifies, "Come". The leaf being touched with turmeric means, "I cannot come". A small piece of charcoal inside the leaf is, "Go, I have done with you". Love songs have they in plenty, called "kapya' . The great place for singing this kind of song is when working in the jooms at the time of harvest. At this time the lads and lasses work in a crowd together. Then some youth will take up the work thus:

The hills stretch in long ranges marshaled by God.
The kramoo flower and dymbyn, Oh, maidens, do not sow.
The cockecomb (kramoo) and the dyn flowers
Even should you sow. Midens, do not wear them:
The kramoo and dyn flowers, if worn,
As they fade, a maiden's heart withers away.

As he finishes, the whole party break into the "hois", hill call; and far away down the mountain, or from an another ridge, call will be repeated and taken up by hill man after hill man, till it dies away in the distance. Then there will be little silence among the girls, and they will say, "Do you answer him, Pynchynde?" No. I cannot sing: I am hoarse today, I have not got my voice, and he is in voice like a koel – bird; and jest and counter-jest will be a bandied among them, until some young girl lifts up her voice and replies:-

A dweller in the mountain is the bumble bee;
He lives in a dead bamboo,
On the hill side,
Then a young man will sing again thus:-
Form a far off I see the waters of the kynsa,
White in the valley
What good have I from gazing on it,
Some other will bathe therein

(All give the "hoia".)

From afar off gazing, I see a maiden;
White and farir is she.
What good have I from looking on her,
Some more fortune one will obtain her love.
(Grand "hoia".)

Or this:-
A flock of birds;
One brid only, on a high tree sitting
All alone.
Of men,only,without a companion,
Has no happiness.

There are hundreds of these songs. The above,which are almost literal translations, will serve as examples.

The marriage ceremony of the Khyoungtha is distinctive and uncommon.[27]

Marriage Ceremony

On a young man attaining a marriageable age, that is, about seventeen or eighteen, his parents look about for some young girl's who would be a good wife to him, unless, as is more often the case, he has fixed upon a partner for himself. Having determined upon a suitable match, a male relative of the family is sent off to the girls parents to arrange matters. On arriving at their village, he proceeds to the house; and before going up the houses ladder, he give the usual salutation with both hands joined and raised to the forehead. "Ogatsa", he says, "a boat has come to your landing place; will you bind it or loose it? A favourable response is given, and he then goes up into the house. On seating himself, he asks, "Are the supports of the house firm"? If the answer is, "They are firm," it is favourable, matters may be then be more fully entered into. The affair is taken into consideration, and he returns to his own village to report good progress to the bridegroom's parents, and request them to fix a day for taking the omens. On the appointed day the parents meet, the young people being supposed to know nothing of all this. A fowl is killed by the fathers, its tongue taken out, and according to certain marks there on, the matter is pronounced good or bad. The bridegroom's parents sleep for the night at the house of the intended bride, and all parties look anxiously for dreams by which to foretell the happines or the reverse of the union. On going away, should every thing be propitious, their intended daughter kneels at their feet for a blessing, and they present her with a new petticoat and a silver ring. Learned persons are then called in, who, by consulting the stars, and casting the nativity of the parties, determine a favourable day and hour when the ceremony shall be undertaken. Meantime the parents on both sides prepare pigs and sprits, rice and spices, unlimited, for the marriage feast. They also send round to all their kith and kin a fowl and a letter giving notice of the intended marriage; in some places a pice or copper coin substituted for the fowl. On the auspicious day, and the hour appointed, the bridegroom and his relatives set out for the bride's house,dressed in the gayest colours, both men and women, with drums beating before them. On arriving at the entrance of the village, the female relatives of the bride fix bar the approach with a bamboo. Across this barrier the bridegroom has to dirnk a loving cup of fraternity, generally sprits. Should the females on the bride's side muster stong, the road will probably be barred five or six times before the entry into the village is fairly made. The bridegroom, however, does not drink all that is given him; but after taking the liquour in his mouth, he is allowed to eject it again upon the ground.

In the village, on some open turfy spot a number of bamboo booths have been erected, adorned with flowers and green boughs, and filled with materials for feasting. Here also sit an oopposition party of summers, and mighty is the row as the bridegroom's party defiles on to this spot. A separate and specially beautified booth has been erected for the young lover and his parents, and there they sit in ate and receive visits from the village. The bride in like manner, surrounded by her near relatives, sits in her father's house. The boys of the village, irrespressible as is wont of that species, make faids upon both parties, for the of chaffing and getting alternate feats of comestibles. They also organize an amateur band of music, and serenade the bride towards evening with fiddles and flutes. Of course, all the girls of the village are congregated at the bride's father's and as license and roit are the order of the day, the fun here grows fast and flourish. Towards nightfall the bridegroom ascends to his bride's house amid a tempest of cheers and hailstorm of drums. After this a outburst a temporary lull ensues, to permit of the ceremony being performed. The bride is brought forth forman inner chamber in the arms of the women.On the floor of house are placed water in jars, rice, and mango leaves. Round these a new spun cotton thread is wound and carried again round the two contracting parties as they stand opposite of each other. The "poorgyee", or priest, now comes forward; he recites some prayers in language that is not understood even by himself (probably Pali), and then taking cooked rice, a handful in each hand, he crosses and recrosses his arms, giving seven alternate mouthfuls to the bride's left. The ceremony is then concluded by more unintelligible mutterings. The bridegroom now takes the bride by the hads, and together they make the circuit of the room, bride together. The wedding guests then come forward and place at their feet, each according to his or her means, some presents of clothes or household furniture.

After this, a saturnalia ensues, of dancing, drinking, fighting and love making. The bride and bridegroom are expected to sit up all night. I should add that the happy man does not consummate his marriage until he and his wife (sleeping apart) have for seven days eaten together seven times a day. After marriage a younger brother is allowed to touch the hand, to speak and laugh with this elder brother's wife; but it is thought improper for an elder even to look at the wife of his younger brother. This is a custom more or less among all hill tribes; it is found carried to even a preposterous extent among the Sonthals. In Man's *Account of Sonthalia* (p.100), in describing a Sonthal wedding, he says, "I remarked with surprise the alarming familiarities displayed by the youthful brother of the bridegroom to the bride, and was told that it was custom for the younger brother, if unmarried, to take the face of his elder brother's bride."

Funeral

From marriage to death is not very long stride. The moment we begin to live, we begin to die. Marriage is generally the half way hose between the womb of our mother and the bosom of Terra Mater.

When a person has died, his relatives assemble. Some one of them sits down and commences to beat the funeral roll on the drum; the women weep and cry; and the men busy themselves, some in performing the last offices to the corpse, of washing, dressing, etc, while others go off to the woods and bring wood for the funeral pile, and bamboos, with which to construct the bier. About twenty four hours generally elapse from the time of death to that of cremation. In bearing the corpse from the house to the burying ground, if the deceased were a man of wealth or influence, the body may be borne on a wheeled car, all women also have this privilege; the plebs, however, are simply carried to the funeral pile on the shoulders of their relatives. The procession is after this fashion:- first come the priests, if there are any in the vicinity to attend; they march gravely at the head of the party, bearing on their shoulders their curved palm leaf fans, clad in their ordinary saffron colored robes, and attended by their disciples. Next come relatives of the deceased, two and two, bearing food, clothes etc., which have been offered as alms to the priests on behalf of the departed. Next is borne the bier carried on bamboos by six men and accompanied by as many drums as can be procured. Behind the coffin come the male relatives; and lastly, the procession is closed by the women of the village, clad in their best. The funeral pile is composed of four layers of wood for a woman, three for a man. The body is placed on the pile; the leading priest takes an end of the dead man's turban and, holding it, repeats some passages of the law, four of the deceased's male relatives standing meanwhile at the four corners of the pile, and sprinkling a few drops of water thereon. The nearest blood relative male, or female, of the dead man then fires the pile. When the fire is extinguished, the ashes are scrupulously collected together and buried over the spot: a small conical mound of earth is heaped up, and a very long bamboo pole, with an equally lengthy flag, is erected over the grave. On returning from the place all parties bathe themselves. It is the master of the house who has died, the ladder leading up the house is thrown down, and they must effect an entrance by cutting a hole in the back wall and so creeping up. The relatives drink, and each contributes according to his means to defray the expenses incurred. After seven days the priests reassemble at the house to read prayers for the dead.[28]

Elopement

It is by no means an uncommon thing for a young man to elope with his sweet heart, should the consent of the parents be difficult of attainment. I remember one young fellow, who, having made a runaway match of this description, came to me sanction it; and his account of the proceeding was very curious, and threw much light on their village life. He said, "When I reached the village, it was nightfall; the village was empty, for the grain was now ripening, and every one was up in the jooms; so I stayed that night in the house of Akra, in his joom. In the morning the house mother woke me, saying, "Hasten, get up; wash your face and make yourself smart, for today the girls of the village come here to reap our crop." I looked down the hill, hearing the hoia (hill call) far away down the slope, and saw the girls coming, and the young men with them; so I hastened and tied my hair behind in a knot and put a silver bangle on my arm and a gold bead hanging at my neck and tied on my white turban sprucely for these are the fashions of the Kowkdyntsa clan; and if one wants to get on with the people, one must conform to their customs. Then they arrived, and we all went out to cut the rice. After a time one young girl said to a companion, 'Pynchainda, sing to us'; so she sang and afterwards she said, turning to me, "Here is a young Plaingtsa come to see us. How bashful he is, and how young ; When is he going to be married, I wonder;' and all the girls began making fun, until I was quite ashamed and could hardly cut the grain; the blood went all into my head. Then some one said, 'Sing to us, O brother'; So I sang, and they said, 'you sing well, sit you on that knoll and sing to us while we work;' So I did so.

"At noon we had to eat and the young girls came round me, and said, 'You have sung much to us, now you must eat';

bu I replied, 'No. I am not hungry'. Then the house mother said, 'What kind of a maidens are you, to let a guest stand thus making exuses?

Why, when I was girl, we should have taken him by the hand and make him eat.' So five of the girls came and drew me forcibly to where the food was and I said, "If you will all eat out of the same dish with me, then I will ate; 'so they agreed, and spread a mighty platter, and we all eat. They tried at first to feed me; but after a mouthful or two, for courtesy's sake, I said, 'No, at that rate I shall never be satisfied.'

"At night one of the young men said to me, ' come, and we will go out for some fun; so I went. We went upto a joom, where there were two houses in which lived a family of two unmarried sisters – a married one with her husband, and the father and mother. When we came there, my companion said to the girls, 'We have come to eat brine grain; and they said, 'Come in, and we will cook for you; and I said to him, I don't want to eat; he said, ' You do not understand, when I said we have come to eat brine, that meant that we had come to have some fun, if they had been disinclined they would have said the brine is not yet ripe; come up, you don't know our customs:' so we went up and saluted the elders. The house father had been drinking, and he was merry, and called to me and said, 'How are you married? And I said, 'No.' Then he said, laughing, 'if you were married, I should look upon you as good company for me; but as you are a bachelor, you are only good enough for the girls. Quite right: we did the same when we were young.' Presently he and the mother and the married daughter got up and went off to the other house where they slept, and then my companion blew out the light and threw water on the fire. We stayed there all night, to eat 'brine' grain that is polite way of phrasing it; but this is Kowkdynsta custom; we have not got in among the Palaingtsa. I stayed some time in the village, and I took a great liking for Pynchainda; so we settled to run away. That night there was to be a feast at her father's house, and she and I were to have a singing match, for she was the best they killed a pig and feasted. Afterwards we two sat in the middle of the room, opposite to each other, with a large tray of fresh flowers between us; and the liquor went round, and we sang. I put much love in my song; so after a time Pynchainda's heart became full, and she stopped singing, and took flowers and put them on may head; and she rose quickly and went away, saying she would fetch water; and I also got up and went after her, at which everybody began to laugh. When we got outside, she left her water picher on the bank of the stream, and we come straight away through the jungle.[29]

The Chukma Tribe

"Although the majority of this tribe do not speak Arracanese dialect, I have classed them with Khyoungtha, on account of their similarity of habit in the location of their villages on the banks of the streams, in contra-distinction to the other tribes, whom I have called Toungtha, from their living on hills in preference to the low lands.

"The name Chukma is given to this tribe in general by the inhabitants of the Chittagong District, and the largest and dominant section of the tribe recognizes this as its rightful appellation. It is also sometimes spelt Tsakma, or Tsak, or,it is called in Burmese Thek. A smaller section of the same tribe is called Doingnak. The name of Chukma, Tsak, Thek, and Doingnak, may all therefore be taken as names representing the tribe of which I now propose to speak. There is a third division, or clan, called Toungivnyas.

"The orgin of the tribe can only be inferred from their traditions and physique, as they possess no written records of ancient times. Intelligent persons among them, however, have informed me that they came originally from a country called

Chainpango, or Champanugger. As to where this country situated accounts vary somewhat. By some it is said to be near Malacca; this would ascribe to them a Malayu origin: While, on the other hand, there are many they assert that Champanugger is situated far to the north in the North-Western Provinces of Hindostan. Those who hald to this latter view say that they are descended from a Khetris family of the name of Chandra. The facial characteristics of the tribe are indicative of Mongolian, and not Aryan ectraction; and it is moreover, only of late years that the use of Arracanese vernacular has died out among them. The majority of the tribe, however, hold that they are descended from a Hindoo family of Tood caste.

"The story they tell is as follow: The reigning King of Champanugger hand two sons; and the elder of these went forth with a picked body of men to attack King of Mogoda. In the contest he was victorious; but on his turning his face homewards news reached him that his old father had died, and his younger brother had usurped the throne, and prepared to resist his return. On this the elder brother determined to remain in the country he had newly conquered, and accordingly settled in these hills. His followers took wives from among the country people, who were Buddhists; and to this it is attributable that they forsook the religion of their forefathers, and have altered also somewhat in complexion and appearance.

The Khyoungtha, again, have another story of the origin of the Chukma tribes. It is this:- of Chittagong collected together an army to attack the king of Arracan; and as the force went traveling over the hills they came to the hut of a poongyee, a holy man in the wilderness. This poongyee begged the Wuzeer to halt and partake of some refreshment which he would quickly prepare; and to this the Wuzeer consented. After sometime, as the food did not make its appearance, he sent a soldier to the Poongyee's hut to see when it would be ready. The soldier entered the hut and saw that the Poongyee had put rice and flesh in a pot, and had placed the pot over the fireplace; but he noticed with asotonishment that there was no wood in the fireplace: instead there of the Poongyee ahd put his foot under the pot, and faames wer issuing form the tips of his toes. So the soldier returned to the Wuzeer and made his report. On hearing the man's statement the Wuzeer become earaged, and said." At that rate the rice will never be ready; and he gave orders for the march to be recommenced. Consequently, when the old man came out of redeem his pledged hospitality, he found his guest and unceremoniously departed. On this the poongyee waxed very wrath, and he cursed the Wuzeer and all his army and sent forth powerful charms after them so that when they met the King of Arracan troops their hearts turned to water, and they were all made prisoners. The king of Arracan settled all these Mussulmans as slaves in his territory, and gave them wives of the people of the country; and they were increased and multiplied. This was the origin of the Chukma tribe. In corroboration of this story I subjoin a list of Rajahs who have known to have reigned over the tribe, from which it will be seen that the names of Khan, a purely Pathan patronymic, is commonly in use among them.

1. Jumaul Khan.	About 1715 A.D. first paid tribute of cotton to Mogul wuzeer Fumuch Shah.
2. Sheremusta Khan.	
3. Sookdel Roy	A.D. 1737 made settlement with English Government.
4. Shere Dowlut Khan	In 1776 he revolted against Government, and two expeditons were sent against him and Ranoo, or Ramoo

	Khan, his relative, and a chief man of the tribe.
5. Jaunbux Khan	AD. 1782 the cotton tribute reduced to 500 maunds. This chief oppressed the tribe heavily, and many of them fled of Arracan. He also revolted against Government; but in 1787 he made submission. In 1789 the Government determined that the tribute should be paid in money instead of cotton.
6. Tubber Khan	
7. Jubber Khan	
8. Dhurmabux Khan	A.D. 1812, died about 1830
9. Kalindee Ranee	The present head of the tribe (a woman).

Mr. Hodgson (*Journal Bengal Asiatic Society*, No.1 of 1853) opines that the Thek (Chukma) of Arracan are of aboriginal descent. In this view, however, I cannot concur.[29a]

Colonel Phayre treats of the Thek and the Doingnak apparently as if they were two separate tribes. In this idea I venture to think that he is mistaken, as the Doingnaks are known and recognized throughout the tribe as a branch of the Chukmas that abandoned the parent stem during the chiefship of Jaunbux Khan about 1782. The reason of this split was a disagreement on the subject of marriages. The chief passed an order that the Doinuing however, are a now staggloing back, village, on their return to the tribe. Several of their villages are found in the Cox Bazar Hills, are they preserve to this day the remembrance of the places inhabited formerly by their ancestors on the Kurnafoolee river, although from long residence in Arracan their vernacular language is the dialect of that country, and they are comparatively, speaking, ignorant of Bengallee, a bastard dialect of which is spoken by the tribe at large. Colonel Phayre (*J.A.S.* No, 117of 1841) says of the Doingnaks- " they call themselves Kheem-ba-nago. On their descent I could learn nothing; probably they may be the offspring of Bengallees carried into the hills as slaves, where their – physical appearance has been modified by change of climate. In religion they are Buddhists."

Whatever opinion may be formed of the premordial origin of the Thek, or Chukma tribe, no doubt can exist as to their having been at one time inhabitans of the province of Arracaan from whence they have migrated to these hills. The *Radzawrong*, or *History of the Arracan King* give the following account of them. It is there written that King Kaumysing, the son of the King of Barbnathi, having been assigned by his father, as heritage all the country inhabited by the Burman, Shan, and Malay races, came to Ramwati, the ancient capital of Arracan, near the modern town of Hindostan, having a variety of languages. They then asking for subsistence; to the first who so applied he gave the name of Thek, and their language being different from the rest, they lived separate. The Thek tribe appears afterwards to have played a part of some importance in the annals of the Kingdom. King Nyamingnaytain, with the help of the Tsaks, is said to have gained the throne in the year 356 of the Arracan Era. Again, in 656, King Mengdi is said to have undertaken an expedition against the Shans and Tsaks, who had become very troublesome.[30]

The tribe is also mentioned by Buchanan in his paper on the religion and literature of the Burmese.[30a]

The Chukmas are divided into 21 Gozas, or clans. In calling to a Chukma, one does not ask him his caste, that is shown by his face and dress; but it is usual to demand "of what Goza are you?"

Over each Goza there is a Dewan, who represents the head of the family, from which his clan originally sprung. Among the Toungiynyas this hereditary head is called the Ahoon. He collects the pool tax (the sole hill revenue), and retaining a certain fixed proportion thereof, pays the remainder to the chief of the tribe, together with a yearly offering of first certain fees, the amount of which is prescribed by custom (of these more hereafter). The Dewan also receives as a right a portion of any wild animal, fit for food, that may be killed by any of his people. When the Goza is a large one, the Dewan appoints several subordinates under him to assist in the administration; these officers are called "Khejas". They are exempt from the payment of revenue, and from the "corvee", or unpaid labour, to which the rest of the tribe are liable; but every year they are bound to present to their Dewan an offering of one measure of rice, one bamboo tube of sprits, and one fowl. Their office does not appear to be hereditary.

Religion

The religion professed by the Chukma tribe is Buddhism. But their propinquity to, and constant contact with, the Bengallees, has caused them to mingle with their pure and aesthetic rites much that appertains to Hindoo superstition. They have not as yet imbibed, I am thankful to say, any prejudices as to caste, but many signs and tokens manifest their gravitation towards Hindooism. They have for the most part abandoned the Arracanese vernacular, they observe the Luckhee and Doorga Poojahs, both purely Hindoo festivals. They consult Hindoo astrologers, and have begun to find out that they are descended from the caste of Khettries in Hindoostan.[32]

Festivals

They observe eight festivals of their own during the year.

These holy times are common to, and observed alike by, both the Khyoungtha and the Chukmas; and it may be that they are followed by Buddhists generally: but on this point I am not able, neither is it necessary, for me to speak the Bishoo is the chief festival in the year. At that time, as I have previously described, all classes, men and women alike, resort to the Mahamuni temple to make offerings at the shrine of Gaudama, to give gifts to each other, and rejoice. This festival occurs in the month of April. In the month of July of Sadhang begins. This is a time of fasting, when persons who wish to do meritorious actions give alms, and bind themselves by a a vow to abstain from some particular pleasure, such as good eating, fine clothes, their wife's society, or the like. The fast continues for three months; and for that period the priests are bound to remain stationary at whatever place they may be, and continuously to recite the law and chant the praises of Gaudama. The Tummungtong is a feast at the close of this fast. Magiri is a time of festival when the rice begins to ripen, and when prayers are offered up that no harm may befall the crop. The Hoia and Nowarno occur in October. This is a season of much feasting, corresponding to our harvest home. The Chukmas at his season have curious custom of suspending seven breast cloths (worn by their women) from a lofty pole erected in the village, at the foot of which sacrifice is offered. This is the time of eating the new rice. The Kheyrey and Tsoomoolang are festivals of minor importance, and of no fixed date. The Shonghasa is the worship of the "nats", or deities of wood and stream. The priests have nothing to do with this, and has been condemned as an unorthodox practice. The sacrifice is either offered by the votary himself in person, or an "ojha", or exorcist, is called in to perform the necessary ceremonies.

'At a Chukma village I was once present when sacrifice was thus offered by the head man. The occasion was childbirth. The offering consisted of a sucking pig and fowl. The altar was of bamboo decorated with young plantain shoots and leaves. On this raised platform were placed small cups containing rice, vegetables, and a sprit distilled from rice. Round the whole from the house-mother's distaff had been spun a long white thread, which encircled the altar, and then, carried into the house, was held at its two ends by the good man's wife. The sacrifice commenced by a long invocation uttered by the husband, who stood opposite to his altar, and between each snatch of his charm he taped the small platform with his knife, and uttered a long wailing cry; this was for the purpose of attracting the numerous wandering spirits who go up and down upon the earth, and calling them to the feast. When a sufficient number of these invisible guests were believed to be assembled, he cut the throats of the victims with his 'dao' and poured a libation of blood upon the altar and over the thread. The flesh of the things sacrificed was afterwards cooked and eaten at the household meal, of which I was invited to partake.

The social customs of the Chukmas are on the whole very similar to those of the Khyoungtha.

Marriage Negotiations

When a child is born the mother is looked upon as impure for one month afterwards. A male child is preferred to a female. On the birth of a son guns are fired, and a feast is given; not so when a daughter is brought into the world. There seems to be no particular ceremonies in the naming of a child; a name is usually given that has been borne by some ancestor. Children are generally suckled by their mothers for a long time; it is not uncommon to see a boy of three years old sharing his mother's milk with a young infant. Girls reach puberty at the age of thirteen, and boys at fourteen or fifteen years. When a lad becomes fit, he goes out to cut his first joom; this is a sign of manhood among them, and the parents are bound in honour to give a feast to all their relatives on this occasion. Child marriages among the Chukmas, or indeed among the hill people in general, are unknown; there is no fixed time for getting married. Some of the young men indeed do not marry until they reach the age of twenty four or twenty five; after that age, however, it is rare to see a man unmarried. Marriage is after this fashion. Father, mother, and son, first look about them and fix upon a bride; this indispensable preliminary accomplished, the parents go to the house where their intended daughter-in-law resides. They take with them a bottle of sprits (this is an absolute necessary in every hill prayer). The matter will at first be opened cautiously; the lad's father will say, "That is a fine tree gowing near house, I would fain plant in its shadow." Should all go well, they retire after mutual civilities. Both in going and coming omens are carefully observed; and many a promising match has been put a stop to by unfavourable auguries. A man or woman carrying fowls, water, fruit, or milk, if passed on the right hand, is a good omen, and pleasant to meet with; but it is unfavourable to see a vulture, or to see one crow all by himself, croaking on the left hand if they are unfortunate enough to come upon the dead body of any animal on their road they will go no further, but at once return home and stop all proceedings. Old people quote numerous stories to how that the disregard of unfavourable omens has in former times been productive of the most ruinous consequences.

By the time a second visit is due, the relatives on both sides have been consulted; and if all has progressed satisfactorily, and there are no dissentient voices, they go accompanied by some of the girls of the village, taking with them presents of curds and "birnee" grain, and "jogra", a sweet fermented liquor made from rice. Then a day is settled (after the harvest is a favourite time), and a ring of betrothal is given to the bride. Now also is arranged what price the young man is to pay for his wife, for the Chukmas in contradistinction to all other tribes, buy their wives. The ordinary price is 100 to 150 rupees. On the marriage day a large stock of provisions is laid by both houses. A procession of men and women starts from the bridegroom present there intended daughter with her marriage dress. No ceremony, however, is performed; and the bride, after a short interval, is taken away, accompanied by all her relatives to her new home.[33]

On arriving all enter the house, and the bride and bridegroom sit down together at a small table–the bride on the left hand of her husband. On the table are eggs, sweetmeats, rice and plantains, all laid out on leaf platters. The best man (sowalla) sits behind the bridegroom, and the bride had a representative bridesmaid (sowalee) behind her. These two then bind a round the couple a muslin scarf, asking, "Are all willing, and shall this thing be accomplished?" Then asking cry out, "bind them, bind them"; so they are bound. The married pair have now to eat together. The wife feeding the husband and the husband the wife and at this stage of the ceremony a great deal of bashfulness is evinced, the bridesmaid and best man raise the hands of their respective charges to eat from each other's mouths to the intense enjoyment and hilarity of every one present. After they have thus eaten and drunken, and elder of the village sprinkles them with river water, pronounces them man wife, and says a charm used for fruitfulness. The couple then retire, and the guests keep it up until an early hour on the following morning. The next day, at the morning meal, the newly married come hand in hand and salute the elders of their families. The father of the bride generally improved this occasion by addressing a short lecture to his son-in-law on the subject of marital duties. " Take her" , he says, "I have given her to you; but she is young and not acquainted with her household duties.

If therefore at any time you come back from the joom and find the rice burnt, or any thing else wrong her, do not beat her; but at the end to three years, if she still continues ignorant, then beat her, but do not take her life, for if you do I shall demand the price of blood at your hand; but for beating her I shall not hold you responsible, or interfere".[34]

All marriages, however, do not go in this happy fashion; it often happens that the lad and the lass have made up their minds to couple, but the parents will not hear of the match. In such a case the lovers generally elope together; but should the girl's parents be very much set against the match, they have the right to demand back and take their daughter from the hands of her lover. If notwithstanding this opposition, the lover's intentions still remain unaltered, and they elope a second time no one has then the right to interfere with them. The young husband makes a present to his father-in-law according to his means, gives a feast to his new relatives, and is formally admitted into kinship.

Elopements

These elopements in the hills are sometimes the occasion of tragical consequences. A case in point happened in the district the other day among the Chukmas.

A young man, named Boopeea, was in love with a girl called Shonia- Mullah. The girl lived with her old father (her mother was dead) and one brother named Heeradhun. It was joom time, and they all lived together, away from the village in the lonely little house which it is the custom for each family to held in their own joom (this reminds one of Isaiah's solitary "lodge in a garden of cucumbers"). An elder brother, named Jocradhum, lived separately down in the village. He was married. Boopeea loved the girl, and could not keep away from her. He was constantly hanging about the house, helping in the joom, and eating and sleeping in the common room of the house. He was too poor to make the legitimate proposals to the girl's relative, for this course would entail numerous heavy expenses, besides a cash payment of at least 40 rupees. For two years he hung about her, and she loved him. At last they agreed to elope. The rest of the story is best told in the words of Heeradhun, the girl's brother:-

Last Friday, when I came home from work, my father said to me, "where is your sister? She went out some time ago to fetch water and has not returned. I suspect she has run off at last with that worthless fellow Boopeea, who is always hanging about the house". On this I went and called two or three other young men who lived closed by, and we went off after my sister. We met her and Boopeea in the valley by the stream. Hand. Then I was enraged, and ran at Boopeea and cut at him with my dao; he leapt on one side, and the blow fell on my sister. She said once, 'Oh brother' and then fell dead. I knew nothing positive of Shonia and Boopeea being in love, although I suspected it: it is not our custom to make public our love affairs. If Boopeea had applied to the family, and been able to pay the usual sums of money, we would have consulted together, and given him our sister in marriage. He would not have spoken himself; he would have employed a third party: but as he was unable to pay the necessary expense, he ran away with her. It is our custom, in elopements, for the young men of the village to go in the search of the runaway couple. If they catch them, they ask the girl whether she leaves her home voluntarily or whether force has been used. In the former case she is let go, but her husband has afterwards to pay a fine. If they not caught, they get off free, and the elders settle it according to custom."[35]

Among the Toungiynya and Doingnak sections of the tribe, the unmarried lads are all assembled at night in one house under the charge of an elder lad, in the same way as in the Khyoungtha villages. This, however, is not the custom with the Chukmas proper. The lads play at "konyon", the game is known to them as "geela kra." They also play a game resembling our English "touch". Pegtop is a common amusement among them. Cards dice, or gambling for money, are unknown. The Jew's harp has, on its late introduction, gained a high place in the estimation of the junior portion of the community.

In one point in particular the Chukmas differ from the whole of the other hill tribes, viz., that they are averse from changing the sites of their villages. From generation to generation the village is kept at one place; but yet they do not aim at any permanency of structure, the houses being built in hill fashion, of bamboo only, thatched with leaves.

The custom of putting a village in quarantine in case of sickness is universal amongst them. The average duration of life, they say, does not run beyond sixty years, but that formerly disease was much less common among them, and it was not unusual to find men and women attain the age of 90 or even 100 years. They insist, in proof of this, three diseases which have appeared among them within the last two generations:- First, a sickness called " tsana pers". This disease appears first in the form of a low intermittent fever; but attacks increase in frequency until the type changes to remittent, the tongue and throat become ulcerated, delirium sets in, and is followed by death. Second, "nos-bees", or the new poison; this is simply a strong remittent fever. Both these diseases are said to have been unknown until within the last sixty years, and I can quite believe this to be true, as the wilder hill tribes, further east, still enjoy immunity from these attacks. The third disease, which has only lately made its appearance among them, is syphilis. They are well acquainted with herbs and simples, and possess a rough pharmacy of their own; but they have no medicinemen, professionally speaking. The dress of the Chukmas is simi- lar to that of the Khyoungtha, save that the petticoat of the women is of coarse blue and red home-spun, and is worn rather shorter. Their jewellery also is somewhat different in shape.

They burn their dead. In the case to man, the body is burnt with its face to the east, and five layers of wood are used; while a woman is burnt face westward, and seven layers of wood are consumed in the funeral pile. Both the Chukmas and Khyoungtha use more wood to burn dead body of a woman than of a man, and this is curious, as one would imagine that from the greater development of fatty and cellular tissue in women, less combustibles would be required.

On the death of a Dewan or of a priest a curious sport is customary at this funeral. The corpse is conveyed to the place of cremation on a car; to this car ropes are attached, and the persons attending the ceremony are divided into two equal bodies and set to work to pull in opposite directions. One side represents the good spirits; the other, the powers of evil. The contest is so arranged that the former are victorious. Sometimes, however, the young men representing the demons are inclined to pull too vigorously, but a stick generally quells this unseemly ardour in the cause of evil. If possible, at the close of a funeral, there is a display of fireworks, and guns are discharged. If a man is believed to have died from witchcraft, the body, when half burned, is divided down the chest. A post, pole, or some other portion of the dead man's house is usually burned with him. The ashes of the pile are thrown into the river, by the side of which cremation invariably takes place. At the burning place the relatives erect a lofly pole with a long streamer of coarse cloth pendent therefor. Seven days after death, as among the Khyoungtha, the priests assemble to read prayer for the dead, and the relative gives alms.

Crime and Punishment

Crime of any sort is rare amongst the Chukmas; the most frequent misdemeanours are those connected with women, and for these a certain scale of fines is allotted. The said fines are divided between the chief of the tribe and the head man or Dewan.

If a man runs away with another man's wife, he has to repay to the injured husband all the former expenses of marriage, and is fined 40 to 60 rupees. Should near relatives (within certain prohibited degrees) fall in love with each other, it usual for both of them to pay a fine of 50 rupees and corporal punishement is also administered.

Divorce is not difficult of attainment amongst them, and can be awarded by a jury of village elders. The party who is judged to be in fault is fined heavily. As a rule, however, divorce is uncommon, and the women make good and faithful wives.

In serious cases, where the guilt or innocence of any person is to be tested, they use the ordeal by rice.

Lewin's Adventure into Lushai Country

The Lushais raided the British territory near Chandradnona: "I started at once on foot, with a party of police, in pursuit of the marauders, but could find no trace of them, they having made their dash and retired as swiftly and secretly as they had come. The exposure, hwoever, that I underwent, and the anxiety of this this fruitless pursuit, the sleeping out in the forests amid heavy rain, combined with scanty food and severe fatigue, brought on a sharp attack of fever, by which I was prostrated for some time.

"The difficulty of adequately defending the long line of frontier, consisting as it is of hundreds of miles of pathless forest, weighed upon my mind greatly at that time, and I found myself day and night reflecting upon the problem. There seemed but two alternatives; we might either, at a great cost, send a punitive expedition and destroy the villages of the raids; or we ought to strengthen our cordon of police posts, and establish an efficient line of defence along the whole frontier. Either of these courses would entail great additional expense on Government, and as the standing paradox was to obtain security without icrease of expenditure, I thought it unlikely that either of my alternatives would be acceptable to my superiors." What other way, was open to me? This was the subject of my reflections; this cud I chewed and rechewed. The main point was evidently to obtain some influence over these Lushais. My predecessor, Captain M— had gained great renown by his lucky surprise of their raiding party, and he was currently reported among them to be invulnerable to shot or steel. Could they be brought to consider this quality as one generic to the race of Hill Superintendents?

Now, in my somewhat miscellaneous reading, I had come across an account of the conjures Robert Houdin's experiences among the Arabs. The French Government had brought him over to Algiers to undertake a contest with the native Marabouta, and he had been completely successful in establishing a reputation as a mighty magician. Among other tricks I remembered one in which he had permitted an Arab to fire a loaded gun at his breast; the gun contained a marked bullet, which was immediately afterwards produced by Houdin from between his teeth.

I was pretty quick with my fingers, and determined, if possible, to reproduce this trick among the Lushais, being quite sure that, if successful, my renown would transcend even that of the famous Captain M— it was not long before the wished for occasion presented itself. At the end of September I went on a visit of Iswan Dewan; one of the headmen of the Chukma tribe, which was situated close to our most advanced police post of Kassalong, a long day's journey from my headquarters up the Karna-Phuli. The main object of my visit was to meet some Lushai messengers who had been sent to me by our old enemy Rutton Poia, and, if it could be managed, I intended to accompany them back across the frontier and pay a visit to the chief in his own village.

The Lushai "Karbaris" (literally " men of business"), duly arrived, and met me at Kassalong. In their interview with me they stated that Rutton Poia was anxious to maintain the friendly relations at present existing between us, and trusted that his people might be permitted to trade, as heretofore, at our frontier markets. He wished also to assure me that he had nothing to do with the late raid on the Bohmong's villages. I listened patiently to all they had to say, and then replied that as the matters they referred to were of the highest importance, it was necessary for me to see I would myself go to him. Also some demur this was at length agreed to.

Ishwan Dewan did all he could to dissuade me from the enterprise, reminding me that it was not so long ago that Rutton Poia had murdered, or caused to be murdered, a sergeant and two of our frontier policemen, who had been sent on a friendly message to his village. I meant going, however, could be none to an official of my exalted position.

I ordered Jemadar Fuzlah, with twenty of my best men, fully armed to accompany me, and the next morning we started in dugout canoes on our journey upstream. About six miles from Kassalong we reached the Burkhul rapids, a grand tumble of water, here it was that my predecessor Captain M., had been let down form lofty over- hanging crag, whch towards a hindred feet or more above the roaring water, to take his perilious swim. Truly a bold and daredevil feat!

The Lushai " Karbaris", like my old friends the Sendus, would not trust themselves in boats, but went on foot. My boats were paddled by some of Ishan Dewan's Chakmas, who acompained me such against the grain, being in fear of their lives; I was however, compelled to employ them to manage the boats, as I found to my astonishment that the hill police were, for the most part, unused to rowing, and quite unable to steer a canoe. We dragged our boats painfully through the rapids, having often to work deep in the water: but above was smooth and easy going, so that we paddled along without further interruption, until towards sunset we reached Utanchatra, where we found the Lushais awaiting our arrival they having traveled on foot through the forest.

Here we drew our boats on to the great flat rocks which formed the bed and banks of the river, and camped for the night. The Chukma boatmen lighted a fire on a sandy place by the side of the river, and the bright flames irradiated a small zone of the surrounding forest, throwing into denser blackness the depths of wood and stretches of dark water that lay beyond. Our dinner, such as it was, speedily dispatched, and the men, tired with their day's work, were soon stretched sleeping round the fire or in the boats. No sound broke the stillness of the night, save the lapping of the water against the side of my boat where I lay smoking a final pipe, and thinking of the day's journey.

Midday, perhaps, was the least pleasnt time in the twenty four hours, for then all creatures were silent all had withdrawn to the shade and shelter of the forest; only the large black forest flies were out settling on one without a sound, and with the softness of a piece of cotton wool, the first sign of their presence being a sting as of a lancet thrust. Once, with a clack of wings like some aerial machine, the great hornbill passed over our heads, to roar from his nest, where doubteless he had left his mate sitting on the eggs, duly plastered up with mud, leaving only room for her beak to receive the nourishment he brought her. The natives will to keep the large bill of this bird in their houses, although they will eat its flesh. They believe to cause discord in families and to promote quarrels between husband and wife.

They came the evening with its chorus of frogs and the shrill horn of the mosquito, while the sun westering in golden stretches of light made the river a path of glory. As twilight fell, I remember, an old tree' we passed on the band was full of fire flies, who sent forth a beautiful silvery radiance, making the whole tree beat, as it were, in pulses of light, fading, and flash-ing.

The next morning we left our boats, and followed a jungle path lead-ing towards a lofty range of hills some ten or twenlve miles distant, on the top at which was situated Ruton Poia's village. Our path for some dis-tence lay over low-lying undulating ground crossing occasionally a rivu- let, or passing through dense forest jungle; then it rose on a hill spur, winding up over boulder covered slopes, among huge trees thickly with creepers and orchids, until a length it narrowed ito a close, rocky defile. Here for a little space we halted, to allow the "Karbaris" who guided us to parley with two wild looking Lushai scouts, whoeach armed with an old fire lock were posted on the summit of a towering rock which commanded the path. Then we passed on again, until at last the path came out on to a sheer precipice several hundred feet in depth, along the face of which the path was led, by a sort of bamboo ladder resting on wooden piles, driven firmly into crevices in the rock. A very awkyard and shaky pathway I found it for my booted feet, and I was heartily glad when I arrived safely at the other side, where we reached a long grassy slope which led to the summit of the hill. On reaching the end of the ascent we were confronted by a crowd of forty to fifty Lushais, armed with guns and spears, and presenting a somewhat truculent and offenisive aspect: I took no notice whatever of these persons, recalling the hill proverb:

If you go into a stranger river take in your flags:
If you enter a stange village, take the strut out of your wald;
Or better still, as my hill servant quoted:
In your own village crow and be a cock; but when
You're in another, you must be a hen.

I sat down on the grass to recover breath after the somewhat stiffpull up the hill, and the "Karbaris" went on to communicate to the chief, Rutton Poia, the advent of his unlooked for visitor.

The Lushai held all of, regarding us in surely, scowling fashion; nor would they respond to any friendly overtures on the part of my men. I ordered Fuzlah to see that our retreat was not cut off; but inwardly I reflected, with some disquietude, how easy it would be to catch us like rats in trap, by simply breaking down the bamboo ladder not far below. I gazed upon the Lushais with much curiosity, as they were, with the exception of the "Karbaris", the first fair sample of the race which had come before me.[38]

They were well made muscular men, of somewhat dark complexion, and with a surly, forbidding cast of countenacee. Their whole clothing consisted of a single long home spun mantle or sheet of cotton cloth, sometimes white with a blue transverse stripe, or of a dark blue fabric, the stripe being crimson or yellow. Their straight black hair was bound in a knot upon the nape of the neck. Some of the youngest and best looking of the braves had small bunches of brilliant coloured feathers, crimson, blue, and yellow, stuck earring fashion through the lobe of the ear. About half of the them carried guns, which as far as I could make out were all Towermarded old flintlock muskets of King George III's time; some of these had been restocked and handsomely painted in red, black, yellow. Two or three among them, I noticed, wore the handsome guyal powder-horns which I had previously seen among the Shandus; and some smoked pipes made of bamboo and lined with copper, similar to one with which Yitchee had presented me.

After a short interval, the "Karbaris" returned, and intimated that Rutton Poia would consent to recieve me; but that, on account of the fears of the women and children in his village, he was unable to admit my armed escort, who would have to remain outside. This did not admit to argument; so, after a brief consideration, I ordered my men to camp where they were placing a sentry on the bamboo bridge, and then, taking with me Fuzlah and my hill boy Adupah, who was useful as an interpreter, I set forth to the village, preceded by the "Karbaris".

The Lushai village lay before me, a confused mass of houses thickly scattered over the hill-side, and nearly all on different levels. The village was surrounded by a palisade of enormous logs, as thick as the leg of an elephant and ten feet high. The entrance lay through a stockaded passage, thickly studded with downward–pointing bamboo spiked, and defended by two heavy doors of tough-hewn timber, so thick as to be practically fire and bullet proof. On passing through the passage I found the stockade was lined with men in readiness to repel any attack. Evidently these Lushais were a suspicious race, accustomed to treacherous dealing.

The village itself was built on no fixed principle, each householder having apparently placed his dwelling where it seemed best to himself. There was, however, the semblance of a main street, and down this we solemnly walked, preceded by the "Karbaris", towards an isolated building standing in the centre of the village, which they informed me, was the guest house, where I was to be lodged. Opposite to this was Rutton Poia's abode, a large barn like structure, a hundred and fifty feet long by forty broad, raised on a low platform about four feet from the ground. It was thatched with wild palm leaves, and its entrance adorned with long lines of skulls, buffalo, pig and deer over the doorway.

I looked anxiously to see if I could distinguish any human heads among the trophy but could see none. This I considered a favourable sign, for I had been informed that the heads of the unfortunate policemen who had been killed here, not more than a year ago, were hanging up over the chief's doorway, and I drew a favourable augury from the fact that they had been removed out of regard for my prejudices.

Another hopeful circumstance was that the village was thronged with women and children, all crowding out to look at the strange white first of all hidden away. These females were stout legged and not uncomely, clad in the scantiest of blue skirts round the hips, the upper part of the body being shrouded in the national home spun sheet. All children under ten were, without any exception naked.

I was shown up the ladder into the guest house, a one roomed dwelling, with walls of bamboo mat, raised on a high platform, to which one mounted by a spoiling log cut in steps.

I asked when it would be convenient for the chief to see me, and was informed that the moment had not yeat arrive, as Rutton Poia had sent out to summon some of the neighbouring chiefs, but that I was to be formally introduced to the family circle on the following day. This information I extracted from one of the "Karbaris", who was affable and fairly communicative, and who had evidently been told off to attend upon men and keep me in a good humour, as he devoted himself exclusively to my service.[39]

Towards sundown some food arrived for us from the chief's house; a rough and barbaric meal of seethed pig's flesh and rice, garnished with greasy capsicums, some rice and other uncooked food had been sent to my men outside the village, as I ascertained from Fuzlah, whom I sent out to reassure the party and see that the sentries were properly posted.

"I was somewhat troubled by the inquisitiveness of the boys and young men of the village, who climbed up perpetually to peep into the guest house. For hours together eyes glistened through every crack in the walls, giving one an uncomfortable sensation; but as the evening came on they retired, and we were left alone for the night. To prevent surprise I was undertaken to watch until midnight, while Fuzlah and Adupah would share the remainder of the night watch, keeping guard while I slept.

"I had brought with me a soft quilted "rezai" to sleep on, and with a rug wrapped round me, and sword and pistol under my head, I lay and thought long and deeply upon my line of action on the morrow.

"The positon was not altogether a pleasant one, and caused me to cogitate much upon the nature of fear, and to wish that timidity or nervousness could be excised by a surgical operation from the characters of those who did not desire these emotion. I have found through life that although one can always force one's body to do the right thing at the right time, yet that to eliminate nervousness from the mind is a much more difficult matter. An old Swedish story came into my head as I lay there thinking upon the curious inequalities of disposition which we call cowardice.

"When Charles Gustavus, King of Sweden, was besieging Prague, a peasant of most extraordinary and portentous visage demaned admission to the royal service offering, by way of qualification, to devour a whole hog in His Majesty's presence. The celebrated old General Konigsmarck was standing by the King at the time, and the although a soldier of proved courage, was rather superstitious. Regarding, therefore, this astounding offer of the peasant as something "uncanny", he remarked to the King that the man was probably a sorcerer, and should be burnt.

"Sire!!" said the peasant, highly incensed at such uncalled for interference, "If Your Majesty will make that old man take off his sword and his spears, I will eat him immediately, before I commence on the hog."[40]

This terrible threat, combined as it was with a preternatural expansion of the hideous peasant's jaws, had such an effect on the old General that he forthwith fled, never stopping until he reached his own quarters, where he continued shut up in a melancholy and desponding frame of mind, brought on by disgust at himself for having given way to panic. It is the unknown and the mysterious which produce the mental tumult which we call fear. *Omne ignotum pro magnifico.*

"During the early part of the night the sounds of rough chating, accompanied monotonously by a drum, reached us from the chief's house; but soon all was silent and the village seemed wrapped in slumber, save a guard of two or three Lushais, who lounged smoking by the chief's door. It was a novel position : on a hill top two thousand feet or more above the sea, everything different, all new. I had no desire to sleep, and Fuzlah also seemed disinclined for slumber and gladly drew towards the fire at my invitation to have a chat. He was of opinion that the Lushais were a murderous looking lot of scoundrels, and that what we ought to have done was to have brought fifty more of our men and burnt down the whole village. Then we talked of our Shendu adventure, and this led to his own previous life, and he recounted many things of wars and stratagems, when as a comparatively young man he had served as a soldier under the Maharaja of Cashmere, at Gilghit. Insensibly my attention wandered. I had so much to think of in the present that I could not give heed just then to the past; so Fuzlah soon wrapped himself in his rug and went to sleep.

At midnight I roused Fuzlah and tried to sleep myself. Myself, I had, however, seemingly scarcely closed my eyes when I was awakened by an extraordinary noise, something between a bull's bellow and a railway whistle. What was it? We started to our feet, and Fuzlah and I were looking to our arms when Adupah said, "It is only the guyal calling, Shaib! Look, the dawn is just breaking, and they are opening the village gates for the beasts to go out to pasture."[41]

These guyals were beautiful creatures, with broad fronts, sharp wide spreading horns, and mild melancholy eyes. There were the indigenous wild cattle of the hills, domesticated by these equally wild Lushais; all day long they were allowed to wander untended, but returning always each to his master's house at night, to receive a handful of salt, of which they are immoderately fond. The Lushais make no use of the milk, regarding that fluid, indeed, as an unclean excrement; but they would slaughter a guyal occasionally, on high days and holidays, for the sake of the flesh, which is esteemed a great delicacy among them.

Making our way through this crowd, who did not incommode themselves by moving out of the way too much, we passed on to the further end of the room, where, in a small partitioned racks with a window looking out over the hills, sat Rutton Poia, with sundry other chiefs.

I looked at the chief with considerable curiosity, and heat me with, I daresay, equal interest. He was a small, dark, athletic man, with a melancholy cast of countenance and large, stern eyes; he wore no ornament or insignia of his rank, save that his mantle was of a finer texture than the ordinary homespun worn by other Lushais. On my coming the chief and those who were with him made no motion of welcome; but the "Karbari" showed me a mat, where I and my two attendants seated ourselves. A pause ensued, during which the chiefs sat like so many brown images, each wrapped round in his mantle. Inwardly I fumed greatly at the rough incivility of these barbarians; but I had not come all this distance in order to lose my temper, so I restrained myself and endeavoured to assume a brown image like aspect, as like that of the chief as possible.

At length Rutton Poia grunted.The "Karbari" translated this sound by saying that the chief wished to know why I had brought a formidable party of armed men to his village.

I replied that my men were armed in order to defend themselves from the dangers of the road; but that, having reached Rutton Poia's village, I had now no need of arms, as my presence showed I requested that the chief would dispose of the contents of a bale which I had brought with me. The said bale was quickly opened and the contents, consisting of scarlet cloth, cotton sheeting, beads, looking glasses were carried off by the chief's retainers; but Rutton Poia and the rest of them still sat like brown images.

"I am glad to hear", said I, "that Rutton Poia disclaims all participation in the outrages which have recently been committed in my country to the south; and I have come here in consequence, to confirm the friendship between us."

No reply. Some brass cups containing a strong sprit were handed round.

"The prevention of such occurrences is my duty". I continued; or, when not preventable, we can punish our enemies and Rutton Poia knows that what I say is true".

This was a side shot at the chief personally; for I knew that he had been himself in command of the party which was so effectually routed by my predecessor, Captain M. On this, Rutton Poia took a big gulp of sprits, and then addressed a remark to the interpreter. I noticed that he shuttered in speaking, but whether this was through nervousness or habit I could not tell. I hoped he was nervous.

"The chief says that Captain M. was a magician. Is it true that he had a charm against shot and steel"?

"All Sahibs", I rejoined impressively, "are alike gifted with this power by Government on their taking charge of the Hill Tracts. If you have a gun handy I can easily prove this to you."

On a sign from Rutton Poia a gun was brought, the chiefs communed with each other in low tones, the drinkers left their post, and a crowd of heads peeped over the partition.

"Now", I said " charge that gun". The "Karbari" carefully put in a measure of powder. "Now a bullet". It was handed to me.

"Lend me a knife". One of the chiefs produced a knife, and I proceeded to cut a cross on the bullet; then, raising it up so that all could see the mark, I said; "You would all recognize that bullet again"? Murmurs of assent. "Then see, I take that bullet and I place it in the gun, thus; then I ram it home in this manner. Now prime the gun."

It was heavy flint-lock musket; the "Karbari" carefully primed it. Rutton Poia rose and carefully examined the priming.

"Now", said I, "fire at my chest". The "karbari" hesitated.

"Do as the sahib tells you", said Rutton Poia.

I covered my ears and face with my ram, and the "Karbari", at a distance of about ten yards, took a carfully aim and fired. I staggered for a moment, as if receiving a shock, and then putting my hand to my mouth, from between my teeth I took the marked bullet.

"Is that the ball that was in the gun"? I asked calmly, handing it to Rutton Poia.The excitement was intense. The chiefs were now all standing, and the bullet was rapidly passed from hand to hand amidst exclamations of astonishment. It was indeed the marked ball!

We resumend our seats. Conversation among the Lushais now became vivid; their immobility had disappeared.

At last one big fellow, Vanlula I think was his name, got up and began to make a speech. I need not further described the pow-wow which followed; suffice it to say, that by 4 o'clock that afternoon I was back to the boats, having contracted a solemn alliance, offensive and defensive, with Rutton Poia and his allied chiefs, the comtact having been duly ratified by the sacrifice of a guyal, with the proper ceremonies, and sealed by infinite potations.

"Skilled magicians, I suppose, are never nervous, or it is at any rate, part of their profession to appear imperturbable, but I confess that, as I lay in my canoe on my way down stream, it was with a shiver of excitement that I recalled the scene at the Lushai village, and thought of the moment when I changed the pewter bullet of the Lushai and substituted for it a waxen ball carefully blackleaded outside, according to Profesor Houdin's receipt, which I had prepared in the gun when remmed home while I concealed the marked bullet under the base of my thumb.

When the "Karbari" was about to fire at me, I covered my face with my arm to keep the powder the pieces of wax out of my eyes, the same movement enabling me to pass the bullet into my mouth, when I was of course able to produce it after the explosion. I went straight down the river, stopping only one day at Chandraguna, and reached Chittagong on the 24th October, 1866, being anxious to report what I had done to the Commissioner. He was much amused and interested at my adventure, but advised me to hold my tongue about if officially, as Government would certainly not approve of what I had done in contracting engagements to assist a Lushai Chief, and my irregular proceedings might incur severe censure if officially reported. I accordingly said no more about the matter, but I determined, nonetheless, that as long as I remained in the Hills I would loyally perform my part of the compact, and would help Rutton Poia and his clan against their savage neighbours, so far as lay in my power. I must add that they too, on their side, did faithfully observe their engagement, and to the last day of my service in the Hills they remained true to the alliance we had contracted.

I remained a fortnight with my friend the Commissioner in Chittagong, not for the sake of the change of air, as also to consult him about the various reforms which I wished to introduce in the Hill Tracts.[42]

Before Lewin could return to the Hill after his trip to Calcutta, the Lushais made incursions into the territory of Bohmongs and for this he had to go away there hundred miles away from his headquarters. This absorbed his whole attention. "The enemy as usual came and went like a fox to a hen-roost, vanishing before and news of their presence could reach me". Lewin established a strong outpost, hoping thus to guard against future outrage.

Lewin had a love for the hill men and disliked the Bengali plainsmen. He goes on wirting in his account that the Bengal the sensation most keenly felt by an Englishman is that he is an alien in a foreign land; but among the hill folk he is among fellow creatures. "Wherever I went among the people, I was hospitably entertained, fed and feted; in return I kept open house for all who came to see me.

"I devoted all my spare time to acquiring the different languages and dialects spoken in my district, being strongly impressed with the idea that no true juctice can be done through an interpreter, and that the only key to the thoughts and customs of the people lies through their language.

"In the Chittagong Hill Tracts there were spoken no fewer than four distinct languages. With the first of these, Burmes, I was fairly acquainted; Bengali I knew before coming to the Hills, and so mastered the Chakma tongue, which is practically the same with the introduction of local words. The Tipra and Lushai languages were quite distinct, and difficult to acquire.

I had parted with all my Bengali "bamboos"; save one, and the people could now undersatand the working of justice in the court-house or kutcherry, my Burmese clerks being in sympathy with them and understanding their customs.

Towards the end of the year 1867 the frontier became much disturbed and I moved up, with all available fighting men at my disposal, to our most advanced frontier stockade at Kassalong. I felt more and more convinced that the chronic state of irritation which existed among the border tribes could not without danger, be allowed to continue, and that sooner or later, the Government must be driven to offensive as well as defensive measures.

The violent and cruel Lushais saw in a pacific policy only fear or cowardice, and would only be convinced of our power by stringent reprisals. Rutton Poia's tribe alone stood staunchly by their alliance with me, and gave me frequently private information which enabled me to frustrate intended or attempted raids on our territory.

Genesis of the Lushais

During my stay at Kassalong I embraced every opportunity of becoming better acquainted with the Lushais, who freely resorted to our market, and learnt all I could concerning their language and customs. They have a curious tradition concerning their genesis, which I heard from one of the principal Karbaris of the Sylu tribe.

"Our ancestors", said he, "came originally out of a cave in the hills. This cavern may be seen at the present day near Van Huilen's village among the Burdia clan. Strange noises are heard to issue therefrom,and no one willingly approaches the spot.

"At first we had great chief whose name ws Tlandrokpa. He married God's daughter and was a very powerful chief. To prepare for the marriage all the animals were summoned to clear a road through the jungle by which to bring the bride home.

At that time, which was longer than long ago, all living things spoke with the language, and all the animals obeyed the call except the sloth, his cousin the hulug monkey, and the earth –woman; therefore it is that to this day these animals are ashamed and hid themselves, not loving the sun-light.

Then there were great festivities. Tlandrokpa gave Patiens (God) his great gun; one can hear the sound of it often when it thunders, that is when Patien goes out hunting up there.

Some time after the sedding Tlandrokpa quarrelled with Patien, and was conquered by means of the great gun and its fire. And the earth took fire and burnt with a great hear, and the whole race of men would have been consumed; but Patien's daughter counseled us, and we came towards the sea, where there was much water and so our ancestors saved their lives.

Here in the new country, there was great scarcity of food, for at that time men did not eat flesh; but at last, by reason of great hunger, they began to kill and eat the animals. Then the creatures spoke and begged for mercy in such pitiful words that it was hard to slay them, until at last Patien's daughter besought her father, and he took from the animals their power of speech. Since then food has been plentiful among us. This we have heard from our ancestors.

The Lushais resemble in many points our own Highlanders. Their chiefs wear mentles woven of a red and blue tartan; their music resemble that of the bagpipes, with a gourd reservoir instead of the skin bag; they are split up into clans, which are often at feud one with another, and they cement friendship and forment strife by free indulgence in an ardent spirit closely resembling Highland whiskey.

Lushai Chiefs

Their chiefs are chosen from one ancient strain of royal blood; but does not therefore follow that every chief's son shall succeed his father. He must first show himself worthy to be a leader before men will follow him. Although his rule may be set aside, the scion of a chief's house (or "Lal", as he is called) is held sacred as being of semi-divine origin, and he must not be ill-treated or killed. The chief directs in war, and must be first to attack and the last to retreat.

Once, in Rutton Poia's village, I noticed a drunken Lushai rudely push the chief out of his way. Rutton Poia said nothing, but gathered his mantle closer around him and continued his conversation with me.

"What is this"? I asked; "do you not punish disrespect in your followers"?

"Disrespect"! he exclaimed, "why the man is drunk and incapable of disrespect! But putting his condition aside, here all are equal. On the warpath, or in chase, if he did not obey me he would die; but here he is as in his own house".

If any man is in want, he walks into the chief's house and takes what he needs. "He is a chief", they say, "and will receive plenty more gifts. All we have is his so also his goods are ours. Who should give to us if our chief does not"?

For public purposes, such as feast days, receptions, the entertaining of guests, the chief sends for anything that may be required to whoever has it. His house is built for him and his land cultivated by the unpaid labour of his followers.

The chief's house is a sanctuary, where all criminals may take refuge. Even the avengers of blood, pursuing a murderer red-handed, may not pass beyond the threshold with arms in their hands. But by thus seeking refuge under the chief's roof –tree the fugitive becomes ipso facto the chief's slave. He has other slaves also of those taken in war; by them he sends orders and messages, their authorization being the chief's own spear, which represents his sign manual. A piece of red cloth attached to the spear means " blood", a small piece of cane attached means "battling", and if to the same is added a piece of capsicum, then an offender knows that his punishment will be hot and pungent. Two pieces of bamboo tied corsswise accompanying the spear is a demand for black, mail the number of head of cattle required being indicated by bends in the bamboo tied crosspiece be burned or charred with fire at one end, great danger and urgency are denoted. This last token is like the old token of the fiery cross on the Scottish border, it admits of no delay, and must be responded to by men fully armed, even if they have to go through the forest by torchlight.

In the house of a chief there is always drinking going on. The "seepah" or "Khoung" (both names being given to the hill beer made from millet seed) is either sucked up through reeds direct from the great earthen jars, or drawn off into mighty horns or great brazen bols, by means of a siphon formed of two reeds joined with lac and thence ladled out ot the drinkers by a gourd spoon. Should there be an extraordinary gathering of guests, auxiliary cups are quickly manufactured from the joints of a bamboo.

Account of Lushai Raid

My interpreter, Ramoni, who had formerly been a slave in Rutton Poia's house, and whose freedom was granted at my at my request, gave me a very graphic account of an expedition he had made with the chief into British territory: the raid was directed on the Bengali villagers of Cachar.

"The Bengali men", said Ramoni, "all ran away, except those whom we met were able to spear. The young women and children also tried to escape, but we caught most of them. We killed all the men we met with, except healthy yong lads of fifteen and under; these with women of not more than thirty or thirty-five years, were tied by the thumbs, their arms being bound behind. The women were kept together by a cord passed through the lobe of their ears; if the hole in the lobe were not large enough, it had to be widened by a knife or skewer.

On the ruturn journey one of the women sunk down from exhaustion and could go no fatrther, her feet and ankles being much swollen. The chief halted, and after a short consultation, he said to me, "Go, Ramoni, and spear her. I will stand by and see that you do it properly". I felt much afraid, for I had never killed a human creature, and I was only seventeen years old.

When the girl saw me approaching her with the spear in my hand she fell weeping and caught at my feet and my garments, entreating me. Then my heart beat and my head became giddy, so that I said to the chief, 'I cannot do it'.

Dog, and son of a slave! Replied he; never again call me by the name of father! And all the young men of the party laughed and jeered at me saying they would tell the maidens in our village how brave I was, and would ask them to make a petticoat for me.

Then I shut my eyes and rushed at her with my spear, but the blow was ill-directed; and Rutton Poia snatched the weapon from my hands and killed the girl with one blow. "Here', said he, giving me back my spear with the blood of it, 'lick this to strengthen your heart'.

"The blood of Bengalis is very salty', said Ramoni; "but since then I have not been afraid to spear anyone".

When going out on a foray the Lushais take with them as food, yam and rice pounded together, and rammed down into tubes of bamboo. On this meagre sustenance they can march enormous distances. They are very cunning in their strategy, sending out spies, and keeping their main body in ambush. On the only occasion when they surprised and destroyed one of my outposts they did so by means of adecoy. Late at night a loud noise was heard at the gate of the stockade, and voices called out that a village of the Khyoungtha, distant some four miles, had been attacked by a party of Lushais, and prayed for assistance. The guard promptly got under arms and headed by the Jemadar went off in the darkness to succour the distressed village, leaving only a few men to guard the stockade.

As soon as the main body of defendant were at a safe distance the Lushai came out of their hiding place and escalated the stocked, killing my men, carrying off the women and children into captivity, and taking the heads of the slain with them as trophies but is to this latter practice that the Lushais owe there name, 'Lu', meaning head, and "sha" to cut; so that "Lushai" would signify a "decapitator". The generic name of the whole nation is "Dzo".

It is customary for young men on their first expedition to eat a piece of the heart or liver of a slain enemy in order to confirm their courage. When successful in a foray, they are careful not to wash the blood stains from their hands until they return home. On reaching their own village, they are met by the women and old men, who escort them to their houses with triumphant songs, beating of gongs, and blowing of reed pipes. A guyal, or two or three pigs will be slaughtered, jars of beer broached, and for two or three days the whole village is given up to rejoicing and feasting.

Thery are, however, on the whole, a grave and silent people, doubtless heedful of the old proverb, "My son, if you be wise, open first your eyes, then your ears, and last of all your mouth; for the Lushai sleeps, hunts, and smiled with his mouth closed. This habit undoubtedly prevents the admission of cold air and consequent tooth ache and early loss of teeth. Also there is among them no croup, no teething disorders, nor lung diseases.

From early childhood they are taught to close the jaws and cover the head and face with their mantle while sleeping, in order to avoid the damp air and malaria of night. The Lushais, like most hill dwellers, are a hardy and healthy race, and suffer mainly from disorders brought on by hard drinking. Cholera (which they call "the foreign sickness") and small pox were unknown among them until the year 1861, when the former was introduced among them by some Bengali captives taken in a raid.

The contagion spread rapidly, infecting village after village and causing dire consternation. Men attacked with the terrible malady, in many and their inevitable desertion by all their relatives. Thanks, however, to this inhuman practice of deserting the sick and dying, the diseases died out after.slaying its thousand, and has not since reappeared.

In ordinary cases of death, all the relatives of the dead man are called together, and a big feast is held. This corpse is attired in a fine mantle, and placed in a sitting posture, with his weapons near him, and is thus addressed by the eldest male relative: "Brother! You have a long journey before you; eat". Then he places food before the body, and the dead man's pipe is filled and placed in his hand, while all present bid him farewell.

On the second day, when all the guests have well drunken, all corpse is placed in a hollow tree by way of coffin and buried in the jungle. Among some of the tribes the curious custom prevails of drying thę bodies of their chiefs or great men, over a slow fire, first sheathing them in pith, and then hanging them up on a tree.

In the Howlong clan, the body thus dried is hung from rafters of the house for seven days, and during this period the widow must sit underneath the corpse spinning. On no account must she quit the spot, not even to take food, being dependent for her nourishement during this period of mourning on the kind offices of her relatives.

I found the idea of my position as a government official conveyed but a vague impression to the minds of these uncivilized people; so I took my standing among them as a chief, paramount in the district, but subject to a yet greater white chief in Calcutta. I had obtained permission from Government to move my headquarters from Chandraguna to Rangamati, a more central spot, a day's journey nearer the frontier, and I determined to test my position as chief, in the local fashion, by calling on all the Toungtha in the vicinity to build me a house.

Accordingly I sent message to all the Pankhos, Mros, and Bujrogi villages for twenty miles round, saying that I was moving from Chandraguna to Rangamati, and desired a house to live in there. I further informed them that numerous jars of beer and three pigs were waiting the consumption of those who laboured.

Within a week some three hundred men had set to work with a will, and built me a large house, Lushai fashion, on the spot I had selected. It was built entirely of bamboo, except the poss, which were huge logs of unhewn timber, and the floor, which was constructed of small saplings about two inches in diameter laid lengthwise.

The positon of my new headquarters was quite central. It was situated on a bend of the river Karnaphuli, which at the place makes a sort of loop. I had the land thus enclosed cleared from jungle. At the narrow part of the bend I placed the police barracks, thus defending the small peninsula from land attack, while the river, which was here very deep, protected the other three sides of the new settlement. My own house placed on a lofty cliff overhanging the river, and commanding a beautiful and extended view on all sides. I names my new abode "Barn House", but had hardly settled myself comfortably in it when I had to start off again in hot haste for the jungles.

My new frontier police patrols had kept the district free from raids for many months.[43]

The Lushai Fair or Mela

Lewin had a love for the Lushais and he suggested to the

Bengal Government a Lushai Fair at Kasalong for the entertainment of the Lushai chiefs. Lewin had been to Chotanagpur (now in Jharkhand) in his early career and saw the tribal fairs there. He, as the Deputy Commissioner, CHT made correspondence with the authorities of Chotanagpur with a view to obtain hints and informations of general nature as to the necessary arrangements for the Lushai Fair (Judicial Proceedings, Bengal Govt., Nov 1868 No.70). The novel plan of Lewin impressed Lord H. Ulich Browne, the Commissioner, Chittagong. However, John Edgar, the D.C., Cachar was the first to suggest the Lushai Fair at Silchar (Cachar) and infact, Silchar witnessed Lushai Fair two years before Kasalong Fair. But there was difference in approach in this regard between the two British Frontier Officers. Edgar's aim had been to amuse the chiefs and also the induce them to establish trade marts in their territory i.e. commercial aspects goaded shrewd Edgar. But Lewin's aim was political. Lewin wrote to the Commissioner:-

"it would, however, I think, be a mistake to suppose that any increased freedom of intercourse between ourselves and these tribes would conduce to any great extension of commerce.

The object, therefore, of this mela is primarily political, to bring about more intimate and friendly relations which were hitherto been beyond our direct influence. The yearly assemblage of a large body of British subjects bringing goods of all sorts and the display of a certain military force, will impress them with the power of the Government, both to reward and punish while the cordial reception given to their childern, and the sports, amusements, and festivities it is to be hoped will supply the place of the undignified money gifts to present them with which they have hitherto been annually called together.[45]

Lord Ulich Browne recommended Lewin's suggestion to Bengal Government and Lewin had been successful in his attempt at friendly communication with the two leading Kuki tribes. Alexander Mackenzie, the towering personality on frontier affairs, then Junior Secretary, Government of Bengal, apporoved of the Lewin's suggestion.

Lewin and the Lushai Expedition 1871-72

Lewin took leave and went home in 1869. He was in England for about two years. He returned to India and reached Calcutta in January 1871. Before leaving Calcutta he had interviews with Lord Mayo, the Governor General of India and also with the Lt. Governor of Bengal he got the information about the impending Lushai Expediton. Lewin writes:

"I confess to having felt very glad that the Government had come to this determination, for I had eaten much dirt at the hands of the Lushais for some time past in carrying out the conciliatory and defensive policy which had been hitherto prescribed. The expedition, in my opinion, might have era to follow and punish all raiders found crossing the frontier; it would have been comparatively easy to deal with our enemies thus in detail and quite in accordance, moreover, with their own customs: but to attack them en masse by a military occupation of their country was a very big thing indeed, and would cost a large sum of money. However, better this enormous cudgel than the perpetual sugar stick which my unwilling hands had previously administered; and so, having received my instructions, by the month of February I was once more back at Rangamati, with the reins in my hands so of yore.

"In November I assumed my position as Political Officer with the Right Column, and made over charge of my dear Hill Tracts to a Bengal civilian, a very Irish man, who inspired me with no confidence whatever.

The Lushai expeditionary force was to assemble at Kassalong before entering the enemy's country, and thither

I accordingly repaired. I had previously send word to Rutton Poia not to be alarmed at any warlike preparations he might hear of, as I would guarantee his safety and thatof his tribe, if they were true to our alliance. I had great hopes of utilising him and his men as intermediaries in recovering the captives from the Howlong tribe. The expeditionary force slowly assembled at Kassalong, coming by steamer from Calcutta to Chittagong, and thence by boats to the frontier. The 2nd Ghurkha Regiment, commanded by Colonel H. Macpherson, arrived first on the scene; splendid little fellows they were, with equally fine body of officers, quite a corps d' elite.

I sent on my assistant, Mr. Crouch, with one hundred and fifty men of the Frontier Battalion to build a stockade and clear a camping ground for the troops at Demagree, close to Rutton Poia's village.

Rutton Poia himself, with two minor chiefs, came in on the 12th November and gave in his adhesion to our cause, offering all the assistance in his power. I introduced him to General Brownlow, with all due from he asked to pay a visit to his village when opportunity served, which the General good- naturedly promised to do.

The great difficulty of the campaign, it was evident, would be the commissariat. All supplies, it was drawn from Chittagong, being carried from thereby boat to Demagree, on a river broken in its upper course by frequent rapids.

The Khyoungtha contingent of coolies sent by the hill chiefs now began to assemble; their chief employment would be to manage the dug out canoes carrying supplies in the upper river. The small Ghurkhas, true hill men, like the Toungtha or the Lushais, were utterly unable to manage a conoe; indeed, as we soon ascertained, some among them could not even sit in dug out without upsetting it.

On the 6th of November, the General, Colonel Macpherson, and I started from Kassalong to Demagree, in sparate canoes, each manned by four hill men. We passed the night in our boats at Utan Chatra, and here I found some turtle eggs in the sand, which were not unacceptable at our frugal mes. We arrived the next day at Demagree, and were delighted to find a good stockade built and as large area of ground cleared for the accommodation of the troops. This had been well and quickly done by the men under Mr. Crouch's orders, to whom the General expressed his satisfaction.

A Lushai look out station was discovered close to the Demagree falls, where the river came tumbling through a groge into a large rocky basin; a cradle of cane, rigged up in a lofty tree on the heights, commanding a view far down the Karnaphuli. The night of our advance party arriving there, the Lushais had tried their vigilance by throwing stones into the camp, but otherwise they had been undisturbed. I had sent out scouts into the Lushais country beyond, and they now reported that the Lushais were in force on the Sahjuk stream (a northern tributary of Karnaphuli), and were preparing to resist our advance.

The men were set to work preparing a timber side up the Demagree falls, as, when once we had passed onward, every ounce of food would have to be dragged up the fall, which was of no great height, perhaps twenty feet.

On the 22nd of November the General vistited Rutton Poia's village in accordance with his promise; he started early, taking a Company of the 22nd Ghurkhas as escort, and I accompanied him to act as interpreter. The village was situated on the range of hills east of our camp at a distance of three miles; and midway on the road the chief met our party and conducted the General to the village, where we breakfasted on provisions which we had brought with us. And were related with hill beer. A guyal also was killed in honour of the visit, and two baskets full of the flesh were sent to camp for our consumption.

General Brownlow and his staff returned in the afternoon, but I remained at the village for the night as Rutton Poia wished me to assist at a great council of his friends and relatives which was to be held there, to decide the course which the clan should take during the coming contest.

There was accordingly a big talk and a corresponding drink. Rutton Poia's desire was to maintain a benevolent neutrality; but this I assured him would not be allowed, and I pictured the ferocity of the General in unspeakable terms. The difficulty seemed to be that if Rutton Poia and his clan should take an active part in our favour, the hostile tribes on the retirement of the expedition would destroy him root and branch.

I promised that at the close of the campaign he should have a detachment of police in his village, if he desire it; and by judiciously waving in the background the warth of General Brownlow, he finally consented to act with us. For the present, I undertook to leave fifteen men to guard the chief's village, as an open sign of British support, while he and his clan agreed to afraid for; and put assistance on whatever way it might be needed during the campaign.

At the close of our long and animated conference, which lasted for to the night, Rutton Poia's wife brought her young son, a boy of about ten years old, and solemnly placed his two hands folded between mine, in token of his recognition of me as protector and suzerain.

On returning to Demagree and repoting what had passed to the General expressed himself satisfied, and took the opportunity to say that, as my place for the future would be with him at the front, it would be necessary to appoint another officer to superintended the work of the hill coolies, and he proposed appointing Captain Hood to that duty. I accordingly assembled the head men of the coolies contigent and harangued them in their own tongue, directing them to work loyally under Captain Hood, and to pay the same respect and obedience to his orders as they would to my own.

We had something of scare in camp a few days later, for news came that a large party of the enemy had occupied the river in rear of us, with a view to cutting our line of supplies and communication. The hill coolies at Utan Chatra (half-way between Demagree and Kassalong) had struck work, and talked of returning to their homes, for the Khyoungtha feared the very name of Lushai, and even a report of being cut of would create a panic. The news reached camp at nightfall, and an hour or so later I was on my way, with twenty men of the Frontier Battalion, to see what was really the truth of the matter. There was no moon, and we had a narrow squeak for it in the rapids, one of the boats being upset and four rifles lost; but no further damage was done, and at daybreak I reached Utan Chatra.

My first care was to reassure the hill coolies who after a while calmed down and departed with a convoy for Demagree. On inquiry I found that a party of armed men, said to be Lushais, had certainly been seen crossing the river by a ford a few miles downstream only the day before, and on going to the spot I soon found a trail. We followed the traces of the party through the jungle for two hours, until we came to a spot where they had halted and cooked food. Here on the ground some rice was discovered which had been spilt, and this on inspection proved of our own commissairiat rice, easily distinguishable from the hill grain; therefore, as none of our grain strores had been plundered, the party could not have been Lushais, and were probably some of our own coolies, who had absconded, with their rations. Leaving my Subadar, Mahomed Azim, to follow the trial farther, I returned to Demagree.

The chief Vanpoia came in on the 2nd of December, and gave in his adhesion to our cause. He reported that the Sylus were killing and eating their guyals, and would most certainly oppose our advance. He, like Rutton Poia, made an attempt to get a guard for his own village, alleging that at the close of expedition he and his tribe would be eaten up by the Sylus and Howlongs for taking our side. I promised him that a strong guard should be left at Demagree when the campaign was over, which would protect him if necessary.

I was much worried by the hill coolies, who would do nothing without my personal orders; and none of the officers of the expedition knowing the language, I had not a moment's rest.

Our force was now augmented by the arrival of the 27th Punjab Infantry, who had marched from Kassalong to Demagree through the jungle. It did one's heart good to see so fine a body of men come down the hill into camp, marching, like our Highland regiments, to the music of the pipes. They gave the "Pathan scream" as they entered camp—a strange noise that stirred the blood as if for fighting.

The captives, whose recovery was one of the main objects of the expedition, were for the most part in the hands of the Howlong tribe, between whom and us interposed the Sylus, and it was clearly desirable to secure the neutrality, if not the amity, of this latter tribe, if it were in any way possible to do so; they were, however, so suspicious and unapproachable that all my efforts had hitherto failed. It therefore became necessary to obtain the services of someone who would act as intermediary, and with this view, on the 18th of December, I went to the village of a small chief named Lengura, who was own brother to one of the principal Sylu chiefs, but who, from ill-luck or incapacity, was a person of comparative insignificance. To my disappointment, I found the village deserted; but my men in routing about discovered a pig, two guyals, and fifty maunds of unhusked grain, so it was plain that the inhabitants' departure was only temporary.

I therefore left a party in ambush, and towards nightfall was lucky enough to capture the chief Lengura himself, who returned to look for the guyals.

I spent a long time in endeavouring unsuccessfully to secure his assistance; he remained obstinately deaf to all proposals, even casting on the ground at my feet the money which I offered in exchange for his pig and guyals. After a day or two of close confinement he at length consented to act as our ambassador, and accordingly I dispatched him to the village of a Sylu chief named Vanlula which was within easy distance of our camp, authorizing him to say that if our advance towards the Howlong country were unopposed we would not harm the Sylu tribe.

In the evening I strolled in the same direction which Lengura had gone, towards Vanlula's village, hoping to gain admission; but I had not advanced far up the slope when a ball came whistling close by my head, and I therefore accepted the hint and returned to camp.

The headquarters now moved up from Demagree, and occupied a fresh camp on the Sahjuk stream close to Vanlula's village. The General was not at all well; but this was not surprising, as the hill climate is very trying until the constitution becomes inured to it.

It was a remarkable sight at the close of a march to see the speedy and dexterous manner in which the hillmen and the Ghurkhas would, in the twinkling of an eye, convert a dusky forest glade into a comfortable village. At sundown we would halt in some secluded glen; the arms were piled, and in few moments there would be filled with the cutting sounds of *dao and kuki;* the tangle of jungle would be cleared; huts built, thatched with leaves and walled with split bamboos; fires lighted, and everyone within a measurable distance of comfort in less than half an hour. There was not a tent of any sort with the whole force; every ounce of dead weight that could be carried was brought along in the shape of either food or ammunition. For houses we depended on our enemies, and in their default we were able to run up very cosy shanties ourselves.

On the 13th of December Lengura returned, and informed me that no less than five of the Sylu headmen with their followers were assembled at Vanlula's and that, in reply to the message which he had conveyed from me, they had desired him to request that the expedition should at once leave the country; on this condition only would they treat with us or assist in recovering the captives; if we advanced any farther they would attack us. Foolish folk! I rewarded Lengura, and communicated his intelligence to the General, whose practical reply was the issue of orders to attack Vanlula's village the following morning.

The advance was made in two parties under cover of the morning mist. The night attack under Major MacIntyre of the 2nd Ghurkhas was a feigned one; and while the enemy's attention was thus engaged, the main body of the 2nd Ghurkhas under Colonel Macpherson, wrested the hill on which the village was built, and charging with the bayonet, took the place at a rush.

The enemy bolted, leaving one man dead, and carrying away with them two or three more dead and wounded. At the very first shot fired Vanlula set fire to his village, which was almost wholly consumed before we got possession of it; among the burnt houses we established ourselves as best we might, and scouts were sent out to ascertain the enemy's movements. They returned at sunset, reporing that Sylus had retreated northward, leaving signs of a precipitate flight in the shape of various articles dropped along the road and a dead body abandoned in the retreat. Among other things was found a coat belonging to a man of the Frontier battalion who had been killed by the Lushais a year before; also a basket and other small things of Bengali workmanship. From this evidence we deduced that the Sylus had been concerned in the raids upon British territory which had caused the expedition; this in some measure explained their persistent mistrust and hostility towards us.

The General was still far from well to the regret of all, for he was a true leader of men, and gained the confidence of everyone who was brought in contact with him; but his indisposition was not allowed to interfere with the work of the expedition, and he marched on foot and directed everything just the same as before.

It was determined to form a provision depot at Vanlula's and parties were sent out in all directions to search for and bring in such hidden stroes of grain and other combustibles as were discoverable, the resources of the country.

My position as a diplomatist began to cause me considerable anxiety, for how was it possible to recover the captives, or to enter into relations of a friendly character with the Sylus, if they absolutely declined all intercourse with us and confined themselves to a sullen hostility. Rutton Poia, who was with me, was apparently on bad terms with them, as neither he nor any of his men could be prevailed upon to undertake an embassy. Moreover, we depended for our food chiefly on supplies from Chittagong, which had to be brought many weary miles before reaching us. What should be done, if, as seemed probable, the ememy retired before us, burning every thing save the standing crops, and carrying with them their livestock and other combustibles?

I went out in the early morning of December 19th to think over some new plan; but sitting on the hill top, some two thousand feet high, so heautiful was the sight before me that for the moment I forgot all my perplexities, and could only rejoice in the grandeur of the landscape spread out below.

The sun had just risen out of a wilderness of delicately purpled peaks, which stretched towards the east and a keen cold breeze from these seemed to whisper a message of defiance from our enemies, whole villages, perched like evries on many an unknown top, could be clearly seen all around.

The whole Sylu country lay within striking distance of our position, no lessen six large villages being within a day's march. Beyond these lay the Howlongs, living on still loftier heights, never trodden by English feet, an undiscovered country, range upon range stretching far away in the distance, even to the confines of China.

Every valley around was filled with fleecy white mist, which , like soft snowy wool, hid all beneath it, and to of this rose craggy eminences covered sparsely with forest trees, while here and there, in the morning sun, some Sylu clearing gleamed golden with ripe corn. The far off horizon was bounded by a clearly defined dark purple range of hills, perhaps twenty miles distant, and as the sun rose the mist came pouring over this ridge and through the clefts of the range like some gigantic ocean, another deluge dashing its waves in foamy cataract on an affrighted world. So real did this seem to me for the moment that I found myself thinking that had this white foam been water, between me and earth there could have been but a short five minutes.

This climate, now that we had got up on the heights, was simply delicious, and the General's health began to mend rapidly. The air was bracing and dry, developing one's appetite to an alarming extent, the more so as from Dan to Beersheba all was barren. After my usual solitary life in the hills, I found the gay sociability of camp life very pleasant and much enjoyed the daily change and adventure, the nightly camp fire with its round of song and story.

We were somewhat harassed by attempts on the part of the Lushais to cut our line of communication. One day they laid an ambush for the party bringing the mail, and shot our Ghurkhas; but they did not escape scathless, for our men promptly retaliated and killed two of their assailants.

On the 21st of December Colonel MacPherson assaulted and took the village of Lal Hlira. We watched the attack with much interest throught field glasses, the village being on the next range of hills, three or four miles off as the crow flies. There was a great deal of firing, and the General was much relieved when Macpherson telegraphed by flag signal that the attack had been made without any loss on our side, although the enemy had suffered, and large stores of grain had been captured.

At the same time, Major MacIntyre, with another detachement, was busy to the northward, where he burnt two villages and destroyed fifty six granaries. One of these villages was strongly stockaded, but was abandoned by the Sylus without any serious attempt at defence. Some cattle also were captured, which proved a welcome addition to the commissariat.

I meanwhile busied myself in endeavouring to communicate with the Sylus. Conversations were sometimes held between us, across a valley, by shouting. The burden of my song was always, "Make submission, and we will cease from troubling you", but received no satisfactory reply, nor was any result attained.

Christmas Day was observed in camp in true English fashion. General Brownlow invited all the officers of the advanced Column to dine with him, and to our great astonishement, among other good things, a miraculous plum pudding graced the board. I obtained the recipe afterwards from Major East, Assistant Quartermaster General, who had evolved the same from his inner consciousness, as follows: one pot of marmalade, one pot of black currant jam, some guyal suet, and a sufficiency of biscuit pounded fine, together with a tablespoonful of essence of ginger, the whole boiled for two hours, and served with a few spoonfuls of burning. Result, beautific!

The next day we moved foreward and occupied the village of the Sylu chief, Van Hbnoya, meeting with no opposition. This village was a large one, consisting of about theee hundred houses, and was remarkable for having in its vicinity a large sacrificial altar of curiously carved stone, decked with a varied collection of the skulls of the different animals which had been offered thereon. I could find no human skulls among them.

Soon after our entry into Van Hbnoya's village, the villages of Van Kunga and Van Hnuna, which were in sight, were set on fire by their inhabitants. I sent on a party of picked men, and some of Rutton Poia's Lushais, to parley with them, and prevent this useless destruction; but in vain.[46]

Day after day passed by as we pursued our course, marching farther and farther into the bowels of the land, until by the end of the month we had reached the great Towrang Tlang range, where the General hoped to obtain some unsatisfactory tactics, they fought as little as possible, but burned their villages on our approach, retiring with all they could carry. They hailed us out of the jungle one day, saying, "Do not destroy our grain".

"Let our chiefs come in, then", I rejoined, "and make submission."

"No, no, no", was the reply. "Go your ways; leave our country. Wea have nothing for you but powder and ball, and plenty of that". Brave words these! but nothing else.

At the General's request I cause proclamations to be prepared, written in Burmese and Bengali, setting for the that our subject invading the country was to effect the release of certain of Her Majesty's subjects, who were held in captivity by the Lushais, and inviting the tribes to send emissaries to at with us. The proclamations were left, natiled up in conspicuous positions, at every place we visited; but as the Lushais could neither read nor write, I did not anticipate much effect from this step. Unless their curiosity should induce them to employ some literate captive to investigate the mysterious magic papers which the invaders were sowing broadcast about the country. Otherwise, the proclamations would certainly be regarded as magical formulae, intended to bring disease and pestilence among the people, and would be looked upon merely as an additional incentive to hostility.

One of our little Ghurkha soldiers was caught, while our scouting, in a Lushai deer trap. The trap consisted of a stout young tree bent down as a spring, with a loop outsperead. Into this loop the man unwittingly thrust his foot, and was at once jerked high into the air, kicking lustily. His comrades soon set him free by cutting the thong which held him, and he escaped with the fright and a bad sprain.

The weather grew colder and colder, the nights and mornings being truly chrismatic; but the general health of the force was good, in spite of a very limited scale of diet.

On the 2nd of January the General and I ascended the Tworange range, hoping to discern some sign of General Bourchiers column; but we gained nothing by our climb, save a grand view of the surrounding country. Sylu SAvung, the largest village of the Sylu tribe, and the residence of their head chief, Savunga, lay in full view not more than ten miles off, separated from us only by a deep valley, which was curiously intersected by the head waters of three rivers, two of which ran northwards to Cachar, and the third bent south to join the Karnaphuli river. Far away to the east we saw the villages of the Howlongs, while about eight miles to the north lay the strongly stockade village of Lal Nagora, eldest son of Savunga, which the General determined to attack and destroy.

The following day, therefore, Captain Battye of the 2nd Ghurkhas, with two Companies of that regiment, was sent to reconnoiter in the direction of Lal Nagora's village, and reported that it was held in force by the enemy, who apparently meant fighting.

The next day the attack was made by the whole of Colonel Macpherson's regiment led the assault, and was the first man over the also was slightly wounded in the attack. The village was burnt and a large quantity of grain destroyed.

At night the Sylus approached our camp in the darkness and held a parley with me. They said that their head chief Savunga wished to come in immediately with a peace offering of elephant's tusks. I replied that he might do so with safety, but that until he did, the progress of the expedition would not be stayed. I added that their villages and crops would be spared if no resistance were offered.

Rutton Poia was with me during the nocturnal colloquy, and he promptly suggested that, if Savunga came in, it would be wise to chop off his head and put it on a pole. So much for Lushai faith! No wonder they were suspicious. We halted all the next day to see if anything would come of this overture, but the Sylus still made no sign.[47]

We advanced upon Savunga's village on the 6th January. The road was very difficult , being blocked by huge boulders, and leading over up and down, rest along a ridge, then plunging down a thousand feet into a valley, where we waded and stumbled for an hour or more along the bed of a torrent, then up once more to the heights, and so on.

On arriving at a "joom", or clearing, within about nine hundred yards of a small outlying village, we saw that it was filled with armed men, and the General thought this a favourable opportunity for showing the Lushais the force of our guns, which had hitherto not been employed. Fifty

Ghurkhas was sent forward skirmishing straight to the front, while the mountain-battery of which Colonel James Hills was the commandant, was directed to open fire over their heads. The small seven pounder steel guns, unscrewed into two pieces, had been painfully carried along on the shoulders of coolies; but now they were quickly put together, and in an incredibly short space of time were making beautiful shell practice at the village, which was crowded with armed Lushais.

Having never seen a big gun fired before, the enemy's consternation was great, and as the first shell burst over their heads all scattered helter- skelter, abandoning the village, and fleeing for their lives in all directions.

"It is wonderful"! remarked Rutton Poia. "You fire one gun out of another. No one could withstand it".

On mounting to the village, we found that the enemy had prepared for us an artful avalanche of rocks, which was to have swept the path leading upwards; and also a goodly store of spears, arrow, and other misiles to be hurled upon our devoted heads; but they had reckoned without our sevenpounders, and their designs came to naught.

The same day some of my men, whom I had sent out scouting into the jungle, in the vain hope that they might capture some Sylu men who would serve as envoy, discovered and brought in to me four fine gongs of Chinese workmanship.

The next morning, early, the great village of Sylu Savung burst into flames. The encounter of the day before had apparently convinced the Sylus that they had no chance against us in fighting; and on the 2nd of January we occupied the site of their chief village without any further opposition.

There was now but one village of the Sylu tribe left standing. That of Lal Jika, the youngest son of Savung; all the rest had been burned by their own inhabitants, or taken by us. This tribe, therefore might be considered as subjugated, and we accordingly turned our attention next to the recovering of the captives from the Howlongs, whose villages were now in full view, and within striking distance.

The Government of India had been pressing the General to avoid any unnecessary destruction of villages or crops, although I confess, I could not see how this could be avoided, or what could have been done other than what had been done. Still the Governor-General's wishes were law, and I determined, at the General's request, to undertake a peaceful embassy to the Howlongs before the first blow should be struck against them.

I started, therefore, on the 13th of January, taking with me Rutton Poia and his Lushais, together with an escort of fifty Ghurkhas, bound for the nearest Howlong village, which was plainly visible from our camp. As we drew near, the inhabitants of the village discovered our approach, and, to my dismay, followed their usual procedure and set fire to the place.

Rutton Poia looked very grave at this unmistakable declaration of hostility, forthwith declined to proceed any farther, saying that the only method of peaceful approach to the Howlongs was by the rear. He proposed that we should at once return to Sagunga's, whence he would pass by a long detour to the south, and only thus be able to gain access to Benkuia and Sangbunga, the two brothers who ruled the Howlong tribe. This proposal involved much delay, but I saw no other course, and to my regret, we had to return to Sylu Sagung, and report the failure of our mission to General Brownlow.

Much against his inclination, the General agreed to halt at Sylu Savung, while Rutton Poia set off on his round about journey, accompanied by subadar Mahomed Azim, one of the most intelligent officers of the frontier Battalion.

This chief was directed to inform the Howlongs that the only basis upon which we would treat with them was the unconditional release of all the captives, together with free access for ourselves to the Howlong's country; otherwise we should attack. We had then to await the result; and indeed, both officers and men needed rest for although the campaign was not very ardous as far as fighting was concerned, still enormous distances had been traversed over the rough ground, the soldiers carrying heavy weights in the shape of clothing and ammunition. Hard fare also had been our porition in this savage and inhospitable country, the English officers, for instance, having subsisted on a diet of chapattis, tinned mut- ton, and rum. The General himself fared no better than the rest of the force, and the general health of all began to suffer for, want of change in the diet.

There was no grumbling, however, unless the universal and heart felt aspiration to make an end of the business could be construed into a complaint. While awaiting the result of Rutton Poia's mission, the General turned his attention to the last remaining village of the recalcitrant Sylus, who had as yet made no sign of substantial submission. This was, as I have said, the village of Lal Jika, youngest son of the chief Savunga, and here, if anywhere, the tribe might be expected to show fight.

General Brownlow, having reconnoitred the palce and determined upon his course of action, delivered the attack on the 21st of January. We started at 8.30 A.M. to avoid the mists of the early morning, land marching along, found our road stopped by a stockade. While the guns were being shot up, an extension was made by both flanks to turn the enemy's position, perceiving which, the Lushais let fall about our ears an avalanche of rocks and stones which they had in readiness, but which fortunately did little damage. They than abandoned the stockade and retreated to their village.

Our advance was continued, and at a distance of seven hundred yards, Colonel Hills' small seven pound rifled guns opened fire with shell and sharpnel. This made a clearance of the Lushai, who fled in dismay before those new and terrible projectiles, and we occupied the place without loss. It was a strong position, most elaborately stockaded, and, but for the funs, we much have suffered severely in capturing it.

Having destroyed the crops and granaries in the vicinity, we returned to our camp at Sylu Sagvung. Here I was met by the glad tidings that my ambassador, Rutton Poia, had effected the release of Mary Winchester, and had delivered the child into the keeping of Colonel Tytler, of the 4th Ghurkhas, who commanded at Demagree, by whom she had been despatched to Calcutta via Chittagong.

Mary Winchester was described as being a pretty child of about six years old, fair complexioned, with hazel eyes and European features. The officer who sent by Colonel Tytler to take her over from Rutton Poia, found the little maid sitting on the log platform of the chief's houses, having for clothing only rag round her loins, and with to a top of small boys were disporting themselves before her.

She appeared, during her long stay with her kidnappers, to have altogether forgotten the English language; but on the officer fumbling in his pocket, and demanding whether she would like to have a sweetie, her memory at once responded to this ancient and familiar question, and she held out her hand, showing that she understood what had been said.

She was duly made over to her friends in Calcutta, and from there was sent to Scotland, where I believe her father's relatives resided. Ten years passed an examination at the Royal Mary College. It was curious to consider that, but for a chain of unlikely events, she might have been the bride of some dusky Lushai chief, wearing a scanty kirtle and an amber necklace.

Further, I was informed that the chief Rutton Poia, having succeeded so far in his embassy, had departed with all speed to the Northern Howlongs, whose villages now confronted us, and he particularly requested that we would abstain from hostilities, as otherwise his safety might be jeopardised.[48]

The General chafed like a charged lion at this forced inaction, which he was compelled to endure; for it would have been but poor satisfaction to undertake a military promenade through the Howlong country, as we had already done through Syluland, and to have to entire without recovering the remainder of the captives; and as, moreover, I had pledged my faith to Rutton Poia, it was agreed to wait for one week more before entering the Howlong territory.

A night or two afterwards, as we were sitting in the General's hut playing a rubber after dinner, we heard two shots fired in quick successsion, followed by the scream of wounded man; then more shots, sharp and quick, as our men fired in reply. The whole encampment was astir in a moment, like a disturbed ants's nest. The hum of voices and the clank of hastily donned account were heard on all sides.

We found that the Lushais has stolen up through the jungle, under cover of the darkness, and had shot one of our sentries, sending a charge of slugs into his chest at twenty pacs distance, and then had promptly scuttled off. Our poor fellow was badly hurt, and at the time it was believed that medical aid could do nothing to save him.

Returning to the hut, we could not resume the rubber, but smoked an angry pipe, grieved at the loss of a good soldier in so cowardly a fashion. I may add here, however, that the little Ghurkha, who was shot through the lung, did not die of this wound, his life being saved by the unwaried attention and skill of Dr. Allen, the medical officer of the 2nd Gurkhas; but, as they say in the East, the lad's "kismet" was bad, for he had no sooner recovered from the charge of sluges in his lungs, than he was attacked by cholera, and died before the end of the year.

The conversation running on night attacks, General Brownlow related some of his experiences of that kind of the North Western Frontier.

During the Ambeyloa campaign he had been beleaguered one starlight night by countless Afghans, who yelled and fought for six hours, in their endeavour to turn him out of a small breastwork of loose stone held by a picquet of his old regiment, the 20th Punjab Infantry, about one hundred strong. The position, on a commanding knoll, was a good one, and the enemy dashed themselves against it in vain, being driven back time after time with much loss. After one of the most determined of these onslaughts there was a lull and silence, which was broken by a voice close to the picked proposing a suspension of hostilities and a song. The object was probably to gain time to carry off the killed and wounded; but most of the men of the 20th happended to be Pathans, and the incident was of much to their taste they broke into a shout of applause and bagged the General to give the order "Cease firing". Which he accordingly did.

Then from behind his sheltering rock the Bajahari (for he gave his name and clan as well as a pledge to enlist in the 20th at the close of campaign) immediately began a wild weird song of love and war, that indicated the throat and lungs as well as the heart of a fire born mountainner. He had so sooner ended than two young Afridis of the regiment sprang on to the parapet of the breastwork, and sitting outlined against the sky, a target for a thousand matchlocks, replied in a duet of equal sound and melody, not a shot being fired at them.

At the last words of the song died on their lips they jumped back under cover, with the plaudits of both sides, and the promise of the order of merit as a reward for their music and their valour.

A few playful remark of mutual defiance were followed by the warning from without that it was time to resume business, and emphasised by a storm of bullets and renewed attacks that lasted until daylight, when the enemy withdrew, and the exhausted picquet was believed and returned to its bivouac below.

This same outpost, known to history as the "Crag picquet", and on which the safety of the whole camp depended, was twice subsequently carried by the enemy sword in hand, and on each occasion its capture and recapture cost the British force upwards of a hundred killed and wounded, Sir Neville Chamberlin (the General commanding), and Colonel Hope, of the 1st Highlanders, being among those who were badly hit in the last of these Homeric contests.

Our Lushai opponents, however, were not of this kidney, but like the mosquito, although contemptible, they were annoying. On other occasion they came creeping up the hill side to the house where I was sleeping, and fired through the floor (the house being raised on piles, Lushai fashion), without, however, doing me any harm. The campaign, we hoped now, would be finished in three weeks' time, for after the expiration of the week for which I had stipulated, the General intended to take a stretch out with a flying column, severing for the time being his communication with the rear.

From Silchar, the Cachar Column or Left Column of the Lushai Expeditionary force under Brigadier General Bourchier marched against the site direction should meet the Chittagong Column at a convenient point.[49] *(Mizoram Under British Rule*- S. Chatterjee). According to Lewin, "The country between us was unknown and unmapped and it was impossible to say what distance apart we might be". Captain Lewin had been resting for a while but was ill at ease". A soldier can endure anything better than inaction, and here, waiting at Sylu Savunga there was nothing to do, nothing to see, nothing to read, nothing to eat; there was not even any news. "But what to do next? General Brownlow ordered advance against the Howlongs.

"We started with our faces set against the Howlongs on the 12th of February, 1872. Our small force consisted of three hundred Gurkhas, with the two mountain guns and half a company of Sappers. The path descended first some 2,300 feet into the valley of the Daleshari stream; then rose for 1,300 feet, leading along a ridge for some distance; then another plunge of 1,000 feet into the bed of another hill stream, whence a final ascent of 1,600 feet brought us out on to a rolling upland the country of the Howlongs.

When we had to march long distance through water it was my custom to go barefoot. This was regarded by the officer of the force merely as eccentricity, but experience, hard stones, muddy water, and long marches combined, proved potent arguments in favour of bare footness versus shoe leather, and convinced many of the expediency of following my example.

We camped for the night soon after our final ascent, and the next morning, Captain East, our Assistan Quartermaster General, and I went out together reconnoitering, after proceeding some distance we saw on some rising ground to our left the smoking ruins of a village, which, in due course, had been burnt by its inhabitants on our advance the day before. The knoll on which the village had stood, however, was now crowded with Lushais , and on our hailing them a friendly dialogue ensued. To my infinite satisfaction, they professed a desire for peace, and said that their chiefs were quite willing to release the captives. "Go then", I said, "fetch your chiefs; let them bring the captives and arrange matters. We will do you no harm then".

Returning to camp, we reported the occurrence to the General, who was as pleased as we were at the turn things seemed likely to take. Our force moved on, however, in spite of fair words, to a village called Chongmama, to the east to which, at a distance of two days' march, lay the villages of Benkuia and Sangbunga, the head chief of the Howlong tribe, and within easy striking distance of four other large villages, aggregating, perhaps, a thousand dwellings.

We found in the jungles round Chongmama numerous huts, which had been erected by the burnt out Sylus, with stroes of grain and other things. These we carefully left untouched, as sufficient punishment had been inflicted on that tribe. It was ascertained from the Howlongs that General Bourcher's column was at a distance about four days' journey to the east; our General, therefore, abandoned all hope of effecting a junction, or even communicating with the left Column, as we were at the extreme end of our tether and lofty range of hills intervened.[50]

On the 15th the General sent out two reconnoitering parties: one under Major MacIntyre; which returned after some hours with full information as to the roads and passes northwards; the second party, under Captain Battye, went east, and soon after back a messenger to the General, reporting that a mile below camp was a stream, the passage of which was barred by large bodies of armed Lushais. Were they to force the passage or not? The General ordered party to return, and sent me down to parley with the enemy. I found the fort guarded by Benkuia's men, that being the direct road to the chief's village. I bade them go and fetch their chiefs quickly, and that I would be personally responsible for their safety. In my own mind I felt convinced that Rutton Poia's embassy by the rear had been successful, and that the Howlongs meant to submit; their own innate treachery, however made them suspicious of us.

Lewin's Daring Adventure

That night, as I lay asleep in my hut, a voice came to me out the darkness. Close to my head.

"Thangliena!" (Lushai paraphrase of Tom Lewin) "Thangliena! Is it peace? Made no reply, the voice continued—

"The great chiefs will be at the Tuldung stream tomorrow at dawn, but you must come alone, without any soldiers. "a pause; the "Thangliena! Do you hear?"

"I hear," I replied, groping for my revolver, and cautiously emerging from my shelter to halt further parley with the mysterious speaker, but there was nothing. All was silent, and there was only the dark night and the keen wind, with the sound of my own men snoring. The messenger, a Lushai evidently had crept past our sentries, done his errand, and was gone; so I lit a pipe, and sat down to think over the situation.

I know that the General would object to my going alone to the meeting as proposed, for if it should turn out to be ruse, and I were captured and carried off as a hostage by the Lushais, the last state of things would be worse than the first. Again, if I went to the rendezvous with a body of soldiers, the chiefs would suspect treachery and probably would not appear.

However, I had been successful before, in my dealings with the hill men, even when I had no avenging force at my back; and now my necessity was greater, for I had my policy to justify. The mere thought of failure was insupportable. My whole experience led me to believe that these people could not understand or realize a complex governing machine like ours. They needed personal dealing, personal authority, personal promises. After all, I had played with my life for much smaller stake, so I determined to go. In the early morning, before the camp was well awake, I set off down the hill path leading to the Tuldung; after going about half a mile I heard a sound behind me, and glancing round, found that I was followed by an armed Lushai. A little farther on, another man issued from the jungle, and joined the first, then another, until at last I was followed by ten or twelve of the Howlongs.

I took no notice whatever of my following, by marched steadily on; down went the path, steeper, until at length I reached a black slow flowing stream, the Tuldung. Across this a rough bridge had been thrown by felling a large tree, the trunk of which lay across from bank to bank a distance of eighteen or twenty feet. On the opposite side of the stream the ground rose again abruptly, and I saw standing there tier on tier of Lushais, in series crowd, armed with guns and bristling with spears.

My heart was beating a good deal faster than it should have done; but there was only one course possible, so I tightened my belt with a hitch and went on steadily over the bridge. The passage of that narrow slippery tree across the deep dark stream, with the rows of strange hostile faces looking down on me, I shall never forget.

As I reached the other side, a venerable white bearded Lushai met me and took me by the hand; two other men bearing light canes, made a passage for us through the crowd, striking the people, and chilling them back; and so I was led to the chiefs.

They were sitting in a circle, a little distance back from the stream, in a small rarest glade, and around them surged myriads of Lushais; the jungle was like ants' nest. As I was led forward by my white bearded conductor, there was a cry from the crowd of "Thanglienna! Thanliena!"

The chiefs rose and received me. I inquired which was Sanbunga; he came forward, and in an agitated manner put his own gun into my hands, while his brother, Benkuia, took a short sward from his waist and hung it about my neck. Fortunately I had on me some valuable arms, a sword and silver mounted dagger taken long before in the Mutiny, and these I presented gravely as return gifts. Then we seated ourselves.

I felt inexpressibly relieved; they were evidently in a great fright, so I consequently ceased to be nervous. The game was won; the campaign was at an end.

I was able to speak some Lushai myself, and the chief's "karbaris" were acquainted with bazaar Bengali, so I had little difficulty in communicating to Slngbunga and his brother the terms on which alone peace could be concluded. It was necessary, I told them, first that they should give up all British subjects, whom they held captive, or account for them, according to lists which I had in my possession; also free and friendly access to their villages both now and in future must be granted to us; and further, I required them to take a solemn oath to abstain from making any raids in future upon British territory. If they complied with these conditions our force would be withdrawn.

After some consultation, the chiefs replied that they had heard my words with satisfaction, and that their desire was to have peace. They promised to send a definitive answer to my demands on the morrow.

Just at that moment I heard the tramp, of our Gurkhas coming down the path on the other side of the stream, and some of the Lushais ran up shouting that the soldiers were coming. For a moment a look passed round the circle, just a glint of the eyes, which gave me a cold feeling down my back. But I explained that the soldiers would not cross the stream and had probably been sent by the great General Sahib to escort me back; and so we parted with many expressions of amity and good will.

On my return to camp I had infinite pleasure in reportıng to the Genearl all that had passed, and he, with the generosity which is his chief characteristic, after expressing his satisfaction at the turn matters had taken was so good as to say that he left the entire management of the affair in my hands. This was just what I desired, for by personally concluding a treaty with the Howlongs, backed by an avenging force, I felt that my influence would be greatly enhanced in any future dealings I might have with them after the expedition was over.

On the 18th February I swore the indispensable oath by blood and steel with the Howlong chiefs, and they presented to Government a peace offering of elephant tusks, home spun cloth, guyals, &c.; and the day following the first instalment of captives was sent in, with the promise that the rest, who were scattered in distant villages, should be collected and delivered up as soon as possible.

The camp now swarmed with picturesque Lushais, men, women, and children, bringing for sale eggs, fowls, cloths, pipes, and other local wares, and gazing with infinite couriosity on their quondam enemies.

In accordance with our newly made agreement, the General at once dispatched a detachment of Gurkhas and an officer of the Survey Department, to visit the village of Benkuia and other in their neighbourhood, and thus assert our right of free entry. The Survey officer took with him the necessary instruments to map the country that was to be visited.

Lewin as the Civil Officer of the Right Column

The aim of the Lushia Expeditionary Force had been to punish the guilty Lushai chiefs who perpetrated raids into British territory and also to display the military force the dreadful fire power of the Government to command obedience from the wild savages. The other aim had been to free the captives including Mary Winchester. The task of the Civil Officer was to negotiate political terms with the chiefs and at the same time to collect whole information about the Lushais and Lushai land. Before the actual operation Bengal Government asked lewin to make a study tour of the interior places of Chittagong, Dacca and Sylhet districts to make an on the spot survey of the base areas that would provide the infrastructure of a large scale military operation. His notes were accepted by the authorities of Fort William.

Lewin from his camp at Savung wrote to the Junior Secretary, Government of Bengal on 24 February 1872, "The Lusahi tribes have no coherence, but seem to be forest Ismails; their hands being against every one and evry one's hand against them. Thus, Sukpilal recommends that we should attack Benkya and Sevunga, while these chiefs advise that Sukpilal should be compelled to give his captives, the object of each being to strengthen himself at the expense of the other."

Sukpilal's Territory

Lewin then goes on defining the territory of the Sylo chief Sukpilal's "With regard to the people and country between Cachar and Chittagong, I am of course only in a position to speak positively of such portion there of as came within the sphere of observation of the Right Column. Ther are no tribes between Sukpilal and Karnafuli river in a northernly direction with whom we have not had relationas."

The limits of Sukpilal's authority are conterminous, -South with the Joom boundaries of the chief Laljeeka, son of Savunga, the head of the Syloo tribe; east with these of Lalbura and Jo- htoma, Howlong chiefs; while to the west his tribne is supposed to join, and have relations with certain Kooke clans living within the bounds of Hill Tipperah. I know nothing of the country north of Sukpilal's clan.[52]

Lewin's Final Report

At the close of the operation of the Right Column of the Lushai Expeditionary Force, Lewin carefully prepared the draft of his final report and dispatched it from Chittagong on 26 March 1872 to the Secretary to the Government of Bengal.

"I have the honour, to submit, as required, the final report on the operations of the Right Column, Lushai Expedition in as far as related to the political aspects of the campaign.

"The object of the expediton against the Lushais, which has just been concluded, was not solely that of retaliations; for althought punishment was, if possible, to be meted out to the guilty participators in the late raids on Cachar, a still more important end to be gained was deliverance of British subjects carried away into captivity; while paramount to both these considerations was the necessity for conducting our operations with a view to establishing permanently the security of our frontiers.

At the commencement of the operation in Nov. 1871, we faced many difficulties, " The knowledge we possessed of the Lushais, of their language and customs, was very impercect; and throughout the whole of the perters. The information possessed by there civil authorities as to the identities of the actual perpetrators of the raids was vague and incomplete, and our knowledge of the paths of the local difficulties before us next to nothing. Never perhaps has an English force advanced into an enemy's country with less knowledge of what was was before it, or with more uncertainty as to obtaining in any way the desired information."

The local officers had no communication with the Lushai's once a year, when some few hundreds of them came to the annual mela of Kasalong. The headquarters of the Deputy Commissioner of the Chittagong Hill Tract were from 9-12 days journey from the nearest Howlong and Syloo village; no direct trade was carried on by our own tribes with the Lushais. The Lushais themselves were strongly opposed to any of our people entering into their territory, for they fear tha new deseases would be introduced to them. "Our ally

Rutton Poia, reaped considerable advantage from being the sole intermediary between us and the other tribes". He prevented us from getting direct information about the tribes.

At the commencement of the operation who had the apprehension which side Rutton Poia would take. His brother-in-law, Vandoola, the southern Howlong chief urged him to go against us. The Sylos, with whom Rutton Poia is not in good terms, sent him threatening if he helped us.

He, of course, chose to help us, possibly seeing the strength of our force assembled at DEMAGIRI near his villages. He tried his best to exert his influence upon the Southern and Northern Howlongs in favour of us and the recovery of Miss Winchester is indirectly due to him. It is due to him "We were met with confidence by the chiefs, and a basis laid upon which terms could be imposed and our future relation regulated."

By offering his cooperation, with us the chief Rutton Poia became unpopular among the Howlongs and Sylos, and he had invited his danger. "Indeed" one of Saipooea's head men, in my presence (ignorant that understood him) charged the chief with treachery in having brought the English forces to their village contary to his pledged word."

I assured him with General Brownlow's concurrence that an possible help be sent to him and a guard would be posted in his village.

The first advance of the force was made on 9th December 1875 against the Syloo for road communication and that they were responsible for the Cachar raids and they possessed Mary Winchester.

Before attacking the Syloos we wanted to have a friendly communication and sent Leinsiloung, a known Kukie sent to us to that effect but with no result.

On 12 December we reached the Vanloola's village and sent Lengoora, a Kookie known to us, to inform our purpose. He came to inform us that the Syloo chiefs were determined to attack us. He refused to go again as our ambassador to them. Soon I waas attacked form an ambused mulsketiers butwas saved luckily. We attacked the village and took in on 14 December 1871.from this date up to the 25th January 1872 the military operations of the force were continuous. "Our attacks were equally rapid and decisive."

Meanswhile I sent emissaries of my own accompanied by Rutton Poia's men to the chief of Benkuia, to hand over Mary Winchester and other captives to beg submission. Seeking the advance of our emissary he delivered Mary Winchester to our men but did not surrender himself, for the thought that the aim of our attack was mainly for the recovery of Winchester. He also thought that we would not be able to penetrate further.

We reached the village of the chief Savoonga and the punishment of the Syloos were complete.

On 12th February the force corssed the Tlangdoong and entered the Howlong Country.

The Howlongs raised the white flag and chief after chief came to make peace with us.

"The terms insisted upon were alike with all. They were briefly the surrender of all captives; an agreement on their part (ratified in the most solemn and binding manner which Lushai customs prescribes) to live for the future on terms of peace and amity with all British subjects from Manipur to Arracan (including Hill Tiperah), with free right of access to our people throughout their whole country. I append a list of the chiefs who have submitted to the British arms during this expedition."

Banking and Sabunga were not punished.

Operations in the northern Howlong and Syloo countries were successful; the General next advanced to the south to make it complete. The tribes living in that country were under the influence of Rutton Poia and the expediton had not faced difficulties.

He submitted the list of the recovery of the captives. He stated that the Lushais treated the captives, particularly the female captives very kindly. Some of the female captives married the Lushais and they did not like ot come out of their settled home and Lushai village. In fact they had to be forceably taken to the camp. His own interpreter's wife and a grown up daughter who were kidnapped by the raids, refused to come ovdr. To exhibition of such unnatural feelings were ascribed by them, as Kookie magic. "Magic it is true, but I imagine that it was the white magic of kindness and human sympathy."

In addition to the captives released, 250 more persons who were compelled to leave Chitagong Hill Tacts came to tekll their villingnes to come back. A considerable member of Syloo tribes and a whole village of Howlongs intended their willingness to come to live under the British protections. The principal chiefs also requested me to establish a bazaar at Demagiri because Kassalong is too far for them.

Result of the Expedition

"The political results of the campaign have in my opinion been great and manifold, fully justifying the magnitude of the expedition and affording every reason to hope that the permanent pacification of the frontier may be attained. The Lushai tribes have ben forced to recognize the existence of a superior power, able alike both to reward and punish, a firm and secure basis has been laid for our future relations with them whether commercial or political; the whole country is open us, ands I believe that any European could now walk unarmed from one end to the other. The severe lesson that had heen taught to them this year would prevent the Lushais to go against us. Soon these fierce tribe would become tame and friendly to us like the Khasis and Jayantias.

In all matters connected with the tribes it should be remembered that they are not a nation but a segregation of villages, a collection of small separate republic having no coherence, we are nto dealing with thte fagot, but the severed bundle of sticks. In our future relation with them we should remember this carefully.

No permanently pacification of this frontier can be hoped for save by bringing these people into closer intercourse with us by encouraging trade and by permitting the Government representatives to exercise as near and direct influence upon them.

It has also been said that another way of dealing with these people would be to strengthen the hands of some particular chiefs, and so consolidate them under one head; and surely it is first necessary to have a more intimate acquintance with both chiefs and people even any such choice could be made."[55]

List of the Lushai chiefs who submitted and swore friendship during the Lushai Expedition 1871-72.

Tribe	*Name*	*Remarks*
Syloo	Savoonaga	Represented by his son
	Lal Nagora	Sons of Savoonga
	Lal Jika	
	Vanhnoya two brothers	Step brother of Rutton Poia
	Van Kenga	
	Vanhnuna	
	Venhoolen	
	Dowtyeyva	Subject of Savoonga
	Vanlula	
	Vanshuma	

(Contd...)

Tribe	*Name*	*Remarks*
Howlong (North)	Sangvunga	These chiefs are brothers
	Benkuia	The former has married Rutton Poia's sister.
	Vasanga	
	Chegmama	Subject to Sangvunga.
	Lien- U-Koom	
	Lalbura	Brothers independent Johtoma Vandoola Represented by this son Sanghena
Howlong (South)	Vnatunga+two brothers	Cousin of Vandoola
	Sanghena	Eldest son of Vanadoola
	Saipoiya	Brothers of Vandoola Brother-in-law of Rutton Poia. T.H. Lewin Captian,Civil Officer Right Column Lushai Expedition.[55a]

All total 83+27 captives were recovered from the Lushais in the expedition, who were taken prisoners from Cachar, Chittagong Hill Tracts etc.

C

The statement of Suree; by caste a *Rajbunsee*; her father's name Sroop, a resident to the village Kalidan, in the pargana of Purulia, district Purulia, 19th February 1822, in presence of T. Lewin.

She states that she was a labourer in a tea garden, Chachar where the Kookies came and killed Mr. Winchester. They took shelter in the jungle. The Kookies killed her husband.the Kookies captured 18 of them include- ing Mary

Winchester. They were brought to a Howlong village and kindly treated. Along with one Banee, another captives she attempted an ecscape but after two months they were caught by strange Kiookies and handed over to their old masters. She was never ioo treated and the Kookies never attempted to violate her. She had to work for the tribes.

The statement of Poonoo; father's name, Golok; caste Bagdee, residence in the district of Burdwan.

"About 3 year ago was at Calcutta, and one day, when I saw in the bazaar, I was forcibly laid of and carried off by an emigration agent. I was kept in confinement for some time till we were sent to Cachar.

I was not told that I should work on a tea garden; the agent said I should be employed at a raja's house. At last I and others were put one day, at about noon, some hundred of Kookies entered the tea garden and commenced slaughtering on us. They made a frightful noise, so that we were all afraid and tried to run away. I tried to run also but was caught, bound and taken away by a Kookie. I saw several bodies of people who had been killed as I was taken along. There were eighteen of us altogether, besides Miss Winchester. I do not know what had become of Miss Winchester, they sold her I think. They also sold four of our people who were captives. I do not know where they went to. Other captives were brought from Cachar, but not by Benkuia's village: the people of the east brought them. In ever saw any. I heard of it from the Kookies and our captives talked of it. Suree knows about it. She can talk Kookiea. Two of our people were left behind at Benkuia's yesterday, because they did not wish to come as they had no parents. The journey from Cachar to Benkuia's occupied ten days. There were many Kookies before and behind. I know not how many. All did not come with us to Benkuia's. Many left us going east, the day before we reached there. I do not know anything more.

The 19th February 1872

Lewin as Deputy Commissioner

Lewin had been a brilliant Frontier Officer but he was also the chief administrative officer of the CHT and that was his substantive post. He was directly responsible to the Commissioner, Citation Division of Bengal. So he had to write to the Commissioner on many important issues relating to the problems of the frontiers. Lewin was a peculiar local administrator hated behaving as opportunist, shying away from the major decisions and to remain constant to dispose of the day's word without taking thought for the morrow which remained the safest attitude in the field of Indian administration.

He suggested certain measures for the improvement of the lot of the Lushais. The Lucia Expeditionary force smashed the backbone of Sailo (Sylo) clan of the ruling Lucia tribe living on the outskirts of the CHT. The Expedition 1871-72 reduced the Lucia to submission but the Lushai country on financial consideration was not annexed to the British dominion; only that was brought under the British Sphere of Influence. The Deputy Commissioner of CHT and Cachar as Frontier Officers were entrusted with the task to maintain the British influence over the Lushai country, the south and north. The Sailos, particularly the Sailos of the southern hills, had to undergo the tormenting experience of the British atrocities throughout the entire course of the advance of the Right Column as the main burden of the Expedition fell on them. From the stand point of their responsibility in raiding the British territory, their share had never been greater than the formidable Howlong, Thanglowas of Shendus (Lakher) but they (Sailos) were primarily responsible for abducting Mary Winchester and enslaving her. Moreover, the other Lushais, who were no less ferocious than the Sailos, acknowledge the British Supremacy with less obduracy and occasionally sided with the invincible advancing column with the avowed aim of weakening the political and military strength of the powerful Sailos. Thus the condition of the Sailos became precarious in the tribal union. They were always under the constant threat of the Howlongs another powerful Lucia hordes. Lewin was aware of all these government policy was unambiguous in this respect i.e., non-interference. The Saiolos were head-hunting maraunding tribes men easily prone to violent activities would swoop upon the British subject on the frontiers causing considerable tension and alert on the borders of the CHT which has relevance to the strategic well being. But Lewin was of opinion that the Sailos could not be allowed to get tormented by the unscrupulous Howlongs. In his report on 29 June 1872 to the Commissioner, Chittagong (vide, BJP) August 1872, No. 521) Lewin suggested that the loyal Sailos be allowed to move to the west of Sirthay, the range of hills to the English side.[55c]

But his suggestions found no favour with the government. So he wrote back, "British friendly relations with the hill men should not be fettered by any condition." Because they would not keep in future. Lewin had been of opinion that the obedience, the Kukie chief commanded from his subordinates, according to this personality. He recorded, " the chiefs have no more social or political influence over them, then the chairman of a public meeting in London has over the assembly of which he is the president.[55d]

Thus, Lewin brushed aside the suggestion of the higher authorities to put any condition on the migrating Sailo chiefs. He pointed out in his missive that it was difficult to exact a treaty obligation from the Lushais, and that 'they are only amenable to rod' and to Lewin that was the only remedy. Lewin further reported that each clan and tribe were enemies of the other and fought against each other but their customs were the same and they also live in composite villages. Lewin stated, "Each chief ring clans intermarry to gain political advantage. Lewin stated, "Each chief among the kookies has his own village, each clan has its own recongnized limits on joom land. In the case of a powerful chief, many villages acknowledge his leadership and his protection.... These villages keep close together and occupy definite limits, within which no outsiders are allowed to come."[56]

The authentic report of Lewin significantly corroborated by his personal experience was forwarded by H. Hankey, the Officiating Commissioner, Chittagong to the Bengal Government in Calcutta for reconsideration and approval. Alexandar Mackenzie, the junior secretary Foreign Department, Government of Bengal considered it highly desirable that the distressed Syloos be allowed to settle in the west of Sirthay Tlang.[57] Thus, Lewin was successful in his mission of assisting a group of friendless wild tribes on compassionate ground breaking the conservate limit of the administration.

Administration Report 1871-72, by Lewin

This small administration report of CHT, characteristic of Lewin's passionate uncontrollable innerself, convulsed the entire government machinery as he criticized the British policy of managing the hills through the selective chiefs and compelling the local British officer to follow that unworkable outmoded prices of policy against his wishes. Lewin considered the administration of the hills with the help of the intermediary of the so called friendly loyal chiefs was not at all satisfactory as it was indirect coupled with the divestment of political responsibility. To demonstrate his conviction he cited the example of the recently concluded Lushai Expedition 1871-72. According to Lewin majority of such 'friendly chiefs' did not cooperate with the expeditionary force during the operation.

Beside, he also pointed out in his annual report that the jhum cultivation which had been basically different from the traditional mode was causing the decline of influence of the chiefs over the tribe. Thus, Lewin advocated a change in the policy of hills administration. According to Lewin 'direct administration' was the compelling need.[58] Up to this extent Lewin was within his jurisdiction as the administrative officer. But soon he lost control over his self and bitterly criticized the preposterous 'centralization' in the affairs of administration of hill areas. Lewin's imagination ran riot and overpowered his rationality. The military officer's concern for the welfare of the hill men made him pensive and with the glistering flow of ideas he put of his valley of impulsive words attacking the system of administration of the British Government.

II

Cog in the Wheel Controversy

Lucia Expedition 1871-72 had been a very costly and a prolonged military operation since the first Anglo- Burmese War 1824-26 in an unknown terrain of the North East India. Initially the Government of India had been unwilling to launch the costly expedition but the powerful tea lobby both in London and Calcutta which had enormous influence over the working of the Bengal Government made the Lieutenant Governor to insist on the punitive expedition of immense dimension. Lewin's suggestion in this matter had been negative as he expedition believe in the soundness of the policy of conciliation. In my opinion, expedition might have been avoided had discretionary powers been granted to the district officers to follow and punish all raiders found crossing the frontiers". However when entrusted with duty of the Civil Officer by Lord Mayo, the Governor General, he discharged his duties sincerely with courage and conviction. General Brownlow who commanded the Right Column of the Expeditionary Force in the face of insurmountable difficulties during the expensive operation privately admitted the correctness of Lewin's view. Lewin of course was a supporter of the remedy of the rod whenever necessary but not total destruction or subject surrender of the tribes. The success of the Lushai Expedition had resulted into minimal control over the wild tribes and the defence of the frontiers did not improve as expected. All these were bitterly criticized by the Home Government in London and the Government of India, for that matter Bengal Government also had been put to the spot. In such a suffocating situation when the stock of the government had been plunging came the virulent attack from Lewin upon the British administrative system. Government of India could not forgive Lewin for the criticism of the frontiers policy but "cog in the wheel" became a byword of British Indian administration. Resolution of the Government of Bengal, Calcutta, 27 August 1872 passed a stricture upon Lewin's remark.

"The complaint made by the Deputy Commissioner is unreasonable....

Government has its duties and responsibilities as well as Captain Lewin, had while quite ready to entrust to its subordinate officers, especially in frontier tracts, generous liberty of action, it must insist upon having satisfactory information of their proceedings and a real control over their operations. It is impossible to acquiesce blindly in schemes, however promising, that introduces radical changes into established systems, or entail upon the general revenues, that is to say in the peaceable taxpayers of India, heavy charges on account of experiments and arrangements that command themselves to the minds to local officer."[59]

The resolution went on "To complain of the restrictive actions of the Government in this respect is to strike at the root of all authority whatsoever. "The resolution further added" while acknowledging fully Captain Lewin's many valuable qualities as a Frontier Officer, the Lieutenant

Governor would be glad to see in him less impulsiveness of disposition, less impatience of control, and more deliberate judgement, than hitherto he has shown.[60]

The "cog in the wheel" controversy did not stop here. British Indian administration inherited the legacy of the East India Company which was in the main a trading corporation unwilling to spend money on welfare measures of the hillmen.

Both the provincial and central authorities could not forgive the rebellious outburst of the volatile District Officer contravening the rules and despite the invaluable services rendered by Captain Lewin during the Lucia Expedition 1871-72. As the Civil Officer attached to the Right Column, the Government of India with the aim to cut Lewin to size deliberately did not recognize his services and John W. Edgar ICS, the civil officer attached to the Left (Cachar) Column found repeated mention in the India Government's resolution. Edgar received award Star of India and promotion but hapless Lewin was short listed and warned, by the Bengal Government of his off the track unreasonable comment of the functioning of the administration. This was too much for the energetic sensitive and daredevil officer. The life which he had led in the hills was one involving the extreme hardship and personal responsibility. Without friends, without society, without the companionship of a fellow countryman he had to work silently and dutifully with the firm conviction that he was assisting the cause of the Empire. But the lack of recognition of his services "filled me with such a chill sense of disappointment that I felt it impossible to renew work on the old terms." Dejected Lewin with his falling health had to leave India to undergo protracted medical treatment in London and when recovered he left the coveted Government job. It is not without significance that Lewin's appointment as the Civil Officer was at the behest of the Governor General, Lord Mayo who had tested the skill of Lewin, and General Brownlow who led the Lushai Expeditionary Force became sad at the cursory treatment meted out to Lewin. He hoped that in foreseeable future the administration would devise some orderly, mutually acceptable way of getting rid of the controversy. General Brownlow privately acknowledged the services of Lewin to him in the course of his lengthy operation in the unknown land and people. His personal letters and consolation were only a ray of hope in an area of darkness during the operation of the Lushai Expedition Lord Mayo, the Viceroy was assassinated at Andaman. Lewin mourned his death as a great loss. Indeed, the demise of the Viceroy created such a void for him that did not fill up. Brownlow had further cause to feel guilty because in his official dispatch he wrote, "It is due to Captain Lewin's strong personal influence over these tribes, his knowledge of their language and habits, added to his patience and sagacity in dealing with them without, that a single chief submitted or a single captive was recovered."[61]

Lewin was intreped, transparent soldier and adventured unaccustomed with the ambiguous norms of civil service and he became a victim of sudden feud often ridiculed as the Calcutta idlers. The sheer administrative necessities, and certain cogent reasons, mainly relevant to frontier strategic well-being, prompted the wounded authorities of Fort Williams to take stringent note of Lewin's report that castigated the administrative policy of the government. At the close of his life faced with unpleasant realities Lewin, however, mellowed down considerably and had to ponder over whether he had actually distinguished himself by confusing social and economic needs with the cherished principle of administrative continuity to steer clear the grievances of the wild savages whose welfare had been his primary concern. He wrote in his memoir, "Looking back now, with the wider philosophy which years have given, I can see that the Indian Government is perhaps wise in not encouraging individual effort. A public servant's idiosyncracy must not be too strongly developed even for the food of those under his charge. Things may go better for a time-for his time-but the difficulty of replacing such an officer, when removed by death or promotion, is an insuperable objection. A high Indian official once brusquely but pertinently remarked in my hearing, "We don't want personal influence; we want men who will obey orders."[62]

Thus came the inglorious end of the service career of a talented Frontier Officer who in clear, unambiguous terms enunciated the foundation of the policy of the eastern Hills, "let us not govern these hills for ourselves but administer the country for the well-being and happiness of the people dwelling there in. What is wanted here is not measure but a man."[63]

T.H. Lewin compiled A *Dictionary of Lucia Words* and was pioneer in this field. The Missionaries of Welsh Mission followed him. Thus, towards the development of Lucia (Mizo) language the contribution of Lewin is also unique. It is Lewin who made the Lucia people and their country, the hills, valleys, brooks known to the outside world. The Lushais, on the other hand, loved him and honoured him like a national hero. His monument exists to this day at Demagiri overlooking the ever turbulent pool called the Tlabung Lieheng, meaning the round pool. This is a site for national pilgrimage of the Mizos. The plaque runs thus:

"In memory of Lt. Col. Tom Herbert Lewin B.S.C., once Superintendent of these Hill Tracts. Born 1839 Died 1916.

He came to these people in 1865 and worked among them and for them for nine years, when loss of health compelled him to return to England.

The people trusted and loved for his sympathy and sense of justice, for his untiring interest in their welfare, and for his intrepid and dauntless courage.

He traveled in the unknown land, visiting their chiefs, their villages. And their homes, alone and unafraid.

He was first to interpret and write down their language preparing the way for schools and progress.

He studied and improved their agriculture and their laws and helped them in their difficulties.

The people knew him as Thangliana (Tom Lewin) honoured him as a Chief. They called him the "Lushais's first white friend."

They built a home for him voluntarily in token of their devotion. Their children now have voluntarily brought stones here near where his house once stood and have helped the one whoever with the people to build up the stones to the memory of

"Thangliana"

Indeed, a glowing tribute, never before in the whole history of the tribal people of the North East India, a man received so much love and admiration.

NOTES AND REFERENCES

1. T.H. Lewin, *Wild Races of North Eastern India,* p. 9.
2. *Ibid.* pp. 9-12
3. *Ibid.* pp. 15
4. *Ibid.* p. 18
5. *Ibid.* p. 20
6. H.N. C. Stevenson, *Economics of Central Chin Tribes,* p. 106-18.
7. *Wild Races,* p. 23.*op. cit.*
8. *Ibid.* p. 24

9.&10. *Ibid.* pp 32,33

10. *Ibid.* p. 35

11.&13. *Ibid.* p. 39

14. *Ibid.* p. 47.
14a. *Ibid.* p. 48.
14b. Wilson, H., *Burmese Wars,* p. 25.
14c. *Wild Races,* p. 48-50.
15. Col . A. Phayre, *ASJ No.* 117 p. 701.
16,17 &18. *Wild Races,* pp. 52-53.
19. *Ibid.* p. 55.
20. *Ibid.* p. 57.
21. *ASJ Bengal,* 1884, No. 1451.
22. *Wild Races,* p. 59.
23. *Wild Races,* p. 64.
24. Plutarch. *Lives.*
25. *Wild Races,* p. 65.
25a W. Hunter, *Annals of Rural Bengal,* p. 217.
26. *Wild Races,* Ante p. 67.
27&28. *Wild Races,* Ante, pp. 69-73
29. *Wild Races,* p. 81.
29a. Col. A. Phayre. *JAS,* No. 117, 1841 Chukma.
Col. Hodson, *JAS,* Bengal, No. I, 1853.
30. Col. A. Phayre, *History of Arracan,* JAS, No.145, 1844.
30a. *Asatick Research,* Vol. VI, p. 229.
31. *Wild Races,* p. 91.
32. *Ibid.*
33& 34. *Ibid.* pp. 95, 96
35&36. *Ibid.* pp. 98, 101.
37. *Ibid.* p. 187.
38. *Ibid.* p. 196.
39. *Ibid.* p. 198.
40&41. *Ibid.* p. 199.
42. T.H. Lewin. *A Fly On the Wheel,* p. 204.
43. *Ibid.* p. 248. Also, *Tribal chief and His People– A case*

Study, Dr. Mahadev Chakravorty, p. 89. *Tribes of Tripura.* Also, *Mizo Chiefs and the Chifdom,* pp 39-41. – S. Chatterjee.

44. *BJP* Nov 1868 No. 70.

45. *BJP* Nov. 1868. 71.T.H. Lewin to the Commissioner Chittagong.

46. *A Fly on the Wheel,* p. 271, op. cit.

47. *Ibid.* p. 273.

48. *Ibid.* p. 277, Also *Mizoram Under British Rule* p. 72, *op. cit.* also BJP March 1872. No. 253, Court affidavit and delivery of Miss Mary Winchester.

49. *Mizoram Under British Rule,* pp 69-70. Also BJP August 1872 No. 220. Weekly despatch from Brigadier General Bourchier to the Secy Mil dept.

50. *A Fly on the Wheel,* pp. 282-83.

53&54. *Ibid.*

55. B.J.P. August 1872. No. 210. Lewin the Civil Officer of the Chittagong Column to the Junior Secretary, Bengal,. Letter dated March 26, 1872. Vide also the appendix A of the same proceedings showing the list of the Lucia chiefs. Also *Misogamy Under British Rule* pp 76-78. op. cit. for the report on Cachar Column's success see Edgar's reports BJP August 1872, No. 120. Strange enough, Lewin in his memoir *(Fly on the Wheel),* has not mentioned in detail of the incidents of the Lucia Expedition in which he was the most important Civil officer. His services were acknowledged by General Brownlow, the over all in command of the Citation Column. Allahabad newspaper, *Observer* also commented highly about the performances for Lewin, But the Government sidelined him which had its impact of the emotional mind of Lewin. He wrote, "Pleasant words of praise were my sole reward, and, as not only the leading officers in the expedition were either decorated or promoted at the close of the campaign, but the Political Officer of the Left Column, who held a precisely similar position to myself, received the Star of India for his services, many of my friends thought and said that

the omission of my name in the role of honour must have arisen from some fault of omission or commission on my part." (*Fly on the Wheel* p. 288). The Political Officer Left Column was John Edgar, the D.C. Cachar.

55a. BJP August 1872. No. 210, Appendix A.

55b. *Ibid.*

55c. BJP August 1872 No. 521.

55d. *Ibid.*

56. *Ibid.*

57. BJP August 1872, No. 91.

58. BJP August 1872 No. 458 *Annual Administration Report of Chittagong Hill Tracts,* Bengal.

59&60. *Ibid.* Also *Problem of the Hill Tribes, North-East Frontier* Vol. 2, p. 1345, H.K. Barpujari

61. General Brownlow's dispatch to the Secy. Milt Dept. Govt. of India intimating the result of the Expedition Also Lewin's *Memoir* p. 289.

62. *A Fly on the Wheel* p. 313. Also Nehru, Elwin Policy of Tribal Development, G. Das. Proceedings, NET History Association, 1993, p. 285.

63. *Mizoram Encyclopaedia* Vol. 3, p 568, Suhas Chatterjee. Citation Hill Tracts. Politico-Historical background by Chandika Basu Mazumdar, pp. 353-61 Proceedings of NEIHA, 18th Session is an illuminating paper although principally based on T.H. Lewin's works. However, she has wrongly mentions the name of the author of the book *Hill Tracts of Citation and the Dwellers Therein* as Lt. Col. Thomas. Ref. No. 7, the book is a famous work of cT.H. Lewin.

3

Sir John Ware Edgar

John Ware Edgar, one of the direct earliest recruits in the Indian Civil Service, had been a god student of Political Economy and History in Cambridge. Despite his academic brilliance and aptitude for the study of Economics he was not attracted towards the grove of muse, the lure of empire drove him to choose his carer in the newly created glamourous Indian Civil Service. Edgar by birth was not commoner. For his blue blood he had better connections with the men at the helm of power at Home. He opted for the service to the Presidency of Bengal at Fort William. Among largest one, He was to serve under the Commissioner, Dacca, the 15th division of Bengal. Dacca had been a very big division extending up to Manipur including Cachar. Edgar developed a special interest in studying the frontier problems of Eastern India. Some of his papers on frontier issues and especially on tea industry in different journals envinced keen Alexander Mackenzie, the influential Judicial Secretary who had been the incharge of the eastern frontier of Bengal since the days of Honorable Company, recommended Edgar to the post of Deputy Commissioner, Cachar. He was a pretty young men to accept the challenge. The Deputy Commissioner was, because of peculiar administrative setup of Cachar, the District Magistrate and Collector, Civil Judge of the district, and also the highest local police officer. Moreover, the DC Cachar was the Frontier Officer to deal with Manipur Lushai Hills and Tripura and in case of emergency with the officers or British Burma also. In short, he was the chief officer burdened with heavy responsibilities to colonise a newly annexed territory for the benefit of the Crown and also to keep the North eastern periphery of India free from political turmoil.

In those days Cachar was far away from Calcutta. Not to speak of the common people, the officers of Fort William also had faint ideas about Cachar, a newly annexed principality somewhere near Manipur and Burma. From Calcutta to Sylhet it was hazardous five days journey. From Sylhet to Cachar it was another days journey. In a wintery night (14 November 1867) Edgar accompanied by the advance guards of the SLI reached his destination Dudpatil, the official residence of the DC Cachar on horse back. The gloomy darkness pervaded the rice fields and the muddy swamps in the foot hills of the Brail ranges. Edgar was greeted by a few Urdu speaking Chaprasees at the gate with flickering earthen lamps and they led him to the hall where Major R. Stewart, the out gong DC Cachar had been waiting to receive them. Sic footer with large away moustache and serene face Stewart was an aged person with fearful physique. Edgar was much younger and handsome but not tall. Stewart shook his hands vigorously. In those days there was no photographic camera or video tape but the meeting of the two imperial giants one from the Honourable Company and the other from the Crown heralded a new era in the history of the North-east. Next day Edgar assumed the charge. Indeed, it was a transfer of power from the military to the civil authorities.

Edgar's Predecessor

Major Stewart a comrade of David Scott, the hero of the Anglo-Burmese War 1824-26 had been close confidant of famous Captain T. Fisher, another hero to the First Anglo-Burmese War and the first Superintendent Cachar. After the F.J. Lister's Expedition into the Morah's country (1850) in the Lucia Hills, Lister recommended the formation of a Kukie Levy for the Security of the Cachar-Lucia (Mizo) frontiers. Stewart was the most celebrated of all the Officers commanding Kukie Levy. The headquarters of Kukie Levy was initially at Lakhimpur near the Manipur border. Because of his strict vigilance he was able to maintain the law and order on the frontiers of Cachar fraught with pillage and plunder . When Captain G. Verner relinquished the post (1857) of the Superintendent, Cachar, Stewart was the natural choice and he succeeded Verner. Stewart was down to earth military personnel with determined military perception and formidable but he was also a shrewd Frontier officer with a discerning views. He had the sagacity to deal difficult negotiations with the tribal chiefs of Lucia Hills.

He had an economic bend of mind which was rare trait among the military officials. He explored the possibilities of Lushai commerce and its possibilities of linkage with Cachar's trade potential. The Bengali and Manipuri traders carried on trade into the Lucia countries during the cold seasons in the inaccessible Lucia Hills. The Lucia commerce was the most important ploy to maintain a viable link between Cachar and the hill men. Stewart conducted a military survey of the river Soni and Dhaleswari up to the point of their navigability. This had been a positive step towards the exploration of northern Lucia Hills. With the aging of friendly Kuki chief, Munjihow who assisted the Cachar administration in chasing and capturing the Citation Mutineers (1857), the local British officers were at a fix to the next course of the Anglo- Kuki relationship. Till then the Lushais were also known as " Kukis". Shrewd Stewart manipulating the reality Sukpilal was ambitious but crafty and far from being loyal to the English and occasionally tried to fish in trouble water to harass the administration. Stewart's predecessor Captain G. Verner had a very low opinion about wily Sukpilal and considered him a drone but Stewart shook off the noble principle of political Puritanism and took a positive step to forge an entente with Sukpilal. He did not succumb to the greater political and economic interest of the government. Taking the advantage of the chief's greed for money Stewart roped him in the diplomatic net. Stewart's newly found shrewd Brahmin Hari Cahran Sharma, whose fluency in the tribal languages and familarity with the tribal customs made the task of the government much easier.[2]

Stewart implemented the Revenue Rule, 1859, settlement for 20 years at the rate of Rs.3/- per hall of land, with right earnest but in his measures he had been very cautious to the sensitive issue of destabilization of population structure of Cachar. His successor Edgar, however reversed his policy.

Stewart was a man of modern outlook and was aware of the utility of education in modern life. Under his supervision some elementary schools and vernacular schools made their headway in rural Cachar and in Silchar town. Under his patronage the Presbyter, Reverend Preys set up the Silchar Government School (Silchar High Grammar School) in 1863. In 1863 when the Wells Presbyterian Mission had been winding up the two mission girls schools of the town (Malugram and Sadarghat) he requested the mission authorities for its continuance in the interest of public good. The Silchar Government Girls School was originally a missionary school. Unplanned Silchar town founded by Captain Fisher had been groaning amid the filth and sqalor. The people were dirty and responded the call of nature on the streets and the stench had been stinking to the high heaven when the wind blew. There was no municipal board. So, Stewart took the stern step and made it punishable to commit public nuisance on the highway. He specified a field on the bank of Barrack to be used to ease oneself. He sought the permission from the Commissioner, Dacca establish a piggery for the pigs, and the jackals to act as scavengers. Stewart's influence and the Labour Act 1863 were behind the establishment of the hospital at Silchar (1864) for the treatment and medical check up. Stewart also established a private market near Annapurna ghat for the benefit of the dwellers of the Silchar town. Stewart had been the Superintendent of Cachar for long ten years and before that he was the Officer Commanding Kuki Levy, Cachar for about three years. His long association, experience and above all dynamism made him the most informed person about Cachar to the authorities of Fort William. His famous successor Edgar had highly praised the out-date to have Stewart as his predecessor.

A Glimpse of Colonial Economy of Cachar before Edgar

The principality of Cachar came under the political control of the East India Company with the Treaty of Yandabo, 1826. The last prince, Gobinda Chandra of Cachar defaulted his promised annual tribute of ten thousand rupees to the Company's treasury (the cost of security) as per Badarpur Agreement and thus incurred the usual displeasure of the local officers. After the assassination of Gobinda Chandra (24 April 1830) the Company officials negotiated with the Libsey Brothers, the traders at Sylhet to lease out the plains of Cachar for an annual rent of Rs 10,000/- but the negotiation did not fructify. Company formally annexed the principality of Cachar by a Proclamation, 14 August 1832 and Captain T. Fisher was made the first Superintendent. The revenue demand for the year 1830-43 was Rs 27,435/-. Thus there had been stagnancy in the yield despite the increase in population. The new settlement was made in 1843-49 had been Rs 13,300/-. The total land revenue for the year 1852-53 was Rs 65,259/- and in the year 1853-54 it yielded more than Rs, 80,000/- Another settlement was made after the expiry of the 15 years in 1859; this time the old rate of Rs. 3/- per hac (nearly 5 acres) was changed to progressive increment of rate when the revenue yield stepped up to Rs. 91,000/.

1859 settlement was made for 20 years. The burden of implementing the settlement, fell on Captain Stewart who discharged his duties with a reformist's zeal. During the Superintendency of Major Stewart Cachar became a viable Revenue district and the Commissioner, Dacca recommended to the Governor of Bengal for the inclusion of Cachar into the revenue category.

"The first rules to be introduced into Cachar for the grant of land for tea cultivation, were the old Assam rules of 1854, which were extended to the district in 1856. One fourth of the grant was exempted from assessment in perpetuity. The remaining three fourths were granted revenue free for 15 years, and then assessed at 3 annas an acre for 10 years and at 6 annas an acre of 74 years more, the total lease being thus for 99 years. Large tracts of land were taken up under these rules, but most of the owners took advantage of the permission accorded to them under the fee simple rules, to convert their leases into a fee simple tenure, and the total area now held under the 99 years' lease rules of 1854 is 25,728 acres.

"The fee simple rules were first issued in 1861 and modified in the following years. Except under special circumstances grants were limited to an area of 3,000 acres, the land was put up to auction, and the upset price ranged from Rs 2-8 to Rs 10 per acre. These rules were in force till 1872."[5]

In 1856 first tea garden was established in Cachar at Barsangan in Jatinga valley.[5c] In 1858 on the advice of Sanderman, the planter, the government agreed to the exportation of labour to the tea estates. Stewart had the vision of Cachar's plenty. He became aware of the potentiality of Cachar. At the beginning the tea planters had to face the hostility of the Lucia Kukies and they contrived their own security. The industry also had to face the temporary recession because of stock market crunch in Calcutta. But Stewart's bid to win over the Lucia chief Sukpilal and Stewart's diplomatic measures to keep the other Lucia chiefs in good humour were intended with the aim of protecting the interest of the tea industry. The tea planters had trust in Stewart and in return he also reciprocated them to overcome their difficulties relating to infrastructure and the problem of defence. Stewart was appointed the Deputy Commissioner, Cachar in 1867 when the status of the district was raised mainly due to Stewart's own effort. In November 1867 when he handed over the charge to Edgar the tea industry in Cachar shrugged off its teething troubles, stood erect to face the challenges of new economy. There was also a steady increase of the revenue and the law and order situation of the new district was fine. Thus, when Stewart left Cachar for Calcutta with his characteristic smile John Edgar stepped into his shoes with greater determination and resolve to transform the newly annexed territory into a tea planters paradise.

Edgar Accepted by the Urban Natives

The aim of creating the Indian Civil Service had been to replace the outmoded system of Company's administration. Imperialism, the foundation on which the Company's empire was based, remained as before it received a facelift with the added glamour of British sense of justice. The men of the service were mostly from the Victorian upper middle class educated English gentry. Born into the limelight those boys were expert in charming manners and English snobbery. They were to replace gradually the blunt and tough servants of the Kampany Bahadur.

John Ware Edgar was a unique representative of the so called "heavenborn" service. He was suave in speech and charming in manner, but firm in resolve. The rustic Cachar's populace always afraid of the Europeans kept themselves at arm's length from the resolute military officers like Captain Verner or Major Stewart but in Edgar they discovered a pleasing personality, a lovable face full of concern for the natives – a trait unknown to them. Edgar ment each and every one of the native employees of the Cachar tahsil and exchanged greetings. They were overwhelmed by strange *sahib*. Indeed, that was the tryst with their destiny.

Silchar Town

"Silchar is the only place in the district which has any pretensions to the name to town. It is situated on the bank of the Barak in 24,49' N. and 92,48' E. and commands a charming view down the river, which is dotted, with the sails of native craft and lined with groves of the area plan, while a little to the north, the purple hills of North Cachar rise sharply from the plain."

"The town itself has a somewhat tumble down appearance, and, with the exception of the church and the new circuit house, does not contain a single building of any size or dignity. The houses of the Europeans stand round a piece of open ground, which becomes very wet and swampy in the rains. The business-quarter lies a little to the south, but there are few substantial merchants in Silchar. There is a considerable trade in rice, European piece goods, timber, and other forest produce. Tea boxes are manufactured by native firms."[6]

When Edgar took the charge of administration of Cachar there was in fact, only one town, Silchar. It was a small town smaller than Gauhati, Tezpur, Jorhat or Dibrugarh. But when he left Silchar the town became as famous as Dibrugarh as a tea town and in administrative importance equivalent to Gauhati. Under the magic influence of Edgar the sleepy town rose from its slumber to a new lease of life. Total area of Silchar town was 2.4 square miles. It was served by 13 liner miles of road 10 of which were metalled by the PWD on 1868. The people during Edgar's time had to drink water from the private or wells and in every summer cholera made hints invariable appearance. There was no municipal facilities except the nine municipal police constables to maintain order in the town under the D.C. The Silchar Municipal Board was set up long after Edgar in 1892.

The Silchar Government School was, however, started functioning at the instance of Rev. William Pryse of Welsh Presbyterian Mission Church in 1863. When Edgar was the Deputy Commissioner, the school was under the head master, Abhaya Charan Bhattacharjee. In 1866 the school became Cachar Zilla school and because of Edgar's recommendations overruling several routine formalities of the educational norms the school was brought directly under the control and supervision of the Inspector of Schools; in 1868 it was renamed as Silchar Government School. Silchar Government School which catered the needs of English education in Cachar, Lucia Hills and Manipur received a new lease of life under the aegis of Edgar, and its impact upon the future training of manpower resources in the region, had been profound and far reaching. The celebrated head master A.C. Bhattacharjee had a good rapport with the Deputy Commissioner and he helped him (Bhattacharjee). Cachar Public Works Department started its function as a branch of the Bengal PWD in 1868. A local Committee was formed to supervise the road construction works of the District Board and Edgar was the first president of that Committee (1868). When Edgar was in Dacca in 1865 he calculated the population of Cachar being 152,000 souls and that of Silchar town five thousand only.

But Silchar began to grow steadily in size and population. Captain Fisher set up his seat of work at Dudpatil but soon it was shifted to Silchar but the administration never used the name Silchar and preferred Cachar in its place. There was no Mouja called Silchar and it was under the Barrack par. Because of flood in 1834, and 1836 Silchar jail was shifted to its present location. The vacant prison (Ratak) complex was reclaimed and declared a market by the administration under Edgar and it was leased out to the shopkeepers. This measure helped a lot to the businessmen during the stockades. But the establishment of tea estates in Cachar boosted the commercial importance of Silchar market. The agricultural products and spare parts of the machinery etc. had good demand among the tea planters. The market also had to meet the requirement of the European tea planters, the managers and their families who had enough disposable income to spend for the luxuries.

The Fatak Bazar of Silchar at present the biggest shopping centre in South Assam owes its origin to Edgar. When Municipal Board was formed in 1892 the Bazar came under the control of the Board. The traders and the business community received great patronage from Edgar. He liberally allowed their settlement in the town. Those traders were mostly Bengalees from Sylhet and Dacca. There were few Marwari merchants also.

The traders and retailers were so moved by the unprecedented welfare measure and largest of Edgar that they christened their own market as John`s market (Johnygunj), John being the first name of Edgar. Edgar often lived in his quarter at Silchar and not at Dudpatil. He frequently visited the Zilla School, heard the grievances of the traders, attended the church services and received the Lushai delegations in his quarters. The Cachar Tahsil was a *kutcha* house Edgar replaced it by a pucca building. This building (at present the Chief Judicial Magistrate's Court) was the first official building in the town. The building had been the seat of Deputy Commissioner's office till the end of the British rule. He improved the civil line where the government quarters were situated. The localities of the natives were also improved. He requested the District Magistrate, Sylhet to send some masons for the construction of buildings. The masons were Muslims and Edgar provided a Khasi land for laying bricks at the outskirts of the town later on named as Itkhola. Till today the masonry in Cachar and Mizoram is the occupation of the Muslims who are the descendants of the artisans brought by Edgar. The brick layers were imported labour. To meet the demand of the drinking water of the increased town population three public tanks and a well were dug up by the administration. A hospital was set up by the tea planters at Silchar for the routine medical check up of the plantation labour under the aegis of Captain Stewart in 1864 which was slightly improved by Edgar. In the SLI stockade (Assam Rifles) there was however, a small medical unit to assist the sepoys and the officers. When Sukpilal, the Western Lushai chief fell ill before his death Edgar sent a native doctor to the Lushai Hills (1871) for the chief's treatment. Sukpilal breathed his last before the arrival of the doctor.

The people of the village Dudpatil where the Deputy Commissioner's Bungalow was situated often had to come Silchar (and they called it Sahar Dudpatil) but there was no ferry service in the river Barak. Only the Deputy Commissioner had his specially made wooden shaft and country boat. Edgar introduced the ferry service from Dudpatil to Silchar in 1868 and the ferry was brought under the Public Works Department. The grateful people named the ferry ghat as Edgar's ghat. Later on it was renamed as Annapurna. Silchar stand on the bank of the river Barak opposite the vast rave course field started from Edgar's ghat and, in fact, the beautiful strand with sprawling bungalows of the Scottish-type–only a shadow of it exists now because of the vandalism of Assam Public Works Department after

Independence was the contribution of John Edgar. Silchar town which had been crying amid reek and squalor was reclaimed put to gear by Edgar. It is Edgar who gave the town a modern shape and dignity. The name of Silchar which was unknown even to the people of Cachar only a decade before Edgar's arrival it became equally famous like Dibrugarh and Darjeeling all over the globe as a tea town only a decade after Edgar left Silchar. In fact, in 1971 local census, Silchar emerged as the largest tea exporting centre in Assam. The sleepy sprawling military stockade Silchar by the touch of the magic wand of Edgar suddenly burst forth into a famous tea exporting centre of international dimension.

Silchar's improvement had been the foremost aim of Edgar. He suggested the Bengal Government the formation of a separate administrative division consisting of the Surma Valley and the hills with Silchar as the divisional headquarters. It became necessary after the abolition of the old administrative unit, Lower Provinces. He preferred Silchar to disconnect hilly Cherrapunji. Silchar's Communication was much better and the emergence of Cachar as the second tea producing unit in India added commercial importance to Silchar. Because of Edgar's advice North Lushai Hills came under the British sphere of influence after the Lushai Expedition 1871-72 and the political control, was to be exercised by the Chief Commissioner of Assam through the Deputy Commissioner, Cachar at Silchar. The Raja of Manipur was also allowed by the Chief Commissioner, to have his out houses at Dudpatil on the other side of Silchar on the bank of Barak and at Lakhimpur. Under the instructions of Edgar the Silchar-Lakhimpur Road, a portion of the famous Cachar-Manipur Road, was improved and the Silchar-Sonai Road of the Cachar-Changsil Road was widened. The aim of spreading the road had been three fold. The above roads were necessary for better communication with the turbulent frontier tribes, to provide communication with the turbulent frontier tribes, to provide communicational infrastructure of the sprawling tea estates in Cachar and also to improve commercial importance of Silchar town.

Edgar encouraged unchecked immigration of the Bengalees from Dacca and Sylhet to Silchar. The people with commercial enterprise were given preference in matters of settlement in the town. This natural selection was, however, interrupted. The baboos with English education, the unproductive draft-dodgers because of their gift of the gab were also settled in the town and in the tea estates. Many baboos taking the advantage of familiarity with Edgar received land grants outside the town and thus became petty landed gentry. The population structure of Silchar town remained materially unchanged long after Edgar as the local people of Cachar were educationally and culturally backward and always afraid of the shrewdness and manipulative tactics of the immigrant town-dwellers, avoided coming to settle at Silchar. Silcahr till today is an immigrants' town and does not reflect the public opinion and culture of Cachar's indigenous people. The culture of the town before independence had been the ipso facto pseudo culture of Eastern Bengal and after independence it is the imperect Calcutta culture. Notwithstanding Edgar's immense contribution towards the development of Silchar town, the claustrophobia of the townsmen had given rise to future problem of dangerous proportion.

Edgar as Deputy Commissioner, Cachar

Before the annexation Cachar into the Company's dominion the feudal rulers here introduced a land tenure system which had been materially different from Mughal India but more or less akin to the Khel system of the Ahom rulers. The Ahoms were the sovereigns of Cachar for long. The King was the lord of the soil and the subjects had no private property rights on land. In the hills, however, the clan ownership was the normal practice. Thus, after the assassination of Gobinda Chandra the land in Cachar was vested into the possession of Company or to be more specific on the Superintendent, Cachar. Edward Gait writes, "When Cachar was annexed, Government stepped into the position of the Raja as absolute owner of the soil. The old rates of assessment were continued till 1839, when a five years's settlement was made. During this period a professional survey was effected, and the next settlement was concluded on its basis for a period of fifteen years; all cultivated land was assessed at a uniform rate of Rs. 3 per half (nearly five acres). Waste land paid no rent for five years and only half rates for the next five. In 1859 a twenty years's settlement was effected."

Bengal Revenue Settlement Rules, 1859

The 1859 Rules of Settlement transformed Cachar from a non revenue yielding to a revenue yielding district and its status was raised. The implementation of the Rules fell on the shoulders of Stewart the task which he attended to the best of his ability but the implementation of the Rules fell on the shoulders of Edgar. Bengal Regulation 1793 popularly known as Permanent Settlement had its application in Sylhet and Goalpara districts in Assam but as Cachar had its own land tenure system and as Cachar was incorporated into Company's dominion along with Assam (by the Treaty of Yandaboo) under the administrative control of the Commissioner, Assam, the old Kachari revenue rules were allowed to continue. But in 1835 Cachar was transferred to the Dacca division and the Revenue Settlement Rules 1835 were given effect to in Cachar in 1839. But population in British Cachar (Cachar plains) had been insignificant only 50,000 souls estimated by Fisher in 1834. Captain Fisher had been a kind hearted man and had sympathy for the native nobility. Thus, when the new land tenure system was introduced a Superintendent of Cachar commented that "every man in Cachar was a mirasdar." But this state of affairs did not continue for long. With the unchecked immigration from Sylhet and imported tea labour already in the process there was substantial increase in population in 1859. In 1865 the population of Cachar was 1,5200 souls (*Dacca Blue Book*— Edgar).

By the rules 1859 the plains of Cachar was divided into several circles. Each circle had been under an influential landlord (misrasdar) who collected the annual rent (settled for 20 years) from landowners on behalf on the government. The rent Rs. 3/- per hall was to be deposited to the Cachar treasury at Silchar. The land include the paddy land, homestead, forest and wasteland, the forest and wasted land had lower rate of rent. As the vatted produce more. But Edgar was aware of the agricultural potential of Cachar. He, like the other Deputy Commissioners in the Brahmaputra valley, was a votary of immigration and encouraged the enterprising Muslims from the overpopulated Sylhet district to come and take up agriculture in Cachar offering the licence quantum libnet to them. In matters of immigration of cultivators of tea garden labour Edgar's zeal had been aggressive. Hailakandi subdivision of Cachar already having a Muslim population became the happy hunting ground of the fortune seekers. Hailakandi was raised to the status of subdivision in 1869 during the tenure of Edgar. The economical immigrants, however, subsequently moved to the Sonai valley.

Regarding unenterprising indigenous Hindu natives Edgar had little sympathy. The predecessor of Edgar out of compassion helped the distressed Burmans, Dimachas and Rajbansis the bulwark of old Kachari nobility but Edgar considered them indolent and had no compassion for their predicament. Edgar also pushed the indigenous tribals the Kukies, Kaccha Nagas etc. for no fault of them to the border and occupied the forest and wasteland. He made the Manipuri settlement in Cachar because he was aware of the law and order problem. Edgar did not hide his aversion to them to the Muslims of Manipuris as traders. The licence to trade were liberally granted to the Hindus, the Bazar mahajans were Hindus. The mahajans kept a book of toll-collection for the inspection of the government. The policy of Edgar was the imperialist policy of Divide and Rule to drive a wedge between the different segments of the population.

The average yield per hall (about five acres) was recorded and the correct measurements were made by the government peadahas and they assisted the mirasdars to collect the rent. Hari Charan Sharma the tehsildar helped Edgar in enumerating and accounting the revenue. There were large number of defaulter of rent. They took the advantage of the inaccessibility of remote regions and often had fled their villages to Sylhet when the peadahas had left the village. The government Muleteers also clouded with the powerful riots to cheat the government. Edgar checked the malpractices awarding exemplary punishments. In selecting mirasdars Edgar used his discretion.

The revenue measures of Edgar ushered in a new landed gentry solvent but not wealthy like the zamindars of Sylhet, stable but conservative, loyal but uneducated and self-contented. Thus, Edgar provided a loyal support base in the countryside and they acted as countermove to any affront to the authority in the most unstable, countrified volatile region. Majority of the landed gentry in Cachar belonged to the Muslim community and they assumed the enormous power in the social hierarchy in rural Cachar since 1868- a privileged status they never had. Sonai and Dhulai valley which were once jejune, barren and the abode of the fierce Kukies soon became the rice-bowl of Cachar because of the toil and expertise of the Muslim cultivators. Thus, the economic impact of Edgar was momentous.

Destruction of Kachari Nobility

The aim of Company's administration had been to

administer a particular tract of territory from the revenue collected from the same. The cost of administration must be borne by the district and the surplus to be siphoned off to the provincial treasury. The Crown's administrative system despite its restructuring and polish was also similarly. The exploitation of land for agricultural and industrial production was the sine qua non of the Crown's policy. The principle of social justice was a ruse and that noble principle yielded to the profitability of the administration very often. The land of Cachar actually belonged to the Kachari nobility and the land devolved to the British Crown through the Company by the happening of an unforeseeable political accident (death of Gobinda Chandra). The English did not conquer Cachar nor it was invested by the Emperor as a grant of Dewani. The lands that were used for settlement of revenue by the British officials were the property of the ruler of Cachar now held in trust by the government. But enlightened and educated Edgar's sense of morality did not haunt him, for a moment that the friendly British Government which was bound by the promise of the Queen's Proclamation had been willingly driving the hapless locals to destitution by his measure –a treatment they hardly deserved. Dethroning of Raja Rajendra Singh of Jaintia to deprive him of his possessions by Robertson, Jenkins and Lister had been an act of gross miscarriage of justice but depriving the indigenous people of their legitimate soil Edgar did not set up any better example. In his reformist zeal to accelerate the speed of economy of Cachar the icon of immigration inflicted a bruise to the already crumbling social structure of Cachar. Edgar, in fact, robbed the locals to pay the immigrants. In lieu of modern economy he denuded Cachar of its heritage, culture and language. Indeed, very heavy price Cachar had to pay. According to the general survey in the North Eastern country the people here give priority to their ethnic identity over their nationality. Edgar's reform struck a death blow to that prevailing system. The old values were thrown to the four winds. The hunting for cash became the goal of life. Edgar planted the evils of brutal modernism a bit earlier. The population structure of Cachar had undergone a sea change in the succeeding decades after Edgar and the Deputy Commissioners of less caliber add to face plethora of vexed problems.

An important result of the commercialization of agriculture in Cachar was the breakup of the old isolation and self-sufficiency of villages and gradual linking of village markets to outside markets in Sylhet, Dacca and Calcutta. The bazaars were no more only local markets for agricultural commodities.

Agricultural commodities started enjoying ever expanding markets depending upon their perishability or durability. Sonai Bazaar thus, a purely village market soon became the transit centre of local commerce to Silchar, Hailakandy, Changsi (Misogamy) and Sylhet. The commercialization of agriculture guaranteed the farmers more remunerative prices, formerly, in Cachar during the days of Kachari rajas and also the four decades after. But Edgar revolutionized the agricultural scenario. The land owners had little to complain. The farm sector offered entirely a different picture in the neighbouring British district Sylhet. The Permanent Settlement of Zamindari system was the prevailing mode of revenue collection there. The Government expected agricultural enterprise, greater flow of capital to land, improvement, cultivation extension, and reclamation of land in the Zamindari system but intermediary ridden system was the lofty aim of the Permanent Settlement. But Edgar's settlement in Cachar was free from any defects of Zamindary system. Moreover, for better or worse, the indeed gentry in Cachar was more or less directly in communion with the revenue administration of the district. It is, however, true that the government officials were generous nor necessarily responsive to the legitimate grievances of the ryots and had not that image of identity of reciprocacity of the zamindars. Thus, during emergencies like famine, flood and natural calamities the Cachar ryots were helpless and had little shelter. The severe 1869 earth quake a had been a pointer to that effect.

Edgar, got the chance to start in a clean a slate in implementing his revenue measures. Cachar seemed to be a lost case to the perplexed East thousand only to any bidder of financial standing but failed. However, with the improvement of law and order during the first decades of British rule, social stability was restored but despite sign of hope the pace of the economic progress was not significant. Edgar like a true imperialist came forward to restructure the colonial economy. In Brahmaputra valley the Deputy Commissioners when they introduced the Rules 1870 they had to show respect to the individuality of the Assamese landlords as there was mounting socio-political pressure on them but in Cachar pressure groups were totally absent; so Edgar had the free hand in applying the Rules 1859. He had the farsight to foresee the bright economic future of Cachar.

He was aware of the vast protentiality of agricultural production of the marshy uncultivated jejune land of Cachar infested with wild beasts and reptiles with the frequent raids of the head hunting Lushais. He had a firm conviction that the virile Muslims were the best agriculturists. He liberally granted the mirasdari to the Muslims and thus built up a reservoir of colonialism in the 22 parganas and 1078 villages of Cachar consisting of 3769 square miles. Being a strong man eager to do something durable he developed a sort of romantic liaison with the strong. Edgar, despite his enormous contribution towards the development of Silchar town is a forgotten person among the dwellers of Silchar but his munificence are still remembered by the rural gentry in the interior of Cachar. The Revenue Settlement rules 1859 at the hand of Edgar became a significant tool to deal with brigandage, drunken brawls and horrendour crimes into a stable, feudal society. Formerly, the economy was amorphous –subsistent economy but he changed it to an agrarian economy of surplus. He gave the villagers home and occupation and peace. The growth rate of farm produce increased considerably during his regime. In fact, the socio-economic rural superstructure built by Edgar, driving wedge between the different segments of the society, continued long after the Independence. The conservative bastion of the reactionary Islamic society of rural Cachar owes its origin to John Edgar. It is true that all used to Edgar, social psychopathology often played its part. But a man with deep farsight, standing on the threshold of time failed to realize that rigidity of his system with its concomitant social malfunctioning might lead to a blockade of social progress.

We notice a glaring contrast between Cachar and Brahmaputra valley so far the buoyancy of the economy of the two regions. The Administrative Report 1872-73 of the Bengal Government indicates sharp rise of prices in the Brahmaputra valley and the increase quota of rice importation (from 0.3 million to 0.7 million mounds) but Cachar was free from that slump. On the other hand, because of Edgar's measure, rural Cachar after feeding her own population could sold its surplus to the tea estates and army commissariat. This was instinctive of the rapid growth of rural economy in Cachar. Local production helped the tea merchants as well as the army stockades were saved from the dependence of imported rice. Edgar's settlement, however, had a social demerit as it upset the pose of the demography of the local population from which the Assam valley escaped unscath. A point, however, is pertinent to mention in this connection that the village Muslim gentry bolstered up against Edgar whatever may be their social clout because of their economic stability came forward to fill in the political vacuum created after the dissolution of British empire in India. As economy is the driving force of democratic political functioning the Muslim rural gentry in Cachar, because of their stable and congent society control, is the safety valve of the political system of Barak valley.

Edgar and the Tea Industry

Before Edgar set his foot on the soul of India tea industry already had its start in Assam including Cachar. But the industry could not over- come its teething trouble. The wild speculation to the companies, unhealthy hostile climate, repeated raids on the tea estates and above all the problem of labour were the obstacles to the growth of the industry. The waste land Rules 1838 provided the tea planters with adequate land so granted was made revenue free for five to twenty years according to the nature of the land. The Deputy Commissioners could order the importation of labour from outside. The local labour was shy as their demand for wages was high. There were also laws to protect the exploitation of labour. The labour charges of the army commissariat was more than double the tea garden labour charges (Rs 4/- per month). Moreover, the oppressed labour had the right of appeal to the Superintendent, Cachar for justice. Under pressure, the Bengal Government passed the Native Labour Act 1863 to legal size the labour recruits through agents. Statutory wages were laid down by the Act of 1865 but this progressive step was aborted by the amendment of the Act in 1870. This was an opportunity not only to the tea planters but also to the resourceful Deputy Commissioner, Cachar.

The aim of Edgar had been to encourage the tea plantation in Cachar to give economic viability of the administration. He opened the doors of the tea estates in Cachar not only to the tea kings of Calcutta but also to the natives who could afford the adequate capital for investment in the industry. Under his direct patronage some enterprising

Bengali Zamindars of Sylhet were asked to invest their accumulated wealth in purchasing tea estates. Majority of the planters were, however, Europeans and they obstructed the Edgar's move, But the British merchants invested Indian capital into the industry and only apart of the total capital invested in tea came from England.

Although political power was transferred from East India Company to the Crown the enterprise of the individual British merchants to dominate and control the Indian money market increased many-fold. A large number of tea companies were floated in Calcutta with their head offices in London. However, the house of the foreign money market was located in Calcutta to facilitate the smooth sailing of foreign capital. Many companies encouraged the tea executives to invest their accumulation on the basis of profit–sharing as investment. Cachar tea fixed 20% annual rate of growth and by controlling the expenditure increased the profit. The Assam Tea Company paid 35% dividend in 1871-81 a phenomenon unprecedented. Lord Mayo and his successor Lord Northbrook were patrons of tea industry and the labour laws were so mended as to help the planters. John Edgar was a favourite officer of Northbrook. Edgar, on the other hand, did his best to help the planters in Cachar in their programme of expansion.

Tea Estates and Lucia Raids

Vast stretches of wasteland of Cachar especially in the backwood southern portion of the district were leased out to the different extensive tea estates on a nominal rent. As the wasteland had many hillocks covered by forests which were a source of valuable timbers, the owners of the tea estates often applied for more land than required for plantation. The planters subsequently settled agricultural cultivators on the excess land. Thus, the owner played the role of planter and landlord both and economically he was the symbol of precolonial feudal economy and fresh colonial imperial economy rolled into one package. The encroachment of forest land by the plantation people (in different phases) which had been the traditional abode of the wild tribes led to frequent border explosions. Edgar initially followed the footsteps of his predecessor, Stewart and ordered strict vigilance of the southern frontiers and occasionally inflicting punishment to the wrong doers. However, he soon, gave up the earlier policy the aggrandizement towards the Lushai Kukies because that lacked comprehension and prudence and attempted to conciliate the Lucia (Mizos) with the help of powerful selected chiefs. The versatile Hari Charan Sarma (Chakravorty) his extra assistant Commissioner, whose knowledge of tribal language and familiarity with their customs and mode of living, came forward to assist Edgar and clever Edgar utilized the service of Sarma to the fullest extent in this regard.

Edgar and Tea Garden Labour

Edgar provided necessary infrastructural facilities to the agro-based tea industry in Cachar for its rapid development. The roads already mentioned which were constructed by the government under the aegis of Edgar helped the goods movement. The planters were allowed to construct their own roads and maintain them as private property where there would be no unnecessary interference of the government.

The planter paid low wages less than what the government paid its own labour force and working conditions of the labour was pathetic. Medical facilities were scarce. Edgar's policy of laissez fair put the labour into awful miseries and made them wage slaves. Edgar was an imperialist of proven loyalty and dedication and believed in economic exploitation of the colonies for furtherance of financial prosperity of mother country. He had very little sympathy and possibly less concern for the oppressed coolies living in the dungeon of tea gardens in utter desperation. The Labour

Act 1863 was amended in 1865, 1870 and 1873. By the Act 1873 government was the only authority to deal with the runaway workers of the tea gardens but to please the planters, Edgar rarely moved to help the labour in distress and often rundown the redressal provisions of the Act unjustly to twist the arm of law. It is no wonder Sir Henry Cotton, the Chief Commissioner of Assam in 1884 confessed that to help the tea magnets under given conditions in the context of priorities what therapy was to be prescribed. The coolie, according to Dewan Cahmanlal (economist) was too precious to be sent out of the tea estates to police and jail custody. However, Edgar had no other options as he was determined to restructure Cachar's economy to support the financial market in Calcutta. For the maintenance of price in the cost of production the planter's only way out was to mercilessly exploit labour. The government had to acquiesce as a matter of convenience. Social welfare measures were a far cry in that distant past. But the only ray of light in the dark tunnel had been Edgar's concern for the indigenous agricultural labour. Unlike his British counterparts in the Brahmaputra valley, Edgar did not rob the peasants in Cachar to pay the planters.

Cachar and Assam Valley Compared

In the Brahmaputra valley the rules 1870 of the Bengal Government effected a thorough change in matters of revenue settlement. The above rules also deprived the Assamese landlords of their ancient rights and privileges yet, the Assamese nobility based on landed property and other movable assets were still powerful almost like their counterparts in Bengal but plains of Cachar offered an entirely different socio-economic picture. The rise of immigrant economy with the commercial culture destroyed the age-old social fabric and the maltreated old Kachari nobility not only lost their earlier grip over the gerontocratic society but were also pushed back to the wall to seek the life of bare existence and many took refuge in the hills. Nowhere in the whole of the North East such nakedness of exploitative British imperialism could be traced in its inglorious history.

Notwithstanding the feudal class character of the old nobility, the landed aristrocarcy was the paramount premium mobile in the direction of social movements. Before Edgar's departure from Silcahr (1874) the educated middle class in Sylhet under the aegis of the rich land- lords gave vent to their resentment of the inclusion of Sylhet into Assam. That phenomenon of bourgeoisie protest, a common political phenomenon in Bengal and Assam did not find any expression in Cachar because the boors in Cachar were the real beneficiaries of the British settlement. From the economic standpoint the feudciaries and their proteges in Cachar had hardly any ground to complain against the government, and, on the contrary, they were grateful to the administration for its lavish distribution. In Assam valley the Revenue Rules 1870 revised the rates of revenue. The priority was given to quicker and larger collection of revenue rather than an increased production. The oppressive rules 1870 equally affected the peasants and the landlords in the Brahmaputra valley. The rise of rajimel and the peasant uprising were the outcome of the revenue settlement. According to R. B. McCabe the landlords along with the priests and dollies were behind the peasant rebellion (1892-93). But in Cachar which was conveniently converted into a perfect colony with a strong murmur against with established mores to lead the ryots to protest against administrative malevolence.

Thomas Fisher and Edgar

It is pertinent to point out in this connexion that there exists material difference between the approach of and measures adopted by Captain Thomas Fisher, the first Superintendent, Cachar and John W. Edgar. Before the annexation of Cachar the princely territory was unknown to the East India Company officials. Fisher had been the only person who had both theroretical and practical knowledge of the country torn by waves of civil strife and foreign aggression. The weak ruler of the principality Gobinda Chandra (already denuded of the standing army for sustainable defence and restoring order) by his political mismanagement and dysfunctioning increased the burden of sufferings of his poor and hapless subjects. Six years before the assassination of Gobinda Chandra (June 1830), David Scott, the Political Agent Assam by the Badarpur Agreement (6 March 1824) took over the charge of the protectorate of Cachar from Gobinda Chandra providing a standing army and the mettle fell on Captain Fisher to clear off the bludgeoning political mess piled up for long.

In that benighted stage of socio-political chaos Fisher restored order in the country and saved the country men from the untold miseries. The people of Cachar were thankful to him and through Fisher requested the Honourable Company to take the charge of direct administration after the unfortunate assassination of Gobinda Chandra. On 14 August 1832, under the proclamation Governor General, Cachar was formally annxexed. Fisher maintained the law and order with firm determination, made a survey of the land, introduced revenue measures (effective from 1835) and founded the town Silchar.

In his reforms he was not aggressive like Edgar but followed a policy of peaceful positive change. He blended the old rules of the principality with the new rules, Following the wait and see principle his administration helped the evacuees from Cachar to come back but he also provided scope for limited immigration from Sylhet for the revival of Cachar's moribund economy; however, his policy of immigration was very cautious as had been natural for the company's first representative and chief officer holding the public property as trustee. He was against the unchecked immigration as that would jeopardize the economic foundation of the indigenous people who had already had to bear tremendous hardship in the recent past to which he had been a mute witness. He could not shake off the idea of British protectorate even after the annexation as his moral integrity demanded him from turning a blind eye to management misdemeanour. His principal concern had been the welfare of the people of Cachar and to retire the irretrievable economy of the Cachar people–the primary task of his official assignment. The carefully thought out innocuous of magnanimous Fisher evolving a competent and calculated strategy incapacited plethora of evils of the unwanted annexation of the principality. His brief but useful administration commands an excellent view of the newly annexed Cachar-the society, topography, demography, ethnicity and economy and beyond for which no one can complain of boredom. The people of Cachar reposed their confidence in him as their benefactor and they were never shy to express support and solidarity to his administration. However, it could still be a painstaking climb for Cachar to its glorious place, having stemmed the rot which had set in overt the last twenty years before annexation. The revivisence should not be achieved overnight. But Edgar's attitude was totally different. He perceived Cachar as legitimate field for economic exploitation to serve the imperialist economy of the British empire. At a time when the rate of inflation had been almost zero Edgar raised the rate of revenue throwing off the policy of fair and square from Rs 3/- per hall to Rs 15/- to 20/- per ha of paddy land. The immigrants had little objection of paying the high rent but many locals lost hold of their paternal properties. Edgar boosted the vault of Cachar Treasury which witnessed enough capital flow to Calcutta but at the cost of the cultivators. Edgar's encouragement to tea industry in the map of emerging tea industry enriched the coffers of the government at Silchar and Calcutta but that hardly helped financially the people of Cachar, on the other hand, the stagnicolous tribals and the Kacharis evicted from their traditional hillocks and wasteland lived a life of penury in the hills and jungles on the frontiers of Cachar. Perhaps immigrant economy is a commentary on post-colonial Assam or rather Cachar. Except for the simple or not so simple fact that the eviction and the concomitant tears some how suggest a human tragedy.

The Naga-Kukie ethnic feud and Old Kukie-New Kukie ethnic feuds on the frontiers of Cachar had been indirectly connected with the dazzling tea policy of the British administration. The Nagas and Kukies who were an important social formation in and around Silchar during Fisher's time had to leave their hearth and home because of Edgar's wrong policy.

Making of Cachar: Edgar's Role

In the annals of economic development of Cachar Edgar occupies a preeminent place. In matters of revenue settlement, infrastructural development, setting up of commercial network and expansion of tea industry Edgar left an indelible mark unparalleled in history. Like a colossus the blue blooded colorful bureaucrat majestically strode on the newly annexed region and uplifted an unknown barren land infamous for its disease, deep-seated malaise and backwardness by his inhuman labour and administrative dynamism. He broke the century old slumber of Cachar and secured a place for it in the map of emerging tea industry.

It is through him that we discover changing mores, manners and economy of Cachar. He lent a universal dimension to Cachar. The annexation of Cachar had a very ominous beginning; apprehending the bleak economic prospect, as envisaged in the early track record, the Sylhet merchant Libsey refused the offer of the East India Company's lease of Cachar on a paltry sum (Rupees ten thousand annual rent) but the same Cachar, only four decades later when the

British rule reached its climax during the administration of Edgar, yielded a revenue of ten thousand rupees in an acre of tea estate. Indeed, by all accounts, this tremendous increase in cash was a miracle. At the most critical juncture of Cachar's history the district was fortunate enough to get enterprising and dynamic Edgar at the helm of its administration whose skill, efficiency augured well for the golden beginning of the British rule in the north-eastern most district in Assam.

Edgar as Frontier Officer

The Superintendent of Cachar was also the Frontier Officer to deal with the frontier tribes living outside the adjudicated British frontiers. He was also to keep liaison with the British representatives at Imphal and Agartala. Before Edgar Captain Stewart was the Frontier Officer in Cachar. Stewart like all other officers in the armed forces was a strong man and initially he followed a hard line to keep the frontiers free from Lucia-Kukie attacks and depredation from Manipuri war lords but soon he realized the diplomacy was more effective than brute force for the pacification of the wild tribes. Though Edgar gets the wholesale credit for the policy of conciliation with the Lushais actually it was Stewart who mooted the proposal first. A brief summary of events leading to the formulation of conciliation is necessary for better understanding of the problems of Cachar frontiers.

Lushais of Cachar Frontier

Lister's expedition opened up the Lucia country and the same time it gave the Kukies of Cachar frontier an insight into the powers of the "Sahibs". They began to think that the powerful "*Sahibs*" had become the sovereign of Cachari in place of the old native kings and the Lushais would not dare to offend the Kukies if the English protected them. This consideration made a considerable headway in strengthening the Anglo-Kukie relationship. The Kukie refugees driven out by the Lucia chiefs easily secured the plots for settlement in the Cachar borders and because of their British citizenship they were granted protection by the Government of Bengal. The Kukies living in the floating colonies were favourites of the local administrators of Silchar. The notable Kukie Chiefs on the other hand did their best to help the English in their times of need.

Abortive Attempt at Conciliation with Sukpilal, The Lushai Chief

By 1840 the Lushais of the Lalul dynasty became the masters of the Lucia Hill driving out the Kukies and in the beginning of the second half of the nineteenth century Sukpilal, the most illustrious member of that family emerged as a powerful personality in the hills south of Cachar.[8] within a few years of the Lister's Expedition he committed raids upon the Hill Tripura and on Adampur, a village in south, Sylhet. At Adampur the Lushais committed gruesome murders and carried off several captives who were British subjects. In this raid Sakpilal was instigated and assisted by Gnoor Shailon, a Pytoo chief, the son of Lalhuklo and also by Rangbhoom and Lal Hoolun, other relatives of Sukpilal. Sukpilal was very clever and masked his offence skillfully. The local officers of Sylhet also failed to detect the real culprit. Sukpilal's complicity in this raid remained untraced to the Cachar authorities till 1864. After the discovery of the real culprit, the Deputy Commissioner, Cachar, sent messengers to Sukpilal to return the Admpur captives. This he refused on the ground that the Kukie chief on Cachar frontier, Vonpilen, had murdered his men and looted the propriety of his subjects. He also informed the Deputy Commissioner that unless justice was done within six moths he himself would commence the hostilities. The boastful bragging of Sukpilal was resented by the local officers of the Government of Bengal but at the same time they took necessary precautions to keep the borders free from the trouble. Stewart informed the Commissioner of Dacca of the existing ill feelings between that Lucia and the

Cachar Kukies, and said that in case of impending hostility Mulla and Vagnoilen would join Sukpilal. And his threats alarmed the authorities of the Fort William. The Government of Bengal requested the Inspector General of Police, Lower Provinces to chalk out a plan to deal effectively with Sukpilal. The authorities of Calcutta were in a mood to send an expedition of Lisher's model immediately. But Stewart pointed out that the idea of sending an expedition should be dispensed with because the month of April was not a suitable month for an expedition in the Lucia Hills, secondly Sukpilal being a powerful chief a large scale military operations would become necessary to subjugate him. The authorities of the Fort William concurred with the views of the Deputy Commissioner and ordered the Inspector General of Police, Lower Province, to put a step to his preparations against Sukpilal.[9]

The Embassy of Vagnoilen

Stewart was a very intelligent frontier officer and an expert in tribal negotiations. He had more faith in diplomacy than in demonstration of force. He endeavoured hard to enter deep into the Lucia problem and attempted to study the grievances of the Lucia chiefs including Sukpilal. A large number of British interpreters were sent to each and every chief of the Lucia Hills. The chiefs responded to the good will of the Deputy Commissioner. On April 2, 1866 the Lucia Chief Vanoilen residing on the south of Manipur came to meet Stewart at his residence at Silchar. Vagnoilen put the question to Stewart whether or not he had made any such demand that Vagenoilen and his master Mulla were to pay tribute to the Deputy Commissioner, Cachar. He further pointed out that Mulla had already demanded from him an amount to be paid off to the English. Stewart could not give a correct reply to the question because he already had communicated the demand to Mulla. Any way, shrewd Stewart replied that the tribute was to be paid by his master and not by him and Mulla could not extort anything from him in this connexion. It is, indeed, very difficult to understand on what basis Stewart demanded tribute from Mulla, an independent Lucia Chief. Possibly he realised his mistake later on and attempted to correct it by giving Vagnoilen the immunity from the tribute. Stewart did his best to entertain the A Lushai delegation and they were accorded cordial send off.

"In the history of Anglo-Lushai relationship the embassy of Vagnoilen occupies an important place because this was the first of its kind. Formerly, the Lushai delegates met the officers of Silchar with different motive. But the embassy of Vagnoilen was a direct response of an independent chief to offer of goodwill to the British Government. C.T. Buckland, the Commissioner of Dacca, admitted that the embassy indicated certain amount of good feelings on the part of the Lushais. The Deputy Commissioner, Cachar, also realised this."

Stewart and the Fort William

But the suspicious officer of the Government of Bengal at first did not attach much importance to the Stewart-Vagnoilen meeting and enquired of the Deputy Commissioner whether Vagnoilen was a spy of Sukpilal, who had come together information regarding the possible Lucia expedition. Stewart dispelled the fears of the superior officers by his negative reply. Moreover, he pointed out that in any case it would be unwise to antagonize the chief, Mulla. He further made it clear to the authorities of the Fort William that there was sufficient justification of the existing ill feelings between the Cachar Kukies and the Lushais of Sukpilal's clan. The Cachar Lushai villages originally belonged to the mother of Sukpilal. In any future advance against Sukpilal the Lushais would form a league against the English.

Mullahs's Representation to Stewart

In the meantime the Cachar Lushai chief, Munjihow

communicated to the Deputy Commissioner that he would initiate negotiations with the recalcitrant chief Sukpilal. In his venture he needed financial assistance to the core of ten thousand rupees. The influence and integrity of Munjihow was open and above broad and the Government of Bengal readily agreed to his proposal. When the arrangements with Munjihow was afoot two Lucia deputations reached Silchar one from Mulla and the other from Sukpilal. The Mulla party expressed their willingness to remain friendly with the English at all costs. The Deputy Commissioner was very pleased with the delegation and a reward of rupees five hundred was presented to the Mulla party. Clever Stewart tactfully following the policy of Bismarck attempted to isolate Sukpilal from a powerful neighbour. The present chief a young lad and because of his minor age he had not absolute command over his powerful subordinates. Stewart took the advantage of this political weakness and attempted to bolster up the guardianless young chief. But this was difficult task because Mulla bore enmity against the English. Only a few years ago Lister launched a massive offensive against his father. But Stewart, from the very beginning of his assumption of the charge of the Superintendent, realised the merit of winning over the minor chief, did his best in this direction and ultimately succeeded. The assurance given by the Mulla party at Silchar illustrated the success of the diplomacy of Stewart."

The Arrival of Sukpilal's Delegation at Silchar

Hardly the Mulla party had crossed the Cachar borders on December 24, 1866, the delegates from Sukpilal headed by his mantry reached Silchar and met Stewart officially. On enquiry, the delegation tried to evade the question of the Adampur captives destined by Sukpilal. Finally, they disclosed that their master was a bit afraid that the English might hold him responsible for the death, marriage, missing or sale of the captives. But Stewart assured that Sukpilal need not be afraid because the Sirkar would duly consider the case of dead and married captives. In case, the married captives decline to come back, they would be allowed to stay with their husbands. The evasion and duplicity of the crafty minister of Sukpilal made Stewart angry and her refused to accept the presents of Sukpilal and informed the leader of the delegation that the sirkar was displeased with his master. Unlike Mullah party this party was nor rewarded.

Although Stewart was very firm in his dealings with the delegation he entertained a hope that Sukpilal would soon be prevailed upon by the embassy of Munjihow and he informed the Government of Bengal to that effect. Sukpilal being the very important chief of the Lalul dynasty, the superintendent was disinclined to show any powerful demonstration against him because that would counteract the policy of conciliation. He considered it better to win him over through diplomacy. In Cachar however, the border affairs were not so smooth, the local authorities did their best to establish a friendly relationship with the Lucia chiefs. Some chiefs responded to the call but Sukpilal, the great Syloo chief of considerable influence living in the close proximity of the Cachar frontier, could not be so easily induced. The sad memory of Lalchukla haunted him and he could not fully trust the English. He began his political bargain. The embassy of Munjihow failed miserably. The law and order situation beyond Cachar frontier further took a very dangerous turn because of the troublesome succession of Manipur Throne. Kanai Singh, a "Manipuri Rajputra" (Prince) who had taken refuge among the tribals of Cachar border, made an attempt to sieze the throne of Manipur by force. The local authorities of Cachar suspected that Sukpilal aided Kanai Singh. During the cold season of 1869 a series of raids by the Lushais. It was widely believed by the local officers that Sukpilal had a hand in those raids. He was an accomplice of Kanai Singh' gang and attempted to divert the attention of the British Government from Manipur to the Sylhet frontier.

"When the situation was thus surcharged with suspicion and fear Kanai Singh and Sukpilal's men jointly raided the Tea Estate of Monierkhal at Cachar in January 1869. Kanai Singh decamped with money and the Lushais with the captives. The emergency of Kanai Singh and his intrigue with the Lushai chief worsened the Anglo–Lucia relationship. The authorities of the Fort William got alarmed. The ambition of Kanai Singh cast a dark shadow upon the frontier of Cachar and the hitherto uninterrupted Policy of Conciliation suffered a temporary setback. The Government began to ponder over to devise means to meet the changing situation."[12]

The Mouierkhal raid affected the security of the tea plantation of Surma valley and it seriously jeopardized the interest of the European tea planters. The government had obviously the obligation to protect the tea industry. This raid was not merely an offshoot of the law and order problem of Cachar but it affected the growing the economy of the area. This raid was followed by other raid in quick secession to aggravate the situation. The tea merchants and the English newspapers of Calcutta raised such a hue and cry over this issue that the government was at the cross-road as to the strict adherence to the Policy of Conciliation at all costs. The basis of Conciliation was the selection of some influential chiefs living in the immediate neighbourhood of the British frontier, commanding the routes of entrance. Those chiefs were pacified with various concessions, like presents and allowance in order to prevent incursions. But when it was found that simple friendly gestures failed to convert a notable chief, whose friendship was considered to be highly desirable, and when it was also disclosed that Sukpilal was going actively against the British interests, the authorities of the Fort William decided to modify the cherished policy.

After proper investigation the local authorities as well as the authorities of the Fort William came the conclusion that steps should be taken against Kanai Singh and the marauding Lushais. Dr. Brown, (the successsor of McCulloch) the Political Agent of Manipur, was directed by the Governor General to advance at the head of a contingent to check Kanai Singh. He was, however, cautioned against any unnecessary violence. The Commissioner of Dacca was also instructed to take effective steps for the capture of Kanai Singh. According to the instructions received from the Government of Bengal Mr. Edgar, the Deputy Commissioner, Cachar, informed the authorities of the Fort William that he would start from Silchar to Sonai to arrest Kanai Singh, further informing them that the Political Agent of Manipur was very anxious to take part in the expedition personally and the Raja of Manipur would send on February 2, 1869 a regiment of one thousand men to assist the British expeditionary force.

This hoping attitude of the State of Manipur encouraged Edgar who was in great pains to convince the Government of India of the utility of a massive attack upon Kanai Singh and his associates. The cold season was almost over the vagaries of nature were looming large on the sky of Cachar. The authorities of the Fort William considered all large-scale military operation in such a time inconvenient. Overzealous Edgar who wanted to capture Kanai Singh forthwith also knew it well but to him a show of military force seemed necessary to strike terror in the minds of the hostile Lushais. The lending of the helping hands by the Raja of Manipur in his venture filled the heart of Edgar with rejoice because the Manipuri contingent along with British garrison would constitute a spectacular showman- ship. But his hopes were soon belied. He received a message from the Political Agent which expressed his unwillingness to move from the capital of Manipur because that would make the Manipuris panic striken.[13] This disgraceful conduct of the Political Agent made Edgar furious.

Delay in the Expedition

Not only the betrayal of Brown but nature also stood on

the way of Edgar's plan of operations. From January 26, heavy rains started and continued till February 3, 1869. The rains cause so much inconvenience that it became difficult to advance in a hilly terrain. In the mean time Colonel Nuthall, the leader of the punitive expedition, fell ill causing a considerable delay in the expedition.

Operations of Three Columns of the Expeditionary Force

The punitive expedition of 1869 consisted of three columns, the West Dhaleswari Column was headed by Colonel Nuthall, the East Cachar Column was headed by Edgar and the Sylhet Column was headed Kimbley and Baker. From the three different directions the three Columns began their march towards the end the February. The Eastern Column surmounting many difficulties reached Bazargha on March 12, 1869. A headman of the neighbouring Lushai village came to report that the Lucia Chief Vonipilal had died a week ago and that his mother would make peace with the English. Further, the headman expressed surprise before Edgar because of his (Edgar's) menacing postures and made it clear that the Lushais under Vonipial's following were not at all guilty of raids. This disclosure of the simple Lucia was a pointer to Edgar who released this mastaskes of using unnecessary force against the unoffending tribals. Considering further advance useless, Edgar retreated to Silchar.[14]

Result of the Futile Expedition

The expedition of 1869 was doomed from the very beginning. The authorities of Cachar wanted the expedition even against heavy odds which the Government of India agreed very reluctantly. The authorities of the Fort William limited the operations to the particular season. It is obvious that a military operation like this, where there was no clear understanding between the local and central authorities, would end in failure. The British Government learn the following lesson from this ill timed, abortive expedition.

The country traversed was very imperfectly known. The wild nature of the country and the rains were responsible for the failure of the expedition.

The expedition undertaken rather late in the reason. That full and complete arrangements were made for the regular transmission of supplies but little or no communication was established between the three columns. Lack of coordination, more so discommunication, sealed the fate of the expedition.[15]

These lesson profoundly influenced the Lushai policy of the Government of India. The authorities of Fort William realised fully well the utility of a systematic and full scale preparation before launching of an attack upon the Lushais. The failure of the expedition 1869, corrected many defects of military department of the government and it greatly helped the Lucia Expedition 1871-72 which was undertaken soon.

The expedition of 1889 failed. Neither Kanai Singh nor daring Sukpilal was taught any lesson for their misadventures, instead the English suffered from reverses. But these reverses were not merely a passing phase of frontier explosions, rather they brought about a radical change in the Lucia Policy.

Edgar's Bid to Conciliate the Lushais: The Historic Tour of Edgar

The whole atmosphere of Cachar Manipur frontier was surcharged with several explosions and it appeared that there was no hope of return to normalcy in the Anglo-Lucia relationship but a desperate bid was made by J.W. Edgar the newly appointed Deputy Commissioner of Cachar. This young and enterprising officer did his best to end the stalemate. Like Captain Lewin he took keen interest in the Lucia problem. He learned the Lucia languages and custom, and made extensive tours in the Lucia country to gather every scrap of information. Unlike Captain Lewin, Edgar was very practical and dispassionate and had the rare ability to convince the higher authorities. By virtue of his labour and imagination this young member of the Indian Civil Service began to assert tremendous influence upon the Government so far the Lucia Policy was concerned.[17]

Edgar made an extensive tour of the Lucia country in the cold season 1870-71 and submitted an elaborate report to the Government of Bengal. In his report he clearly stated the geography and location of the principal villages of the Lucia Chiefs. He also gave pen picture of the history of the Lucia Hills. He said that all the Lucia chiefs were the descendants of the Lalul. At first they lived in a single village but later on their villages extended from the Hill Tripura to the nominal frontier of Burma and from Cachar and Manipur to Chittagong Hill Tracts. But majority of the inhabitants of those villages were not Lushais. Except few cases the chiefs were all loyal chiefs and the ministers were also Lushais . In short, the nobility of the land consisted of the Lucia royal blood. But the rest of the people were Thadores, Thalngums, Waiphis, Pytoo, Hralits of Kukies of various tribes. Edgar made it clear that the Lushais were a family of great Kuki tribe. This observation removed the vagueness of the term "Kuki" and the "Lushai" so long confusing the officials of the Government.

Cricumstances Leading to the 'Sunad' of Sukpilal

In his tour Edgar made Punchangkai, a village down Sonia valley, as the permanent seat of his camp wherefrom he sent messengers to Lal Bura Sukpilal and other chiefs. He met personally many of them: his knowledge of Lucia language made him very close with them. He did his best to assert his personal influence. He convinced Sukpilal the utility of a well defined boundary of Southern Cachar and his dominion and a "Sunad" was given to him for that purpose. On January 14, 1871 Sukpilal and his officers came to the camp of Edgar. Edgar explained the terms of the "Sunad". Sukpilal agreed to take Bhariabi Chura a point where the boundary should cross the Dhalleswari.

In the "Sunad" it was expressly stated that Sukpilal and his people should not attack Cachar of Sylhet. In case of any attack from Cachar they should immediately report it to the Deputy Commissioner for redress. Should there be any dispute of Sukpilal with the "Rajas" of Manipur and Tripura the Deputy Commissioner, Cachar should be informed. When the Deputy Commissioner or any British officer would come to his country, Sukpilal or his "mantris" should meet him. Sukpilal was to send delegates to the Deputy Commissioner at his Dudpatil (Silchar) residence if no Government officer visited the Lushai country any year.[18]

Edgar did his best to win over the most influential chief against whom he personally led a column and it was really a very difficult taste but he behaved with Sukpilal liberally which was unexpected of any British officer of his time. He was definitely, a contrast to his predecessors like Sally and most other. The sheered frontier officer had a firm a conviction that a knowledge of the people and country with whom the English had to deal was more important than military science. His aim was to gather information of the Lushai without provoking Sukpilal. This attitude of Edgar was bitterly criticized by the English newspapers such as the *"Observer"*, *"Pioneer"* etc. but it would be seen later on that he was right.[19]

Motive behind the Treaty with Sukpilal

During this tour Edgar came to know that the village of Dharmagpi had been entrusted with the task of guarding Cachar from Lushai raids. But to him the arrangement did not seem to be satisfactory. He also noticed intense ill-feelings between one group of chiefs with another and also found a reign of chaos dominating the eastern region of Manipur. He put all the blame on Manipur. Under these circumstances

Edgar made a truce with Sukpilal. It is really very difficult to assign the cause that led Edgar to make peace with Sukpilal. Edgar, it seems, did not expect much of "Sunad" but was a shrewd frontier officer, he realised, immediately after a futile military expedition against Sukpilal, that in case of a future large scale military expedition in the Lucia Hills the assistance or in the worse, the neutrality of Sukpilal was a military necessity. The death of Munjihow, the great friend of the English created a vacuum which should only be filled up by Sukpilal alone. Powerless Dharmangpi was no substitute for Munjihow. Sukpilal was not merely a great chief of the Western Lucia clan but his territory occupied a position of strategic importance. He and his subordinate chiefs were, in fact, the gatemen of the Lucia Hills and Edgar was opposed to the idea of antagonising the keeper of the gates. Very likely this motive was the main force in following a policy of appeasement towards Sukpilal and after him towards his son, Lenkhom, till the time of annexion.

A Series of Border Explosions

Edgar was shrewd and clever but no less was Sukpilal. He did not go directly against the English and during the Lushai Expedition 1871-72 he assisted the British Government but he never allowed to jeopardize his own interest. He was indeed very tactful, but the other Lushai chiefs whom Edgar also trusted, duped him. Immediately after his return from the tour when the negotiations with Sukpilal were going on, Edgar was startled to know of a series of daring raids on the borders of Cachar, Sylhet and Chittagong. The ferocity and magnitude of these raids were unprecedented in the history of the Eastern frontier. In January 1871, the Cachar Village of Ainarkhalin the south of Hailakandi valley was attacked, twenty five persons were killed and thirty seven persons were made prisoners. The Lucia hordes swooped upon the Alexandra Pur tea garden and destroyed it, and, though the proprietor Mr. Sellar succeeded in making his escape, Mr. Winchester, neighbouring Planter who was breakfasting with him, was brutally killed by a gunshot and his little daughter Mary Winchester was carried off. A few hours late, an attack was made on the neighbouring garden of Katlichaerra. Here the Lushais were driven out but they caused substantial damage to the garden establishment and personnel. Encouraged by the repeated success the Lushais raided the following day, on the same estate but they were beaten off. Three days later Monierkhal which is situated on the Sonia near the eastern border of the district, was attacked. The Frontier Police made their last attempt to ward off the aggressors. In a trenched encounter the Lucia sustained a terrible loss of fifty seven men. While the attack on Monierkal was going on, another party of Lushais raided the Tea Estates of Dharmiakhal and Nugdigram, killing both the Nagas and the Bangalees of the last mentioned village, and also carried off the captives. A convoy was sent from Silchar to relieve the people at Monierkhal but, in spite of the gallantry of the troops and men, the Lushais overran the army stockades and made their safe escape to the hills. In face of those violent and organized raids the British authority completely lapsed for several days in those Tea Estates. The news of death and destruction reached Calcutta. The European community all over India got excited over the savagery of the wild hordes. When the sad memory of the abduction of Mary Winchester was still fresh, the recurrence of a series of depredations harassed the Government of Bengal.

The occurrence of these raids, in spite of the efforts of friendship by the frontier officers proved the futility of the Policy of Conciliation. The policy recommended by the local officers was of punishment.

Sir William Grey, the Lieutenant Governor of Bengal, proposed a fresh expedition against the Lucia but his proposal was rejected by the Government of India. The Policy of neutrality of Lawrence dominated at that time in the meeting of the Governor General-in-Council. The Government of Bengal was not satisfied with the unhelpful attitude of the Central government. There started a stormy debate between these two Governments. The Government of India refused to admit that it was necessary to chastise the offending Lushais by following them into their own fortresses and hills. But the will of the Government of Bengal ultimately prevailed.

In the mean time a large number of memorandums began to pour in into the Secretariat of the Government of Bengal from the local officers urging a punitive expedition against the Lushais. The pillars of the British administration were those local officers, the District Magistrates or the Commissioners, and it was really difficult for the Provincial Secretariat to turn down their proposals.

Edgar who was highly optimistic about his mission in conciliating the Lushais was also baffled by the repeated raids, submitted a memorandum urging to reduce the tribes to complete subjugation.

In the Lucia Expedition 1871-72 Edgar was the Civil Officer of the Cachar Column. At the close of the expedition he was asked by Alexander Mackenzei, Junior Secretary, Bengal Government to submit a report on the expedition which Edgar replied on April 2, 1872.

Wide Coverage of the Report

Edgar pointed out that his review "will be in the main confined to the operations of the Cachar Column and its dealings with the tribes with which it was brought into contact; but I shall have incidentally to take notice of the political results of the action of the Manipore contingent, and the present and future relation of that state with the tribes on its southern frontiers. I shall also give a brief preliminary sketch of so much of the history of the Lushais since we first came in contact with them as may help to explain the objects at which the commander of our column aimed and to show the amount of success he had in attaining those objects.

Savage Tribes South of Cachar

From earliest times about which there are any traditions in Cachar, the high range of hills to the south of the district and Manipore have been inhabited by tribes who, though very wild in some of their characteristics, and constantly engage in fierce disputes amongst themselves, or with cognate but still more ferocious tribes living east of them, seem to have long ago advanced for and a state that could fairly be called savage. These tribes seem to have been practically independent as long as they were able to maintain their position in the higher hills. The Raja of Tipperah, indeed, claims supremacy over all the villages west of Tipai, but practically his authority was never acknowledged east of the Chatterchoora Range up to which he used to exact a partial and probably fit full obedience. Neither the Cachar nor the Manipore chief had the slightest authority in the hills south of Tipai Mukh, and it is from time to time villages or group of villages, grew strong than its neighbours, and reduced the latter to subjection, or forced them to take refuge in the hills, which were acknowledged by all to belong to Manipur or Cachar or Tipperah. The newcomers theoretically become the subjects to the state within the limits of which they had taken refuge, and in the case of these who took refuge in Cachar and Manipore Hill territory previous to the Burmese invasion, the facts agreed pretty well with the theory. But as mentioned above this does not appear to have been the case with Tipperah. It seems to have been the custom with the conquering villages, at least for many years back, to encourage the families of the wilder tribes to the east to settle down in the places acted by the refugees, and in this they seem to have been tolerably successful. Meantime, the old feud did not always cease when the weaker chief and his people took refuge in a neighbouring state, he was often followed up and attached in his new position. Less frequently he was able to make a successful raid and do much harm to the stronger village. But it is probable that previous to the Burmese invasion both Cachar and Manipore were able to protect their own people, and possibly to assist them in attacking their enemies; but for many years previous to the death of Gobind Chunder, Raja of Cachar in 1830, neither state was able to afford any protection against the independent hill men. Each movement of the tribes in the direction of Cachar or Manipore was followed by horrible massacres of the refugee, and at last the Bengali settlers in the south of Cachar were attacked and driven out of the cultivated low lands near the hills.

The Kukies

During the entire period of which we have any record or reliable tradition, the tract above mentioned, at least as far south as the present north-boundary of the Citation hill Tracts, has been held by families of the great tribe known to us as Kookies. Colonel McCulloch, indeed, states that there are traditions both tamong the Kookies and Nagas which seem to indicate that the latter tribe a tone time occupied the southern Hills, but I have not been able to find any corroboration of this tradition. The name "Kookie" has been given to the tribe by the Bengalees, and is not recognized by the hill men themselves; and I have never found any trace-of a common name for the tribe among them, although they seem to consider different families as belonging to a single group, which is certainly co-existensive with what we call the Kookie tribe. This tribe is again subdivided by the Cacharees and Bangaless of this district into "old" and "new" with reference to the time at which the people of this district first came in contact with each family of hill men. The "old Kookies" are democratic communities with very doubtful traces of having been once organized under chiefs. The "new kookies" are subject to chiefs whose families are regarded as almost sacred, and whose power is only limited by the possibility of malcontent transferring his allegiance to a more popular chief of the same or some other semidivide race. The difference between the political organization of the old and the new Kookies probably accounts for the fact that the former communities were driven out earliest and that there are new to traces of them in the villages of the Lucia and other new Kookies who occupy the hills from which they were driven. On the other hand each family of new Kookies that took refuge in Cachar of Manipore left behind many of its members in the villages of its conquerors, many of whom again when their turn came had to submit to live under some chief still stronger than their own.

Coming of the Lushais

When we took possession of Cachar, and for many years afterwards, the families whose feuds attracted most attention, and from whose raids we suffered most, were the Thlanums, Changsils, Thadoes and Paites. But somewhere about 1840, the Lushais (a new family) made its appearance, which by degrees has reduced to submission, or driven out all the others and for the last twenty years has kept all the possession of all southern hill. The first chief of this family of whom we have any mention was named Lalool, his village seemed to have been originally further south than most of those of his defendants, and he is said to have come of the same stock as that from which the Howlong and Sylhoo chiefs are descended, but all the earlier traditions are very vague. We know, however, that he had at least four sons Lalingbhoom,, Lalsavahoonh, Mongpri, and Bhoota. The last, who was probably the youngest is said to be still alive, and it is likely that at his father's death he succeeded to the original village, as often happen among the Kookies. Previous to this the elder brothers had each started a village on his own account, and being, undoubtedly, capable men had widely exceeded the influence of the family. At this time about 18400 Mongpir's villages were situated on some of spurs of the Chatterchoora, from which the Lushais were rapidly pushing out the Paite chief who had previously occupied the hills on each side of the valley of the Gootur. Lalingvhoom's villages were situated on the hills east of the Dhaleswar, a considerable way south of the peak (Nisapwee) of the great trigonometrical survey: all the hills north of this and west of the Sonia were held by Thadoes, who, however, were beginning to be hard pressed by him. Lalsvaoong had pushed further east, and was struggling with the Singsol Thadoes for the Chaumfai valley and the range to the north of it.[22]

Cachar Manipuries and the Lushais

"About this time the Paitoos applied for assistance against two Manipuri Rajputras, who had been settled by us some years previously in south Hailakandi, to protect that part of the district against the Paitos themselves. In consequence of this application, the Manipories with their armed followers made a sudden and successful raid on the village of Mogpri, which was than situated on a hill near the Pukwacherra, somewhat to the south of the Chatterchoora range. The chief was taken prisoner by the Manipooris, but released on his payment of a ransom, and making a promise that he would not attack Cachar of again to trouble the Paitos, after this the Lushais withdrew towards the south, but they kept up friendly relations with the Manapuree Rajputra, and after the death of the later, with their descendents there seems to have been the origin of connexion between the Lushais and the exiled Manipooris, about which so much was heard in 1869 and again last year. The promise to refrain from attacking the Paitos was not possibly without some effect. For although they were ultimately driven out by the Mungpir and his son Sukpilal to relation between Mangpir's family and that of the Paitoo chief of a kind different form those existing between the other Lucia chiefs and the chiefs disposed by them. A more detailed account of this matter will be found in my report C of the 13th March 1871.

Chief Lalula's Family

"Meantime Lalingvhoom, Lalsavoong and Vonoel, son of the latter, was prospering even more than Mongpir, Lalsavoong, having driven out, or subdued, all the chiefs north of Chumfai valley died before 1894, leaving at least there sons all of whom became powerful chiefs. One of these Lalpong was head of the great village of Sellam, and the other villages own belonging to his son Poyboy; but he seems to have been not some extent subordinate to his brother Vonole, who undoubtedly the ablest and most powerful chiefs that the family of Lalul has yet produced. In his youth he seems to have been constantly fighting, and always more or less successful. He fought various tribes to his south known as Poi, and carried of, he settled down either in the villages of his own Kookies. He followed the policy towards the Soktes, another family of Kookies, whose head is Kamhwo, the powerful chief of Molbehm, and we found hundreds of Sokte families settled among the Lushais. He made about 1850. Col. McCulloch remained in Manipore. He seemed to have avoided quarrels with the other chiefs of the Lalul family, over whom, however, he had great influence and by whose people he was invariably spoken of as the " great chief".[22]

"In 1849 Lalingvhoom was the chief next in influence and importance to Vonolel. He had driven the Thadoe chiefs from the Rengti and Noongari ranges, and had made a village for himself a little a south of the gulf of Nesaqwee (peak Z). This seems to have been a larger village than even Vonolel's. He is said to have been preparing to occupy the sites from which the more northern Thadoe villagers had been driven, when he died in 1849. His death was followed by a raid conducted by his son Mora or Mulla, against the Thadoes of

Kaimong, a chief whose village had been situated on the hill south of B Nongkiung, but who had some years previously taken refuge in Cachar and settled about ten miles south of the station. He had taken with him two sets of gongs. Claimed by the Lushais, and it was on account of this dispute that his villages were chosen for attack. Lt Col. Lister. Political Agent, Khasi Hills, was directed by Government to find out and punish the perpetrators of this outrage and some others were committed at about the same time in Sylhet and Tippearah.

Effect of Lister Expedition

The detailed account of Col Lister operations are described by A. Mackenzie in his memorandum on the North East Frontier. It is sufficient to mention that his little force marched under the guidance of refugee Kookie along the junction with the Noongrai range. From where Col Lister with a portion of his force made a rapid march east- ward, crossing the Rookni near its source, and surprised Mora's village. Most of the inhabitants had the time to escape but some were killed and the village burnt. Col. Lister remained there some time but the Kookies annoyed him and his man so he had to withdrew.

"The addict of destruction of Lalngvhoom's village was very great. In the next cold weather the messengers came from Vonole, his brother Lalpoong, Bhoota, Sukpilal and other small chiefs to had for our friendship and assistance against the Pois. Probably, their principal immediate object was to gather information while and further operation against was contemplated by us. They all seem to have come from the Sukpilal's village and among them were a Manipuri who seated there. He went back to a short stay at Cachar and came with Sukpilal. But the chiefs denied the leaving of Sukpilal. It is possible that the Maniporis contrived to impersonate Sukpilal to receive presents, because Superintendent of Cachar refused to present any body other than Sukpilal. Anyway the friendly relation continued between the Lushais and Cachar and in the tea garden of the south they came to work. A friendly charter was interchanged. But we received less knowledge about Mora's village.[23]

Mistake of British Administration

"Though the Lushais showed the desire of friendly relationship they seemed to have feared and suspected us. Sukpilal who before 1849 advanced another of Chatterchouras retreated towards south very close to the Sylhoos. Mora died sometime after the destruction of his village, leaving an infant son Vonolial, whose mother Impanoo eventually removed the chief village to the site called "old" Kholil which is very much further from the Nisapwee (peak Z). The intention to taking up the village sites abandoned by the refugee Kookies was given up; but what the Lushai's called guard villages were established on points commanding the different routes from our frontier to the chief Lucia villages. All intercourse between our Kookies and the Lushais was discouraged by the Chiefs of the latter and traders and wood cutters were obliged to go by water to certain points fixed by the Lucia from which they were occasionally allowed to go to the villages of the chiefs. In this way, in course of time, the Lushais succeeded in putting between the frontier and their villages a tract of forest which not only unexplored by us, but to a great extent unknown to our Kookies, except a few old men who had not been over the grounds for years. It was a mistake on our part to allow this to happen, particularly as far many years after 1849.[24]

Emergence of Sukpilal to Western Chief

For some years after the Lister's expedition no raids either in Cachar or Sylhet took place. But in 1862 Sukpilal made raid on Hill Tippaerah and some villages on south Sylhet in which several British subjects were killed and carried off. He was transported for similar outrages in 1845. And also instigated by Rangbhoom and Lal Hoolien, Sukpilal's relatives. Sukpilal's role in this raid was not suspected till 1864 when four captives escaped from his village to Cachar. He was asked to hand over the remainder of the prisoners. Ultimately, he surrendered four prisoners and the remainders he stated to have married the Lucia girls and had become their inhabitants who were not willing to come back. Thus, a punitive expedition did not take place which the Government thought of.

In course of those negotiations an agreement was made both the representatives of Vonpilal and Sukpilal, that each of these two chiefs was to receive an annual sum of Rs 600 on condition that they could preservé peace and order in the frontier area and they would pay tribute on some specified articles to the Government. Soon the messenger from Vonpilal complained that the tea gardens encroached on their grounds. The suggestion of Stewart, the D.C. Cachar that the tea gardens to be extended to planters resentment. On extension of the tea gardens meant the narrowing the belt of the impregnable jungle belt.

Major Stewart, the D.C. Cachar

In the beginning of 1867, Major Stewart, the DC Cachar induced Sukpilal to meet him at the Pollycherra tea garden but failed. In 1867 the Sonai was surveyed as far as it was navigable but for the hostility of Manjihow's people the survey of the country of Sukpilal was cancelled . An uneasiness was created in the situation. The messengers said that the Lushais intended to be friendly with the Government but "the truth is that inspite of these negotiations and messages and trading and payment of tributes and police allowances we know much less about the Lushais and what in much more dangerous state, as far we are concerned, that they had been at any time since Col. Lister's expedition. I do not think that the district officers were altogether to blame for the state of things.

Doubtless we had made mistakes; the local officers did not act wisely in recommending to Government to do way an establishment of Kooki secrets kept up since 1849, for the purpose of collecting intelligence connected with the Lushais. I think that Major Stewart was wrong in the way he treated the objection made to the advance of tea cultivation."[25]

"... Our chief fault was not calling the attention of the Government to the evils which we saw clearly."[26]

Edgar then narrated that almost all the officers who had any practical knowledge of the frontier, Col. Lister, Col. McCulloch, Major Stewart and he himself thought that there should have a constant watch over the Kookies in the British territory and Manipur and had correct information about their activities abound the frontier. 'This was one of the chief object of the Kookie levie. This was the leading principle of Col. McCulloch's Kookie Policy. Major Stewart and Col. Vener always told me to look well after our Kookies'... But I remember that when I Came here by the end of 1867 he (Stewart) complained that our Kookies were slipping out of my heads." The abolition of the establishments of the Kookie Scouts in 1860 had been the beginning of the serious change and had weakened British hold over the Kookies. The waste land came under the possession of the tea planters who had been granted the lands for tea cultivation and consequently the hillmen living on the grant-lands, paid taxes to them and had been passing from the official head of the district to the grantees of waste lands.

The Tea Estates

At present the district authorities receive cordial support from the tea planters but in 1863 the general attitude of the non-official community was markedly hostile to the district authorities, and the planters disliked any interference of the district authorities on the Kookies and they instigated the Kookies to disregard the extra-judicial orders of the DC with the result in south Cachar villages moved from garden to garden without our knowledge. In spite of the discouragement of the Lushai chief there had been a lot of intercourse in between their people and our Kookies. But we became ignorant about the affairs of Kookies, living in the gardens. For the information of our Kookies we had to depend upon them and after the death of Manjihow because our messengers often misrepresented and the Bengalees and Manipuris, ignorant of their languages and politics, failed to give us correct information."[27]

Next, Edgar in his report commented that the creation of garden estates had direct bearing upon the Kookies. "The Kookies as I have more than once pointed out, seem to be enable to conceive any political system differing in essence from their own, and they look upon the district of Cachar, for instance, as a group of villages held together by the superior power, natural or supernatural of the European head of it. The formation of tea garden on unoccupied ground by Europeans would appear to them analogous to the formation of new villages by the sons of chiefs, and they would instinctively look upon the owners as a rather dependent on the greater central chief than subject to him. Soon they would think that the power of the central chief had declined and that of the frontier chief under whom they live had become supreme. They would take the advantage of the situation by creating trouble. Our Kookie agents coming to the sadar station and elsewhere would see certain changes in the power of the DC had would think the decline of the central chief. Thus, extending the tea gardens to the south border by the suggestion of Major Stewart, the Kookies had become benefitted and the condition of Government had become dangerous."[28]

It is pertinent to point out in this connexion the opinion of Col. W. Shakespear an experienced soldier and a pillar of the Assam Rifles. He writes, " At this period the Cachar of

Surma Valley Frontier Policy had a considerable number of Kukis in their ranks, who had been retained on disbandment of the old Levy for special duties such as trackers, sharpshooters, scouts, guides, collectors of tribal information, etc., most of whom formed the detachment under Mr. Daily with General Bourhaeir's force, and on whom Mr. Edgar his Political Officer, an inadverted strongly in his report. He found that though much individual bravery came to notice during the expedition, they were useless for the work expected of them, all aptitude for the essence of their tribal habits when at war having been drilled out of them by overzealous Police officers in the past. "Those officers evidently had attached more importance to uniformity of action and the finish needed to produce smart soldiers, which the Frontier Police in general and certainly their Kuki element were not supposed to attain to." "No attempt," he says "had been made to keep up and learn in his boyhood, consequently this expedition revealed the uselessness of these men with us." He recommended that, if they could not be trained for the specific purposes for which they were originally enlisted, and as soldiers they did to shine, they should be eliminated from the Frontier Police. This later was carried out, their places being filled by Goorkhas and Cacharis."[29]

The foresight of Edgar saved the British administration from many harassment in future expeditions relating to annexation and consolidation of the British rule in the North Lucia Hills.

Edgar in his report next dealt upon the change that took place in the Lucia socio-political setup in the immediate frontiers of Cachar.

Changes in Lushai Polity

Important changes took place in the mean time among the Lushai communities. Mora's widow after Mora's death shifted to new Kholle hill east of Tipai. She still claimed the superiority over the villages between the Soni and Dhalewar. Sukpilal's son when grew young pushed further north towards the Sonai with the consent of Voniplal's mother; however, Vonpilal disfavoured it. But when became old he lost his hold upon the fellow Lucia because he was hardly pressed by the Skotes, Howlongs and Pois, he made a contract with the Pallein chief who agreed to assist Vonolel against his enemies. Thingong a son of a dead brother of Vonolel, had a village in the direction of Manipore. Vonolel's son Kenkom started a village twenty miles north of Champai valley.

The young chief intended to fight and eager for fighting but they thought they could merely defend them from the tribes of the south and east. They, however, left the Paittos of Tipperah and Sylhet, and the Naga villages of the Manipore. The old people particularly the old women who witnessed Col. Lister's expedition advised them to enter into the British territory but the warriors born after 1849 or infant at that time, were unable to understand the fears. And probably they thought that the "Cachar chief" had become weak within the course of twenty years and they knew much farther of Mora's village where the force of Cachar could not reach them.

Edgar on McCulloch's Transfer

Edgar in describing the evil effect of McCulloch's transfer on the Kukies of Cachar-Manipore frontiers wrote that Colonel McCulloch had left Manipore at the end of 1867 and was succeeded by the inexperienced Civil Assistant Surgeon who failed to understand the intrigue of the Manipori officers and on their advice handed over the task of managing the Kookie affairs on them.

"The Lushais soon found that the firm and judicious head which had kept them in order for nearly twenty years was withdrawn, and though that they might with safely attack the Manipore villages.

Naga Kukie Feud

"In Nov.. 1868, the Naga village of Mentha, in Manipore territory was attacked and burned by Vonpilal and Poyboy, and several captives carried off. In December of the same year some of Sukpilal's people encountered and killed some of Rungbhoom's Paitoos in the jungles of Hill Tipperah. They afterwards took Rungbhoom's village, which I think was in Sylhet but were driven out of it by the men of a neighbouring police guard. On the 10th January 1869, the garden on Nowarband was plundered and burned, and some of the coolies killed by Lalroom. On the 14th Deowte attacked the garden of Moniarkhal, where there was a police guard, which however, was unable to prevent his plundering the garden and destroying the buildings. Early February great attack was made on the Akala Vaga stockade, among whom Lenkom was prominent. The stockade was taken and a Manipore officer and several sepoys killed. Some Naga villages were attacked and destroyed about the same time.

"We did not find out rough were the actual perpetrators of each raid till long after but we suspected Voniplal and Sukpilal from the first and a small column of soldiers and police up the Dulleswer, in the direction of Sukpilal, while it was if possible, to meet another small force advancing from the south of Sylhet, along the return tracts of the raiders. Another small body was to go up the Sonai to Lushai Bazar, and then across through Manipore force working across from the point taken up by the Manipori contingent this year.

These plans were materially altered and were not carried out successfully in their new shape.

"The parties sent up the Dullessur were forced by the weather to turn back. The party from Sylhet came up to the neighbourhood of Sukpilal's village but had to come back for want of provision. The Manipori contingent was also prevented by the hard weather. We came to know from the

Kookies of Vonpilal was dead and that the outrage on Mulla in November had been made by Poyboy and Vonpilal. But he did not dare to dash on Cachar because of his mother's influence. The other Lucia chiefs promised to do all in their power to induce the principal offenders to come to terms with us. They denied of any prisoners with them.

After the return of the expedition there were much discussion about the measures to be taken of the future protection of our frontier. I suggested that an well organized but small force to be sent to punish Sukpilal for, although he was not responsible for raids in Manipore and Cachar, he was an old offender and in the success of the fellow Kookies might embolden him in future. Here in lies the political importance of the expedition.

I also proposed that while the military expedition was operating against Sukpilal I should go up the Soni with a guard sufficient for defence and made an effort to prevail on the Eastern Chiefs to make a voluntary submission and in this I hoped to be aided by vigorous pressure exercised by Manipore in communication with me on the village of Poyboy and Vonolel. Also stated that after finding Sukpilal into season we should advance eastward to punish the villages of Deowte, and Lalroom. After all the tribes had been reduced to submission we should follow a policy which had been commenced after 1849, which not been fairly tried since the adoption of the policy. I suggested that the Kookies be induced to settle on inhabited land between their tract and our frontiers and by fostering trade and commerce in between their and our Kookies. They should also be encouraged to join in the regular Kukie levy to be prostate for the protection of the frontier. I also proposed to lay down a boundary line between the Cachar district and the Lucia Hills.

Edgar's Tour in the Lushai Country

Edgar made an extensive tour of the Lushai land in the

cold season of 1870-71. Hari Charan Sarma, Extra Assistant Commissioner, Cachar accompanied him. It was a Herculian task in those days in the unknown dense forest and dangerous hills infested with savage tribes. The courage, valour, stamina, sagacity and knowledge of Lushai language and custom of Sarma and especially his pleasant personality to face the delicate tribal issues squarely made the publicized tour of Edgar a complete success which drew admiration from all concerned. In his report to the Bengal Government he gave a detailed description of the geography and location of the principal villages of Lushais. He pointed out how Lalul's clan, the ruling Lushai dynasty, established their hold in the Lushai Hills by defeating the other clans and tribes. Except the few cases the Chiefs and their ministers were Lushais but the rest of the people were Thados, Thlangums, Paites, Hmars or Kukies of variours clans and sub-clans. He made it clear to the government that the ruling Lucia houses were the family of great Kukie tribe. The report of Edgar removed the vagueness of the term "kukie" and "lushai" so long confusing the officials of the British Government. Like Edgar, Captain T.H. Lewin, the Superintendent of Citation Hill Tracts, made a similar tour and suggested to the Government of Bengal a large scale military expedition against the Lushais.

Lord Ullich Brown, the Commissioner of Citation raised a bitter controversy over the cherished policy of conciliation of the Government of India. Edgar's suggestion " the real policy should be of severe punishment for raid, conciliatory and kind treatment afterwards" convinced the Government of India to give up the Policy of Conciliation and adopted a "Forward Policy". The Commander-in-Chief came to Assam and he (Napier) was highly impressed by Edgar's dynamism, Along with Napier came the young officer Robert, who later on became the Commander-in-Chief and whose books are the source books on the military history of India. On the recommendation of Napier the Government of India sanctioned the historic Lucia Expedition 1871-72.

Importance of River Tipai

The Lushai took upon the Tipai as the boundary between the clans, which had been to use their own phrase, the Manipore Raja's men and those which were with the Cachar Sahibs." It is not easy to define exactly the idea of the relation indicated by this phrase; but the clans west of Tipai certainly consider that they are in some way connected with Cachar, and those to the east, with one exception, have the same feelling about Manipore. The exception is the village of Kholle, which thought now situated on the east of the Tipai, still is considered to be one of the villages of Cachar. East of Kholle, at the distance of about one day's journey, is the village of Poyboy, son of Lalpoong. He is at present very much dissatisfied with Manipore and according to the statement of the Lucia chief Dorpong, forwarded to the Commissioner of Dacca with my letter of 6th, he accuses Thadoe subjects of the Raja for having murdered seven of his people this year. In spite of all this, all the Lucias of his village, whom I saw, spoke of their making friends with the Raja, ultimately as a certainty, and the chief and his headmen did not seem to wish to have anything to do with Cachar.

"In the same way whenever I spoke about Vonolel or any of his sons, except Dowte I was told that they sent Muntries and presents into Manipore, and that they wished to be the Raja's people.

"But while I think Manipore is in a better position than Cachar to gain an influence over the clans east of Tipai, it is nearly as important for the latter as it is for the former that friendly intercourse should be kept up with these villages. The chiefs are all nearly related to those south of Cachar. They are continually intermarrying and their people keep up a constant intercourse for trade and other purpose the result of this close connexion is that the minds of the Cachar Lushais will be unsettled as long as Manipore continues on bad terms with the Eastern clans."

Dorpong in his statement had made a reference that Poyboy had asked the assistance of Kholle people to attack the Manipori territories. That was refused but in future the Kholle might take the side of the Poyboy which might lead to disturbance in Manipore and Cachar. The chief complaint of the Eastern Lushais against the Raja of Manipore was that the Thadoe Kookie of Manipore territory had captured and murdered some men this year. If the Kookies got excited over the matter they would attack the villages inhabited by the Manipories in the Cachar border who were British subjects and they would treat any Manipuri by race as their enemy.

Edgar Meets McCulloch

With the permission of the Lt. Governor, Edgar advanced to meet Lt. McCulloch, the Governor General's Political Agent to Manipore to establish a good relation in between Manipore and the clans of its south (in 1867). At that time the Lushais were in good terms with Manipuris, the Thadoes and other Kookies living in the state. Messengers were sent time to time to the Lushais from Manipore under the supervision of Col. McCulloch. "He never allowed any Manipories to mediate in those affairs, fearing their inveterate habit of inventing, which would bring mischief... Occasionally, also, influential Lushai went to see Col. McCulloch and I believe that when his messages carried with his silver mounted Burmese day to any of the nearer villages, the headmen looked upon it as the summon to appear before him. Which they were bound to obey. The Manipore Kookies used at that time to shoot over the hunting grounds of the Lucias near the great salt spring called Chiboo, and when they killed anything they left a hind leg at the spring for the Lushais, who in their turn when lucky, used to league a leg for the Thadoes.

Manipur after McCulloch

"All this is changed. It was at this very spring of Chiboo the Thadoes this (1871) killed Poyboy's men, four of whom were hunting and three making salt. Manipore messengers were sent by the Raja to negotiate with the Lucia chiefs but the Lushais were angry with the reported bad behaviour of the Muntrees of Manipur Raja and refused to come to terms with them. They said to me in case of a "good" Muntree they could begin a fresh talk."

Edgar thought that a change in the relations of the Lushais with the Manipore must be improved. Col. McCulloch, the Political Agent, did his best to handle the Lucia affairs in his own hand. Of course he did all in the name of Raja but never allowed the Manipore officers to interfere in that affair. He could freely talk with the Lushais and had a great knowledge about them and their land but his successor was not so competent. Raja and his officers interfered with the Lucia affairs resulting the present unhappy condition of the frontier. The officer of the Raja hinted to punish the Lushais and they induced the Raja to send an expedition and they expected that the English would help them. But hey forget that in case of attacking the clans living beyond the Cachar frontier the government would confuse a tranquil and calm border. "So, the remedy is that the Political Agent of Manipore should not allow the Manipore officers to interfere into this. The Thadoes near the Chiboo valley be refrained from fighting against the Lushais any more. Chibo should be carefully guarded.

"Trust worthy messengers be sent to meet the Eastern Lushais and induce their chiefs to come to meet the Political Agent at Manipore and if they refuse to come to Manipore it is advisable that the Political Agent should come to meet them."[34]

Grievances of the Eastern Lushais

Edgar had the reason to believe that the Eastern Lushais of the Lucia country had suffered real or fancied injuries from the hillmen who were resident of Manipore and they were eager for a permanent boundary." Each village has its limits and are known and respected by the tribes and any attempt to dishonor except in times of hostilities it is condemned by all. If the Raja of Manipore fixes a boundary and tell the Lushais, that would be respected as long as they behaved well, this would be no small security for him. The effect could be greater if the Political Agent goes there personally.

"It is expected that the Raja who favours the policy of friendly relations with the Eastern Lushais for the Lucia are not the only tribes that cause trouble in the southern frontier. Kamhow of Molbhem, the great Sokte chief is also the enemy of the Manipore who attacked Moirang this year. This Lushai Kookies are also advancing towards the Manipore. Had the Political Agent been in December 1870 at Chibo valley the Kookies could be protected from committing the outrage."

Edgar on Lushi Raids

Towards the end of 1870 the news of death of Vonolel was confirmed and Edgar met Sukpilal at Changsil and fixed the boundary with him. He heard that Vonolel's family was on the way to attack Cachar. Vonolel's son Lal Bura attacked Moniarkhal and Tangdong, the nephew of Vonolel, reached Nugdigram. But during the absence of Tangdong his village was destroyed and his wife and others were taken as prisoners. Some days later, Howlongs under Benkhooya and Sanghoong, sons of Lalptang, had attacked a garden south Hailakandi and had killed European and Indians and had taken away a European girl. Edger heard that the Howlongs were debating of giving up the girls either with the assistance of Rutton Poea or Sukpilal. Edgar, from the Lushai Bazar, attempted to get informations as to the perpetrators of the outrages, Khalkom, Sukpilal's son, came to assist him but the exact location of the perpetrators could not be found out. According to Edgar, the raids, on Manipore, Moniearkhal and Nugdigram had been committed by the relations of Vonolel, and those in South Hailakandi, Sylhet and Tipperah by the Howlong of Lalpitang's family, possibly assisted by Sylhos and guided by the Paitoos. The at- tacks on Nugdigram and Maniarkhal were different from the attack on Alexandrapore, Cutleycherra and Jhalnacherra.

Raid of Alexandrapore T.E.

The garden of Alexandrapore was attacked all on a sudden; the people awe-struck by surprise ever Weinchester before loading his gun was killed in his breakfast table. Bangshaw and Cooke being warned drove the Howlongs but the Howlongs came next day and they were driven out with the assistance of the police. The manager of Moniarkhal got the information and with the help of 37 soldiers and police and again by 39 soldiers under Daily, the Lushais were driven out. The Lal Bura's Lushais bescized the stockade for two days and after a great loss they could be driven out. Government had to suffer the loss of seen armed men and one severely wounded. Five men were wounded previously.[36]

Tangdong's party killing some Nagas and Bengalees came to Nugdigram and attacked Daily's rearguard consisting of 7 soldiers and a police constable. The soldiers fought gallantly but were overpowered and ultimately all were killed excepting one soldier. The Lushais got possession of the thirteen muskets of the dead soldiers. This greatly exalted them.

"The above statement states clearly that although the Howlongs carried a large booty and prisoners they could not withstand the government gun but the eastern Lushais triumphed over out troops."[37]

Edgar's Suggestion

Edgar suggested two punitive expeditions to punish the perpetrators of the crime of 1871 by next cold weather, one would advance from Cachar to the village of Lal Bura and Tangdong and the other from Citation to the villages of the sons of Lalpiting. Between Tipai Mookh and the villages of Lal Bura were situated Kholel (Vonpilal) village and Sullen (Poyboy's) who would side with the government. The people of Lal Bura's village could be severely dealt with.

He also suggested that armed pickets be posted at Chattarchoora, Rengti Pahr and B Nongkong, and the Raja of Manipur be requested to send a large force to some points south of Moirang. That would prevent the Kemhows to aid the Lushais even though that was unlikely (for they were enemies of each other).

Lushai Expedition 1871-72

In July 1871, the Governor General-in-Council decided in sending an expedition into Lushai country. In a letter of the Quarter Master General Edgar found in September that the Commissioner-in-Chief had recommended the point of departure of the Cachar Column be the Tipai Mukh as suggested by Edgar but there was no instructions to attack the Eastern Lushais. He came to know that the Government was not desirous to attack the Eastern Lushais because of the change in the relation of the Lushi with the Raja of Manipore. But the change in the direction of attack might lead to danger so, Edgar made enquiries on the question of the point of departure. The matter was referred to Brigadier General, Bouchier. Edgar came to Shillong to meet the Brigadier General but the General advised him to concur the Tipai Mukh route.

Advance of the Cachar Column

The expedition started from Silchar through the dense

forest and hilly ranges. Edgar came to know from Korpong, a person known to him since 1869 as a man of Vonpila, who was now a man of Poyboy, that the British force would not be able to advance beyond the Tipai Mukh for sometime at least. " And if we go beyond Tipai Mukh and go up to great Mothilen political grounds to advance immediately up to Moothilen of Longton, dense forests and small streams. It was also difficult to carry the provisions in those jungly country.

"Though the actual distance of Chumfai is only 94 miles from Lakhipur it took the actual a length of the our journey was 167 miles. The column got the assistance of the friendly Lushai chiefs and all the hostile Lushais were brought to book by severe punishments inflicted upon the villagers. The Cachar Column was attacked at places by the Lushais but they were steadily repulsed. The Manipore contingent also helped the Cachar Column. "All the military implications and other political implication indicated according to Edgar," " the connexion between the Political Agent of Manipore and the DC Cachar would be very close afterwards. Our relations with the people of Sellam, Toolchung and Enkhom's villages were satisfactory to the end. They assisted us. At last we reached the Chumfai village and the village was destroyed. We said that the immediate object of the expedition was the recovery of the muskets and we came to know that the muskets were broth and then distributed among the hillmen. The drastic measure was taken and only the villages of Vonolel's widow was spared for the people gave two muskets to us. The Chumfai villagers for fear of life subdued and became friendly to us and three headmen accompanied us as guide up to Tipai Mukh. On 8th of March the expedition was over."

Manipur Kukies

"Swarms of Kookies during the expedition took refuge in the Manipore territory. The total number who passed over from the Lushais was 2,594 up to the 23rd March and they took with them 156 muskets. They were Thadoes and Waiphies. These Thadoes say that some thirty years ago they belonged to a powerful village under a chief of their own family, named of Lalchokla's family pressed hard on them and at last they took refuge with Toosong, the head chief of all Thadoes who was much more powerful than the Paitto chiefs. But while some Mungpilal's Thadoes accompanied their to Toosongs village. Many more took refuge with the Lucia chiefs, who were then getting powerful, and who soon drove the Paintoes westward to the Charachoora range. Some time after their, when Toosong, who was father of Koodingmang, the chief who massacred the Mungpilal and the people who had accompanied him to Toosong's village again formed a separate village under the protection of the Lushais, moving about from place to place until this year, when they left for Manipore. But those of this people who had originally taken refuge among the Lushais remained in the villages of the latter sometime living in the villages of Lalpoong, sometime in those of Morah until three years ago when they went to Chipowee. The reason for roving from land to land in the hills are over joomed and no more land left for cultivation. The younger chiefs for four years continued raiding the Cachar and Manipore but the Government expedition had taken away all the faith they had on the power of the Lushai chiefs.

"The Manipore chief, I believe, to settle the people that have taken refuge with him in the hills south of the Manipur valley, and in the north-eastern portion of the tract marked " uncultivated and uninhabited" in the under Lushi chiefs and settled in that portion of the same tract which lies south of the Cachar boundary, and which is much better suited for cultivation than the more eastern hills. It is quite probable that the Kamhow and the Poise will still continue rather attacks on these Kookies, and the Manipore state will probably have to take measures for their protection, but it is probable that these people will not be satisfied with restrictions and burdens of Manipore supremacy, and then they will follow Kodingmang into the Naga Hills, where they would be a constant source of problem both to us and Manipore. There can be no doubt that the villages to the east have of later been pressed hard by Damhow and others, so harsh, that the people have taken to stockading, which they never do unless when they feel weak; but it is to be feared that unless the Political Agent can direct Kookies who have this year moved into the Raja's jurisdiction will now be much less exposed to attacks in future than they had been while living under the Lucia chief.[39]

Result of the Expedition

"The aim of the Expedition was neither annexation nor retaliation but to strengthen the former policy of conciliation after a powerful demonstration. The British Government south to impress it upon the Lucia that they welcome their friendship but at the same time they were their master."[40]

The political result of the expedition were manifold. The Lushais were forced to recognize the existence power, able both alike to power and punish. A firm and a secure basis was laid down for the future relations with the Lushais whether commercial or political. Moreover, the whole country became open to the English.

The success of Cachar Column destroyed to powers of the Eastern Lucia chiefs who posed challenge both to the Cachar administration and Manipore State. The loss of strength of Poyboy restored the balance of power in the hills south east of Cachar.

Another notable result of the expedition was that the power of the Western Lushia clan was bolstered up. The leader of the said clan was Sukpilal and he showed overzealous attitude to get close with the English during the Expedition. In sprite of the sordied past the British officials considered his help necessary for the future. He and his eldest son Khalkom since 1872 acted as the etymon of the southern frontier of Cahar bolstering up of the power of the Western Lushais was necessary otherwise they might have suffered a natural decline at the hands of the Howlongs or the Eastern Lushais endangering the security of the Cachar frontier. Whatever may be demerits of the policy of Edgar he was justified in upgrading the Sukpilal' clan. After all, the Western clan enjoyed a unique postage among the Lushais. Sukpilal' friendship helped the English in exploring the Lushai country west of Muthilen range. The expedition expected the fears of the Cachar Kookies. They did to Aberdeen any future danger from the Lushais and became determined to establish villages between Kolosib and Cahatarchaurra.

The English crippled the powers of Poyboy, the Eastern Chief, whom the Cachar Kookies dreaded much. The Kukies of Cachar realised fully that in future Poyboy would never dare to support his sister who was also greatly frightened and felt that her villages were absolutely under the English. The local officers of Cachar could not foraged the valuable series ordered by the Cachar Kookies and began to help them in all possible manner. After the establishment of the tea estates, Cachar Kookies lost all connections with the Government owing to defective Land Regulations but after the Expedition their confidence in the government was restored *(Ibid).*

The expedition greatly damaged the morale of the Lucia chiefs. The superior military might of the English adversely affected the military prestige of many Lushai chiefs. A large number of Lucia chiefs gave up their old allegiance to their masters and began to placate the British officers of Cachar with a sheer selfish motive. Darlong, the Lushi Minister of

Poyboy, actually helped the English during the operations against his master. Many ambitious chiefs followed his example after the Expedition. Edgar also did his best to assert his personal influence to break the solidarity of the Lushi community.

With the exception to the delivery of captured guns and the captives, especially of Mary Winchester, the success of the Chittagong Column was not so decisive. The Sallows who were less guilty suffered much but the LelaLaiptin Howlongs, living in the south east of Chittagong Hill Tract, who were more guilty, escaped coming punishment. The powers of the Sailoos were crippled but the strength of the Howlongs remained almost intact and this affected the power balance in the Lucia verily dealt with but the Howlongs on the other hand posed frequent threat to the distressed Sailoos endangering the security of the frontier again and again. Moreover, the very dangerous element on the Chittagong frontier was the Sihndus, thus, became stronger. The Shindus of the Arcane side gave lot of trouble to the English in the eighties and nineties of the last century.

Hill Tripura and the Lushais

"It is difficult to mark the western limit of Sukpilal's territory. He say she has no influence in the west of the range in which Chattarchoora is situated. The country west of Sukpilal is nominally the subject of Tipperah Raj but the eastern boundary of the Tipperah Raj's territories uncertain. According to Pemberton and other the Independent Tipperah territories extend up to Tipai Mukh. But some years ago the "Independent Tipperah" had been substituted by "Hill Tiperah" creating a confusion and all the hills between the south of Cachar and Chittagong Hill Tracts seem to have been at about the same time silently included in the Cachar district. I should think that the best geographical boundary between Hill Tipperah and Lucia Hill would be the continuation of the watershed that divides Sylhet from Cachar."[42]

According to Edgar the Raja's (Hill Tipperah) authority over the hills west of Sukpilal is merely nominal. The Kookies of those places belong chiefly to Dorlong and Paite families. The Darlongs lived on the south and Paites near the Sylhet. The Paites of Lalchukla's village were connected with the Thadoes. Lalchookla, the famous Paite Chief was transported in 1845.[43]

Defence and Protective Measure

"I should prefer delay to my final report on the defensive and protective measure to be adopted on the Cachar side and the means to be taken to cultivate friendly relations with the tribes until I have had an opportunity of clearing of all that is known about Tipperah Kookies, as well as about the present and future position of the Howlongs and Sylhet."[44]

Edgar wished to get the information of relation of the authorities of British Burma with the tribes on the Kolodyne. " have long had a conviction, which was steadily deepened as my experience in frontier matters had increased, of the impolicy and uselessness of attempting to deal in detail with the Kookie difficulty. We cannot hope for success, or even for safety, if we allow ourselves to be misled by what really are accidents of political the geography, and treat the relations of each district or dependent state with the Kookies on its border as a separate question, in dealing with which measures can be taken without any reference to any to the others, even though the measures may be based on principles diametrically opposite, perhaps hostile, to these adopted elsewhere, and may possibly have a most injurious effect on the relations between some other district or state and the tribes without looking simply to the interest of Cachar, and if I could herewith safely leave out of sight the considerations which must influence our treatment often parts of the question in which other districts are concerned I should at once submit a detailed scheme based on the principles which I have advocated consistently during the last four years. But I feel that such as scheme only be a provisional one." Edgar also stated that there a had been many informations to receive of the Tipperah Kookies, the Sailoos, the Howlongs, the Xhindoors, and the geography of the tracts where they inhabit. And only after that as final policy could be chalked out.[45]

Cachar Citation Road

Edgar with reference to the letter dated 9th April 1871 no. 64, by the Commissioner Dacca division stated that he was on opinion that the Cachar and Citation authorities should maintain close contact and a Cachar-Citation Road be constructed through Chepowee. He disfavoured the route through the Chunfai valley for the geography of that place was not fully known and besides the use of Chepoowee could not be ignored. If the road of Chepoowee could be undertaken it was to be divided into four sections. Their first of these sections would be from Lakhipur to Mayndahur tea garden, the second would be from Maynadhur to Tipai Mookh, the third from Tipai Mookh to the Tooweebhoom, and the last from the Tooweebhoom to Chepoowee.[46]

He then submitted an estimate receive from the Superintendent of Roads that the cost of construction of the road from Lakhipur to Tipai Mookh would be Rs 65,000 and keeping it in repair nearly Rs 16,000 a year. He further pointed out that the coolies were to be imported and hence the cost would be more. A contignet of 50 policemen could be required to guard the road construction work.

"The third section of the road would be less difficult and would require very few bridges; but one of these, that over the Tipai would be very expensive. This road would facilitate the trade in Tipai Mookh of the Lushais and would frost good relationship with us. The military and political considerations make up to insist upon the construction of this route." Edgar further said the Citation Road would be less costly. " though the Lushais are a nomadic race and move from place to place and it is learned that they intend to leave Chepoowee, still the utility of the road remains.

Edgar's Tribute to His Assistants

Edgar's acknowledged the help of McWilliam, the officiating D.C.. Cachar in his operations in the Lushai Hills. He also praised the service of Ram Ratan Endo, the collectorate Nazir. Edgar paid his rich tribute to the active services rendered by Hari Charan Sharma in the expedition. General Bourchier also acknowledged this help as the most important one and according to him "he deserves special notice".

Edgar wrote, "Here, I may add one qualification for dutch word in a rare degree. He seems absolutely dived of physical fear. I have had the opportunity of seeing him more than once under fire, and each time he was as calm and self-possessed as if he had been in his tehsil cutchery."[48]

John W. Edgar and T.H. Lewin: A Comparison

There are similarities and dissimilarities between the two famous Frontier Officer T.H. Lewin and John W. Edgar. Both of them were rafted into the service of the Government of India immediately after the transfer of power (1858) to consolidate the British rule in India. Lewin, however, had a brief stint in the services of East India Company as a soldier during the Mutiny (1857-58). Lewin joined the military service (police) and Edgar was drafted into the Indian Civil Service (1862) of Bengal cadre. Lewin was a student of Linguistics and Classics in the Royal College, London; Edgar was student of History and Political Economy in Cambridge. Lewin was a writer and had very good command over the

English language. He was basically interested in anything related to literature which gave him immense pleasures to indulge his thought in the literary world like reading and writing. He was also a scholar and his thirsty for knowledge continued til the end of his life.

Edgar was not a scholar, took greater interest into the file work. Although he had the calibre he rarely took interest in publishing his accounts. He was very clever and was that his published views might offend the administration. He knew very well as a pioneer in the Indian Civil Service he was to set an example for the future functioning of the service to the paramount task of consolidating the British empire in India. Entity whose loyalty to the Crown and devotion to duty was the summum bonum of his career. As an interacting person in the development process could not be sourced by the endeavour of the government alone. The administration must encourage the private bodies engaged in furthering the colonial economy for which the British empire was founded in India. He was aware that the progenitor of British capitalism in India were not all morally elevated persons and that they aimed at economic exploitation of India but he cleverly desisted himself from playing the role of avenging angel, not withstanding this struggle against the irregularities of the commercial houses or the corporate sectors to uphold the dignity of the administration. Primarily the "steel frame" was the political tool to expedite the economic inter- est of the empire. Secondly, he willingly merged his personal views as a unlike Lewin, his ego to clash with the administration. As an instrument of government he was conscious of his obligation and responsibilities to the government.

Edgar suggested certain measures but when the situation so deemed he did not hesitate to admitting frankly his mistakes. He hardly felt slighted if his superiors ever admonished him for his lapses. He criticized his colleagues some times bitterly but always within the framework of the administration and never stressed the limits of his jurisdictions. In his famous memorandum relating to the defence of the Cachar frontiers to the Lieutenant Governor of Bengal he politely says, "In trying to explain my grounds for this belief, I fear that I shall appear to touch upon military matters to a great extent that I care to do." (B.J.P. April 1871 no. 27).

Lewin was a voracious reader, intrepid explorer and expert in the art of adjusting himself with the ways and lives of the wild people. He could pick up easily their language and customs and had the rare quality of mixing with them freely. He believed like an ideal neutral bureaucrat each and every word of "Queen's Proclamation" (1858), and was convinced that the empire was for the good of all categories of Indian people.

To him the end and not means mattered. His altruistic views never allowed him to cloud his vision that he was the imperialist ruler. Unlike Edgar who kept his bureaucratic distance from the Indian, Lewin was a thoroughly unassuming person freely mixing with the Indian police constables and the Lushai chiefs. He was always against the lax attitude of the administration. Administrative delays appeared to him to be the lax attitude. He was also against the red tapism of the bureaucracy because he was basically a soldier interested in quick action. Made him often restless and for their reason he failed to hid his negative feelings against the civil servants. Before assuming the charge of the Civil Officer he handed over the charge of Deputy Commissioner, CHT to a civilian. He writes, " In November I assumed my position as Political Officer with the Right Column, and made over charge of my dear hill Tracts to a Bengal Civilian a very Irishman, who inspired me with no confidence what soever."[49]

He was also against the senior civil servants of higher echelon in Calcutta fed on control on the district administration applying the remote control device. He did not mind to scorn them by using the contemptible epithet, 'Calcutta idlers'. Being a person endowed with intellectual brilliance and a strong sense of individualism he failed to accept urgrudgingly the official concept of the administration, discreetly venerates as a symbol hollow and disembodied of British pride. For this Lewin himself was of Government. To be a writer or an intellectual in England is to be inexorably called upon to pronounce on, and even intervene in events that mark the historical destiny of the country. But he failed to realize that he was not at Home and in the bondage of service.

Lewin had a love for nature and had the romantic liaison with the natural beauties of the CHT where the sea sang and birds slept. He was asked by the government to serve the Upper India which had been close to the capital and where amenities of life was much better than the distant unknown eastern frontiers but he had no interest in personal comfort. The Chief Commissioner of Burma, Colonel Phayre was so enamoured by the success of Lewin's high risk exploration of the interior of Lower Burma that he personally requested Lewin to take the charge of the post of Superintendent of Kolodyne valley. This offer came to him before that Bengal Government elevate him to the rank of the Superintendent of CHT. But service carer was secondary to him. He developed in himself a missionary zeal to work among the wild tribes of the CHT. Their welfare was his principal aim. He wrote, "They were the simplest, the most kindly folk, these hill people; truthful, and capable of strong attchments; having also a great appreciation of straight and evern-handed justice. I found them ground Bengali usurpers, and oppressed by the constant dread of Lucia or Shendu raids."

If Edgar is the real founder of Silchar town and architect of modern Cachar, Lewin is also the founder of Rangamati (Bangladesh) and formulated the administrative design of CHT which remained intact a century. Edgar's settlement restored precolonial reactionary feudalism in rural Cachar but Lewin's measure helped the wild hill men of CHT to free themselves from the shackles of the medieval bondage. Like Lewin, Edgar also had but his approach was totally different from Lewin. Lewin was interested in that permanent good of the tribes. Whereas Edgar followed conciliation as an expedient to administration. It was an administrative ploy, a manïpulative contrivence unconnected with any altruistic motive.

Lewin had a moral perception of the Queen's Proclamation and considered the administration as a means to achieve the end of durable peace and prosperity of the Queen's subject. So he geared up the administrator for the upliftment of the tribals. Edgar was a shrewd administration, had an economic perception of British imperialism and considered administration as the necessary tool to further the interest of the British empire in India and as a civil servant he was to protect the interests of the ruling class. He never hesitated to bend the rules whenever necessary to encourage prospective entrepreneur in industries to keep buoyancy in the sluggish capital market. Because of his administrative measure Cahar became the cynosure of the tea magnates and there had been unprecedented investment boom in the Cachar's tea industry; money in tea always an attention grabber, provoking envy and disgust. However, in colonialism relationship between money and administration is more straight forward. Later on Edgar became very powerful as the Divisional Commissioner of Dacca and finally as the Chief Secretary, Bengal Government, the most powerful economic bastion of British imperialism and a member of Governor-General in Council. He controlled the administration to serve the interest of economic development in Bengal on the colonial line. As a clever bureaucrat with a keen historical perception was conscious of the fact that the root of independent British enterprise in Bengal was embedded in the civil service. Formerly, the Company's servants and now the Crown's servants invested their savings into indigo, jute and tea industries. Tea industry became the most attractive field of investment of the rich British bureaucracy to which Edgar belonged. The chambers of commerce in Calcutta raised the alarm and when their interest had clashed with the bureaucracy they cried foul and the English Press, the mouthpiece of British capitalism, supported them. But unflappable Edgar remained infused as he was expert in walking a metamorphically tight rope between reassurance and panic. However, the most significant contribution of Edgar towards Indian economy this time had been his theory of aggressive marketing of exports as an effective means of financing the Indian imports. This led to market growth. Edgar was rare civil servant in the 19th century who took keen interest in India's economic development and attempted to give direction to it according to his knowledge and capacity.

Edgar was a civilian with characteristic imperialist mud and always kept a significant distance from the natives including the native junior. But this he did with the dignity of a shrewd administrator. In fact, he had high regard of his Bengalee juniors like Hari Charan Sharma, etc. About Hari Charan Sarma wrote Edgar, "he deserves special notice he has I may add, one qualification for such work in a rare degree. He seems absolutely devoid of physical fear. I have had the opportunity to seeing him more than once under fire, and each time he was as calm and self-possessed as if he had been in his tehsil cutchery."[50]

Despite his attachment of Burlan, the Assistant civil officer to the Cachar Column in the Lushai Expediton, he unequivocally praised the service of Sharma again and again, but Lewin had a pathological bias against the Bengalees and had no confidence in a Bengalee's martial capabilities. It is really strange that a man of Lewin's benevolent compassionate nature with such a tolerant bend of mind possessed a positive aversion for the Bengali natives. It is true that Bengali litigant lawyers made his life full of worries but Bengali lawyers of moneylenders were only a part of the Bengali society, and to pass an adverse judgement on the whole of the natives for the fault of a section does not conform with the norms of justice. Edgar despite his bureaucratic snobbery often bordering obscurantism was free from such personal idiosyncrasies.

The greatest contribution of Edgar as Frontier Officer had been his suggestion to an integrated Lushi (Mizo) policy of the Government of India. He criticized the existing Lushi policy as picemeal, ineffective and an "impolicy". In his famous report at the close of the Lushai Expedition he wrote, "we cannot hope for success, or even for safety, if we allow ourselves to be misled by what really are accidents of political geography, and treat the relations of each district or dependent state with the Kookies on the border as a separate question, in dealing with which measures can be taken without any reference to any of the others." His suggestion was that Manipur, Tripura, Citation, Sylhet and Cachar's authorities must act in unison for the defence of the frontiers touching the Lushais country. He also wanted to involve the authorities of British Burma into the process. This concrete suggestion had been the coup de grace of his Lucia policy which had further spin off effect on the Government of India's North East Frontier policy.

The extension of cooperation of Cachar's administration to the tea gardens of Cachar was the outcome of the policy of the defence of the British frontiers. The tea estates were established in Cachar in 1855 but up to 1863 the tea entrepreneurs managed their own affairs according to their own effort and resources and did not cooperate with the local administration resulting into deterioration of the much needed frontier security. Major Stewart, the peredecessor of Edgar realized it and requested the tea planters to cooperate with the administration so that movement could be reciprocated in return. The industrial and administrative cooperation which had its beginning during the regime of Stewart received its finishing touch at the hands of Edgar. The Lushais on the Cachar frontier now could directly intercourse with the Deputy Commissioner, much more important glorified person than the individual planter. The planters were also happy as the administration provided the adequate security to the tea estates at government cost. Thus, Edgar kept both the Lushai chiefs and the tea magnates in good humour. The talented civilian by the stroke of his diplomacy developed a participative culture among the parties involved leading to a change in the attitude of the private entrepreneurs and the wild tribes, neither of whom had been friendly to local administration. The increased payment of dividend by the tea companies from 12% to 35% was pointer to the success of Edgar's diplomacy.

The conspicuousness of the Assam and Jorhat tea companies led to the extravagant prospect of tea plantation. According to Edward Gait, "The result was a general collapse." Many new companies were wound up. The Government and Gait admitted the service of Edgar in this time of the temporary depression. In a sense his measures were directed to set on foot the crippling tea industry.

Gait states:

"In 1872 about 27,000 acres were actually planted with tea in the Brahmaputra, 23,000 in Cachar, and 10,000 in Sylhet, the out turn in these tracts was respectively six million, five million, and a third of a million pound."[51]

The rate of wages of the labour in Cachar tea gardens had also been slightly less than the Brahmaputra valley tea.

Despite the apparent success of all the administrative measures of Edgar in Cachar his farm settlement generated many social evils which he could not foresee. Decades before the settlement became a legislative laity the farmer's social order inherited largely from Kachari Kingdom had relocated the farm workers and fishermen to their perpetual under-class status. Under the Edgar's settlement a counter- culture developed among those under-class working under harsh conditions resulting into gangsterism in the stretch of scrub covered swampy marshes throughout the Cachar's east and south. His settlement intended to introduce feudalism of the olden days in a new bottle. But he became a racially inspired-social engineering combined with profound lack of insight. Notwithstanding Edgar's aversion to communalism, his land measures sown the seeds of the communalism in Cachar. The rural gentry to perpetuate its economic hold used the communal card every now and then in Sarma. But Sarma being the son of a poor village priest lacked the social experience of a landed gentry and was also ignorant of the afflictions of the under-class. Sarma's theoretical knowledge of agricultural arithmetic made the task of revenue collection easy and quicker but the system gave rise to many socioeconomic problems. Other than communalism crime became the dominant characteristic of British Cachar (1874-1947). Better communicational network meant for economic development and greater mobility of police force was utilized on the country by the gangsters to their own advantage. Rule of law, the pride of British administration, had to be put on back burner as the machineries to tackle the crime had been weak and the eastern and southern periphery of Cachar remained more or less outside the legitimate holds of the administration. The government had to reconcile with the existing reality.

Lewin's measures in the CHT on the other hand had never been so pervasive as that of Edgar but they never gave rise to leave socioeconomic issues in future. He assisted the poor tribals gerontotherapy. As an administrator he tried his best to save the hillmen from the exploiting Bengalis of the settled districts in one hand and from the doom of internecine administration.

Edgar's approach towards the farm sector of Cachar's economy, like his crystalline tea policy had been sluggish one. He sought rapid industrialization and gave inadequate stress on agriculture; he did not set any target of the growth rate of foodgrain production though he was aware for Cachar's agricultural potential. He also did not fix his mind as to the export of surplus foodgrains from Cachar to Sylhet, the prosperous grain market. Inadequate investment in agriculture was the bane of Cahar's farm sector economy. The agriculture sector in Cachar had largely been rid of any inflow of capital either from industrial or any tertiary sector. Capitalist transformation of agriculture with private investment and involvement was unknown. The poor capital formation was the result of the non availability of the resources let alone the slobbering of the administration. The Government machine although aware of this malady was reluctant to redress it. There was no attempt to subsidize the inputs as in the case of the industry nor there was any step to support the price structure of the foodgrains. Government collected revenues by squeezing the farmers but public expenditure or attention for improvement of farm land or farmer's lot was lacking.

An important result of the commercialization of agriculture of Cachar was the break up of the age old isolation and self-sufficiency of villages and gradual linking of village markets to outside markets in Sylhet, Dacca and Calcutta. The bazaars were no more only local markets for agriculture commodities. Agricultural commodities started enjoying ever-expanding markets depending upon their perishability or durability. Sonai bazaar, thus a purely village market soon became the transit centre of local commerce to Silchar, Hailakandy, Changsi (Mizo Hills) and Sylhet. The commercialization of agriculture guaranteed the farmers more remunerative prices. Formally, in Cachar during the days of the Kachari kings and also the four decades after annexation, there was very poor demand for marketing the farm produce. But Edgar revolutionized the agricultural scenario. The land owner had little to complain. The farm sector offered entirely a different picture in the neighbouring British district, Sylhet. The Permanent Settlement or Zamindari system was the prevailing mode of revenue collection there. The government expected agricultural enterprise, greater flow of capital to land, improvement, cultivation extension, and reclamation of land in the zamindari system but intermediary ridden system was far from the lofty aim of the Permanent Settlement . But Edgar's settlement in Cachar was free from many defect of the zamindary system. Moreover, for better or worse, the landed gentry in Cachar were more or less directly in communion with the revenue administration of the district. It is, however true that the government officials were neither generous nor necessarily responsive to the legitimate grievances of the ryots and had not that image or identity or reciprocacity of the zamindars. Thus , during emergencies like famine, flood and natural calamities, the Cachar ryots were helpless and had little shelter. The severe 1869 earthquake had been a pronator to that effect.

In case of irrigation the situation was more disturbing. The irrigation facilities in Cachar, unlike Brahmaputra valley had always been very poor. The percent of the arable land was dry and non- irrigated and that land remained neglected while the rest eighty percent was rainfed land but its mitigation had never received any subsidy despite the increment in rent. Thus, the cost of production could not be kept in a reasonable level as the food production of rainfed land depended on the vagaries of nature. The price always fluctuated.

The system of procurement of rice was out mode of like that of the olden days. The operational cost (cost of carriage of goods in Cachar 1871 goods. In Brahmaputra valley it was twenty percent of the cost of the goods. In Sylhet it was fifteen percent only. Thus, the government took the advantage of the low cost of transport (bullock cart was unknown; only means of transport was country boat) and fixed the purchase–price of preretinal price of agricultural goods, explicitly foodgrains and meats invariably deprived the farmer in the field and the cattle grazers of the remunerative price. The export of agricultural produce outside. Cachar because of transport bottleneck had been slow. The rural gentry in spite of their elevated social status were not affluent people. The cash crunch of the petty village landlords had been a disincentive for capital investment in agriculture and thus retreading the growth rate of agriculture in one hand making the rural areas a citadel of reactionary forces on the other.

When Edgar came to Cachar population was sparse and land was plenty. If he distributed the land in a planned way as the British govern- ment had done in Sindh and Punjab, there would have been no fragmentation of land with the increase in population and probably modernization of agriculture would have started earlier here. In Assam Valley because of accumulation of capital some village landlords invested the capital in the tea industry but in Cachar that did not take place. Edgar's settlement of the migrant Bengalies in the urban center of Silchar in trace and services (who were relatively wealthy) created a dangerous and unbridgeable rift between the rural gentry and the urban elites who for their sophistication in education, consumption and culture remained an alien class to the rural mass. Unlike Assam Valley the indigenous rural people of Cachar always kept a significant distance from the sophisticated, circumspect, culturally advances but mawkish middle class of Silchar. But this is not true in case of Jorhat of Tezpur in Assam or any other district headquarters in Bengal. Thus, proliferating socio- economic evils in a large measure had been bequenate by Edgar to the people of Cachar. But this is only one side of the picture. The merits of Edgar's measures outweigh the demerits. He did his best, under the trying circumstances, to uplift the people of Cachar, a melange of different socioeconomic quoma with divergent interests and hidden prejudices. The peasantry in Cachar deprived of their legitimate dues were not an impoverished lot to boot and famine did not visit Cachar during the entire British period. Newly annexed Cachar was frightfully complicated terra in contagia by any standard and some of those complications already had surfaced during the administration of Edgar. So in the existing economic ambient he had no other option left to him excepting industrialization and he laid less emphasis upon agriculture and encouraged tea industry as the premier capital formation of Cachar. Thus, it would be singularly wooden comment to make that he did not square his practice with the principle. Between the ideas and reality falls the shadow.

Much of the acts of omission and commission of Edgar as Deputy Commissioner is blissfully lost in the bosom of the past but his transparent frontier policy has been adjudged by the experts as the best in the prevailing context. As an experienced administrator the new Deputy Commissioner had the foresight to read the sign of the times. He unequivally pointed out that annexation of Lucia Hills should be the aim of the administration and the integrated approach towards the Lushai problem be the essence of the frontier policy.

Edgar, reticent and never over effusive, was self-possessed, reserved and dignified and this manners characteristically fitted to the heaven born noble service of which he was a singnificant member. He hated exuberance of emotion as it was against the professional ethics but Lewin was emotional and passionate. The 'cog and the wheel' controversy was the outcome of Lewin's emotional self. Edgar would have shudder to express such a view that would denude the administration of its sheet anchor. Edgar's duty and devotion to service like Cachar's wife was above suspicion. In Lewin despite his rigorous training in the army as a disciplined soldier the Kentish boor frequently lurked in his heart to destabilize the poise in him. Unlike many other administrators Lewin like to think and also to express and share his thoughts. This knwack for individual and intellectual freedom goaded him to strike occasional stunning blows to the battered ego of the centralized Indian administration. To him this freedom was a "fundamental and distinctive sign of an individual when interacting with the institutions and the collective." This is an inalienable privileged relationship between administration and its members.

Lewin is a luminous example of the Western tradition of geographical explorer. His unique courage, self-confidence and quest for unknown identity him a la the Stanley or Livingstone Lewin was original but not Edgar.

The waddle of administrative bindings made Lewin a sad lot. He deeply studied the tribal problem and dedicated his life to save the tribes in their distress and work for their upliftment unhindered by instructions from the neccessitarian higher authorities whom he considered incompetent for the task. His spirit of independence was repugnant to the higher authorities who repudiated his free thinking by issuing strictures. But Edgar's perception of professional functioning, in fascinating contrast, was entirely different from Lewin and thus, he always had his smooth sailing with the Calcutta mandarins and one day reached the top of the administration to guide it. The originality of Lewin's work, his awe inspiring depth of knowledge, the universal appeal of his tribal policy and his dedication for the cause of the Lushais move every body. It is difficult to avoid comparisons with the other giant in this field–Edgar, but one must begin by observing the Lewin had rather limited parameters—the former being the Chief Secretary of the Bengal Presidency, in the absence of the legislative wing, the de facto "Nawab" whereas Lewin was merely a local officer, Deputy Commissioner of a hilly district. Edgar's epic work embraced a vast canvas, a much larger area of India's socio-economic and political history and the gave Sir John W. Edgar's performance a kind of complexity that Thomas Herbert Lewin could not even try to strive for.

Lieutenant Colonel Lewin was placed in a hostile political climate in the Chittagong Hill Tracts and had grown out of his innocence to becoming the principal antagonists of rasimks that was as much a part of white man's consciousness as it was of the government. The limitation of the short- compass of Lewin notwithstanding, our observations do not fail to trace the mind and manners and the intense ethos of a man who became a leader of the Lushais almost by accident. His frame of reference is necessarily narrower than Edgar's but that does not prevent us from adding layers and nuances to a personality that becomes intensely absorbing. Edgar, despite his brilliant success, is a lost talent but Lewin is very much alive in the minds of the Lushais as a demigod till today.

A few words are necessary to discuss the Lewin's remarkable success as scholar. Unlike Edgar, Lewin derived great pleasure in publishing his experiences in reputed scholarly journals and newspapers and his memoirs are a good source of contemporary history and, on the other hand, they display profound scholarship of Lewin which overwhelms us. He was quite at home with the classical Greek, Latin and Persian poets. The philosophical doctrines of Buddhism, Hinduism, and Islam. His quest for knowledge knew no bounds. In a forlorn rock-cave in Sylhet he held esoteric discussion with a tantric dealing with dead bodies. When the tanrtik scorned him and said that he would not discuss with mundane person. Lewin politely replied that he was a seeker of truth. His study about the tribals reveal that he had read intensively the authentic books in English, German and French and the related best articles published in standard magazines. He was conversant with the customs and modes of living with all the "South East Asian and West Asian tribes and making his assessment of the north-eastern tribes of India he often made, to our pleasant surprise, a comparative study. He was as conversant with Voyage aux Regions Equinoxials due Nouvean Continent –Bumboldt, as that of Sir A.P. Phyare in his papers on the Indo-Chinese Borders in the *Journal of Asiatic Society of Bengal*. His range of study and the vast compass of his knowledge are aweinspring.

Nothing missed his watchful evy. His descriptions about the Chakmas, Bohmongs, Lushais and Tipras, their origin, history, social custom are still regarded as the most authentic accounts. By training he is an historical descriptivist rather than a natural synchronic prescriptivist; the Anthropologists, Social Scientists and Linguists often quote Lewin in their works. Without the help of Lewin it is well-nigh impossible to have the understanding of the tribals in their proper context. There are voluminous writings on the tribals of north-eastern Indian and foreign but ceteris paribus the descriptive analysis of Lewin surpasses the others in content and style, let alone philosophy.

Lewin's *A Dictionary of Lucia Words* although a small book it is a monumental work. He is the pioneer in this respect. He compiled the dictionnary before any missionary could take up the important project. Lewin as in the midst of the Lushais (Mizos) for few years only but the linguist in him goaded him to compile the dictionary. His dictionary gave a future shape of the Mizo language, and immernse contribution to the formation of not merely a lexicon of words but it is a remarkable attempt to sum up Lucia knowledge about every thing from its origin to modernity. One of the most heartening qualities lies in its readiness to discuss little known aspects of Mizo life. Such inclusions give the dictionary a constantly refreshing air. The over all presentation is sober, based on solid research most difficult of balancing acts, satisfying specialist while at the same time remaining accessible to the general readers. The dictionary teems with many such similar pleasures, enlivening the scholarship and ensuring that each page is entertaining as well as instructive.

4

R.B. McCabe

R.B. McCabe originally belonged to Assam Civil Service. Soon he became a member of Indian Civil Service. He was at first the Assistant Commissioner of the Naga Hills district, Assam and in 1884 became the Deputy Commissioner of the same district. Naga Hills district was a small district with headquarters at Kohima. The Ao Naga country was outside the *Political Control Area.*

"The boundaries of the Naga Hills district at this time were the Doyang river to the north and north east, the Kopamedze range to the east, Mao thana and the Barrack river from below Bakema village to the south and south west, and most trouble came from the tribes beyond these lines."[1]

The Ao Nagas often committed raids into the British territories. The most daring of such raids had been the Baladhan tea garden (North Cachar) in January 1880. The raid was a rapid and daring one resulting into the death of the manager and a larger number of coolies. Naturally, this created a panic amongst all the tea gardens in that part of Cachar. To combat the situation there was reorganization of defence units. All frontier police units became Military Police Battalions in 1882. The strength of the military police was considerably increased; it had more fire power and modern equipments and better intelligence network. McCabe provided able leadership to the Naga Hills Military Police in its formative period. He was a great leader with boldness of mind, aggressive resources and quick movements and had the unique calibre of stimulating the minds of the security personnel. He became very popular to his subordinates and colleagues as well. He was unassuming, calculating but free and frank. His attempts both military and diplomatic in the direction of pacification of different Naga tribes bore fruits and he became indispensable to the Assam administration. The Deputy Commissioner of Naga Hills district was also an important Frontier Officer having some bearings on the Indian Administration also.

McCabe's Visit to Angami Country

In July 1884, owing to the Ao Nagas of Manmatung having cut up and looted a party of Lhota traders within the settled border, a punitive outing of 50 Naga Hills M.P. and 40 of the 44th B.L.I. under Lieutenant Tieman took place. With them went Mr. McCabe, the Deputy Commissioner. Manmatung was burnt without opposition through strengthly defended, and the murderers were given up. Lieut. Tieman and a few sepoys were injured by "panjis" while passing through the defence. The following January McCabe with an escort of the N.H.M.P. and Captain Plowden made a tour through the country lying between the Kopamedza range, the Lanier, and the Tizu rivers, it having been under discussion to bring the eastern Angamis occupying that area under direct political control of the Naga Hills district. No revenue was to be taken from them as in the case of the other clans in the settled area. Their route lay via Mao Thana to Keza Kenoma, the chief village of the Kazami clan, thence across the Kopamedza range (7,400 feet), British official boundary, to Razami, Tetcholumi, Lozephehomi, where friendly deputations from villages lying in independent territory beyond the Lanier and Tizu rivers were received. The party returned through Khromi and Purbami, and

McCabe recorded the pleasantness of the tour, throughout which they were well received.

"In the winter of 1884-85 it was found necessary to make a show of force in the Ao Country to punish the Sema village of Ningtang for murder of a British subject, to bring home to the Trans Doyang people the fact that they were politically subordinate to our Government, and to determine the limits of the Naga Hills control towards Sibsagar. The Deputy Commissioner of which, Colonel Clarke, was to meet the party. Accordingly Mr. McCabe and Dr. Bora, C.S., escorted by Captain Plowden and 100 rifles from Kohima and Mr. Broaderick from Wokha, crossed the Dyang river on the 15th January, 1885, reaching Ningtang next day. Some resistance was experienced, there was some firing a few Semas were shot, and the place was destroyed. The Column then visited Nankam (Ao) Lopphemi (Sema), Ungma, and Longsa (Ao), the latter village together with Salachu having to be fined for various misdemeanours. At Bor Haimong, on one of the outer ranges, Colonel Clarke was met and the limits of the two spheres of influence and political control were discussed, as also was the desirability of locating a strong post in these hills to check raids and inter-village fighting. The tour was concluded in the end of February, and a year later the Government of India sanctioned the suggested limits of the Ao Naga Political Control area to include all the country west of the Dikkoo river to the Sibsagar border on the plains, this area coming under the jurisdiction of the Deputy Commissioner at Kohima."[2]

Expedition to Ao Naga

"Two years later it was necessary to make an extended tour through the north east of the Ao country to visit and punish certain villages for raiding. Taking Lieut. MacIntyre and 100 of his men, McCabe accompanied by Muspratt from Wokha left on 13th March, 1888, reaching Waromong village ten days later, where investigation into murder and raiding cases was begun. Tamlu and Kanching were then visited and fined, and Kongan across the lower Dikkoo river was proceeded against. On this march the baggage guard was attacked. One sepoy and several carriers being wounded. Camp was formed in Kongan village and, during the night, the tribesmen crept up and managed to fire the houses over the Column's head, the place being entirely destroyed. After visiting Jakhtung, one march further east, the Column returned to Tamlu and recrossing the Dikkoo paid the first visit among the independent Nagas (Changs), who were guilty of raids over the border.

"Yasim, a large village, was found strongly defended by deep ditches bristling with bamboo stakes and stout stockades, and as it was seen to be crowded with armed Nagas who barred all approaches, Lieut. MacIntyre attacked under showers of arrows and spears, and forces his way in. A number of dead were found inside and on our side many sepoys were injured by bamboo stakes and 2 received spear wounds. It was seen that these tribesmen were using a large kind of cross bow firing its arrow up to 150 yards or so, a weapon not met with as yet in these hills. Forming camp near Yasim, a portion of the force was sent to Chihu, not far away, which was taken and burnt, and while this was in progress a message came saying the camp and its guard were being attacked. Hurrying back, MacIntyre was just in time to beat off the attack of some 1200 tribesmen who were all round McCabe and the camp. For two hours they persisted in attacks, and only drew off with heavy losses, while MacIntyre's casualties were several with slight spear wounds. From Yasim the villages of Nokeen and Litam were visited, opposition being met with only at the first named place, where six Nagas were shot, and both villages were burnt for raids and murder. The column thence made for Mokokcheng and reached Kohima on 1st May.

"Again it was strongly urged that the whole of the Ao Naga country should be permanently incorporated into the Naga Hill District, the people themselves being desirous of this and quite willing to pay revenue, and so have an end put to constant liability to raids with loss of life and property.[3]

The boldness, courage and skilled diplomacy of McCabe made the impossible possible. His suggestions on administrative changes were accepted by the Government. He solved the chronic problem of Naga insurgency with iron hand and restored peace in Naga Hill district and also in the adjoining frontier areas of Sibsagar district, Cachar district and Manipur state. The area of Naga Hills district was increased considerably. McCabe appraised the Assam administration with information and notes which proved invaluable. Towards the consolidation of British rule in the Naga Hills McCabe played a very dominant role. The Government had high regard for his dynamism and effective political acumen.

McCabe and Lushai Hills (Mizoram)

The sine qua non of the frontier policy of the British Government had been the security of the adjudicated frontiers. Lushai Hills like Naga Hills was another chronic source of trouble to the Assam administration. North Lushai Hills was under the political jurisdictions of Assam. South Lushai Hills was within the control of Bengal's administration. In January 1888 the Sailo chiefs, Zarok and Leingpung of North Lushai Hills committed the daring raid into the Chengri valley on the border of Chittagong, killing 101 people and carrying off 90 people as captives. Sir John Edgar was the Chief Secretary, Bengal Government. Bengal Government recommended a punitive expedition against the offending tribes. Thus, the Government of India sanctioned the Lushai Expedition 1889-90. The three pronged blitzkrieg advance of the Expeditionary Force overran the Lushai country. Marching from Chittagong side Colonel Skinner destroyed Leingpunga's village and captured the Chief (January 1890) but cunning Leingpunga duped the English by his manoeuvre and escaped. The Lushai country already under British occupation was, however, brought under the hilt of the administration. Fort Aijal (Aizawl) was constructed on a ridge of hill under the fifes of Khalkom as the site of military stokade. Captain H.R. Browne was appointed the Political Officer of North Lushai Hills. Leingpung's overlord, his elder brother, the Western Lushai chief Khalkom, instructed his subordinate chief Thansuma to kill Captain Browne in complete breach of trust of his oath of loyalty to Browne. On 9 September 1890 on his way to visit Cnangsil military post Browne was ambuscaded and treacherously murdered along with 17 men. Khalkom's men overran the Aijal post putting the security position of the administration out of gear. The dispatch of military police from Silchar to relieve Aijal under Lieutenant Swinton failed and Swinton lost his life in the inaccessible hill.

On hearing the death of Browne the Chief Commissioner of Assam sent the wire at once to McCabe, whose service in the Nagas Hills were well-known to the Government of Assam realized that the assumption of political duties in Lushai Hills would be of special importance at least for a time and McCabe was the best officer. At the head of garrison the newly appointed Political Officer left Silchar for Aijal to restore order. He pacified the chiefs to some extent and compelled the surrender of the offending chiefs including dangerous Leingpunga. Leingpunga was deported to Hazaribagh jail where he committed suicide.

Captain Browne, the Political Officer, was under the misconception that the Lushai Expedition 1889-90 had completely subjugated the Lushais and that they would no more rise against the British authorities. He was not to be blamed. The Lushai Expedition 1871-72 wrought pacification in the Lushai country for 14 years. Browne, to consolidate the British rule, concentrated his attention to the construction of roads which was essential in that landlocked country. But the Lushai labour was so disobedient, he had to adopt coercive measures as his last option. He antagonized the Lushai chief Khalkom and in consequence Browne was murdered.

Meanwhile, McCabe, the new Political Officer reached Aijal at the head of a strong military contingent, the Surma Valley Military Police Battalion from Silchar, captured Fort Aijal, effected unconditional surrender of Khalkom including his 15 subordinate chiefs and immediately began his march to the eastern direction to capture Leinpunga, the principal villain of the episode and the strongest eastern pillar of the Sukpilal's House.

Capture of Raja Khalkom

On 23 November 1890 McCabe wrote his famous letter to J.W. Quinton, the Chief Commissioner of Assam to relieve his worries. Under the instructions of McCabe on 19 November 1890 Lieutenant Watson with 140 soldiers and 200 coolies left for Changsil from Aijal; *enroute* they destroyed the chief Khama's village. They restored the military post on 20 November. On 22 November along with his subordinates Khalkom surrendered unconditionally. Khalkom, the paramount Sailo chief was arrested and his statement was recorded by McCabe. McCabe set conditions before Khalkom that (1) he was to give up 20 guns at once, then his *joom* be spared, and (2) that he must accompany McCabe to Aijal and when all the *rajas* (chiefs) come in, the government would pass order according to the merit of each case.

Statement of Raja Khalkom before McCabe, 23 November 1890

"I took the oath of loyalty with Browne Saheb, and he told us that we would have to pay revenue. We did not like this, and subsequently when Leipung, a mantri of Lenkhunga, told me that he had heard the *Saheb* was going to collect revenue from the Western Lushais first, and then from the Eastern Lushai's and that we would not even be allowed liberty to hunt in the jungles, I lost my head, and resolved to fight. We came definitely to this resolution about 1st September. A meeting was held in my *Jolbuk* (guest house) Lenkhunga, Lalrhima, Minthang and Rankupa were present.

Thansuma sent me a special messenger when the *Saheb* left Aijal, and I sent runners to Thangula, who forwarded the news to Lankhunga. The 30 men of my village armed with guns who went to Thansuma's on the 6th September were on a shooting excursion. I do not know what *loot* was taken.

"Lalrhima has the Sahib's two double barreled guns and two revolvers, also six Government guns (taken as fines from the Lushais). Four heads were brought to my village (I do not know what has become of them). Lenkhunga has four heads and Thangula one. My men, 100 in number, with 100 of Thangula, 100 of Lenkhungas and ten of Tolera marched to Changsil. Lalrihma's men were detailed to attack the coolies on the road, while Thanruma and Sailenpui looked after Saireng. Changkunga, Browne Saheb's Chaprasi was seized by Tahlien at the instigation of Lalrihma's mother, and brought to me. I was only chaffing when I said that I would kill him. 20 men of my village have been killed, eight wounded, the wounded men have all been carried across the Sonai to Poiboi's.

"The Western Lushai chiefs may be arranged in the following order, as regards the extent of authority they exercise:

1.	Khalkom	Second son of the elder *rani*
2.	Leingpunga	third son of the elder *rani*
3.	Sailenpui	fourth son of the elder *rani*

4.	Thansuma	fifth son of the elder *rani*
5.	Lenkhunga	grandson of the elder *rani* (Dausuma lives with him)
6.	Rankupa	son of younger *rani*
7.	Lalrhima	son of younger *rani*
8.	Thangula	son by mistress
9.	Lalsavuta	son by mistress
10.	Tahlien	*raja* Sukpilal's *mantri*
11.	Lalluia	son of Sailenpui
12.	Minthang	married Sukpilal's daughter
13.	Lenkhai	son of *mantri* attached to Rani Baniathagi, sister of Sukpilal.
14.	Thompong	brother of Sukpilal
15.	Tolera	son of Sukpilal by mistress.

.....R.B. McCabe"[6]

Capture of Leinpunga

McCabe used to keep, his diary with him and recorded the events of the day. From Aijal he advanced to capture Leinpunga. Leinpunga was the ring leader and the flame of Eastern Lushai rising could not be extinguished because of him. But the fall of Khalkom disheartened him. He realized his miserable end. McCabe continued his ruthless operation (25 November to 29 November 1890) and effected Leingpunga's unconditional surrender. Immediately after his arrest he was put under strong guards. McCabe did not repeat the mistake of Browne. The statement of Leinpunga was recorded before McCabe. In his statement he admitted that he had acted under the instructions from his paramount chief Khalkom. He came to know of Sahib's (Browne) departure from Aijal to Khalkom (village of Khalkom in between Aijal and Changsil Bazar). He had with him three heads but they were thrown into the river hearing the advance of McCabe. He also admitted that his men fired on the boat carrying the sepoys. The diary is brief but to the point. McCabe sent his dirty to the Chief Commissioner. Leingpunga was deported to Hazaribagh jail where he met his lonely death by committing suicide."[4]

"Hardly the first death anniversary of Sukpilal was observed peacefully, his country was trampled upon by the British soldiers and a large number of his followers, including his several sons and grandsons, made their way to the grave to follow the obsequies of their master in the under world a very favourite mundane aspiration of a Lushai chief."[7]

The letter and the diary of McCabe addressed to the Chief Commissioner, reached Shillong late. The Secretary to the Chief Commissioner, Assam wrote to the Secretary, Foreign Department, Government of India intimating the achievements of the British forces in quelling the Lushai rebellion and reacting on the suggestions of McCabe on reinforcement of the troops to suppress the Eastern Lushais'[7a] But the Assam Secretary point out.

"That it was impossible to adopt Mr. McCabe's proposed methods of increasing the garrison in Lushai land for the purpose of enabling him to deal with the Eastern Lushais" on defence considerations of Sylhet frontier. Moreover, Assam Government hesitated to approach the military authorities for more ammunition when a column of the 43th GLI with two guns and an adequate supply of British officers was already on its way to Lushai land.[7b]

"It has therefore been arranged with the concurrence of the General Officer Commanding, in communication with the Political Officer, that from the column now halted at Silchar, only 400 rifles of the 43rd GLI, shall proceed to Changsil, and that they should accompany the political Officer to Eastern Lushai land, where 100 rifles will hold a stockade, to be erected there on a site to be selected hereafter, while the remainder will escort the Political Officer in a promenade through the part of the country, the forts in Western Lushai country being garrisoned by Military Police."[8]

Eastern Lushai Rising

The Eastern Lushai chiefs did not offer any concerted aid to the Western Lushais in their rising of September 1890. They were happy to see the power of the Western chiefs broken. But the foolish chiefs of the Eastern clan also took it for granted that the English would never control their actions or attempt to collect any tribute from them. During the rains the British Administration had very little intercourse with the Eastern Lushais. Of course, McCabe informed that in the next cold seasons 1891-92 he would collect revenue from them at the rate of one rupee per house. In October 1891 he came to know that the Eastern Lushais had made up their mind to make one bold bid for independence. In November 1891 McCabe wrote in his diary that the English would have to deal with two separate groups of village, which were antagonistic to each other. First the Poiboi, Lal Bura, Bungteya and Lenkham, second the descendants of Vutas. He anticipated no combination between these two groups. Lenkham and Bungteya were dead, Poiboi ruled by a minor only powerful chief was Lal Bura. McCabe decided to advance and set up a camp at Lal Bura's village and to use it as a base where from he would collect revenue. Considering the position insecured he soon abandoned the idea of using Lal Bura as the base of his operations. Captain J. Shakespear, the Superintendent of the South Lushai Hills, promised all help to him and McCabe, at the head of an expeditionary force, advanced to Shakespear at Kairuma's new village on January 30, 1892. On the next day at a *Darbar* the future policy of the British Government was explained to the assembled chiefs. A boundary dispute between Kairuma and Dankhoma, which at one time threatened to embroil the

Northern Howlongs with Vuta's descendants, was settled and certain villages* were made over to the Assam Administration. Attitude of the Eastern Lushais with regard to the payment of house tax and the supply of "coolies" was not hostile excepting those of Bungteya and Lal Bura. McCabe came to know that Lal Bura sought defensive alliance with Vuta's family but failed. Lal Bura refused to supply "coolies" and on February 28, 1892 McCabe at the head of a garrison accompanied by Lieutenant Tytlar, Captain Malville marched towards Lal Bura.[9]

Destruction of Lal Bura and Ruthless Suppression of the Rebellion

The British garrison forcibly entered the village, immediately occupied it and took a strategic position. The Lushai burnt their houses with the intention of blockading the British Force inside a hilly ravine. Instead of getting panicky at this, the British garrison maintained calm which was the need of that grim hour. The valour and courage of the soldiers saved the situation. Constant vollies of guns from the central British stockade scattered the disorganized Lushai bands. McCabe attempted to isolate the Pois from Lal Bura's but failed. He sent categorical instructions through heliographic message to Captain Loch, the Officer Commanding, at Fort Aijal to inform the Western Lushai chiefs not to shelter the Eastern Lushais. The operations at Lal Bura continued from March 3-17, 1892. The Lushais adopted the tactics of guerilla warfare and ambuscaded the transport every now and then, causing enormous loss to the English. British soldiers wanted to meet them face to face but in hill fighting their expectations did not materialize. At times the position of the English became very precarious. The Government of Bengal sent urgent telegrams that Shakespear was ready for a march from Fort Lungleh. In the meantime the 18th Bengal Infantry from Aijal reached Lal Bura to relieve McCabe. Under the strict orders of McCabe the able bodied Lushais were hounded by the troops and villages after villages were effected from the face of the earth. As usual the granaries were the principal target of attack. The Eastern Lushais could not withstand the brunt of the superior arms and made a desperate attempt to secure the help of the Western Lushais- their traditional enemies. Kairuma (Vuta's most influential son) sent *mantries* to Sailenpui (Western Lushai chief) but he refused to share the fate of Khalkom and Leingpunga, his deported brothers. The security forces inflicted a crushing defeat on the Eastern Lushais and took a terrible revenge on them. Lal Bura, defeated and humiliated, surrendered along with his subordinates. Triumphant McCabe then advanced to the east of Sonai to capture Bungteya, Lalruya, Tankama, Vangpunga and Poiboi's mother. The operations were conducted from April 10-June 8, 1892 and it was complete at the point of bayonets, to accept the demands of forced labour and they agreed to supply the "coolies" daily for the construction of the roads. A fort was established at Lal Bura and the defeated chiefs surrendered their arms. McCabe's file fulfilled the unfulfilled aspiration of Edgar who as the Deputy Commissioner, Cachar, planned to crush the Eastern Lushais long ago.

McCabe's Administrative Measure

McCabe, the Political Officer, had been a many-faceted personality. He was an ironwilled bureaucrat and had absolutely no compassion for the enemies of the Raj. His dealing with the revolting chiefs had been extremely severe. The Lushai chiefs trembled before the iron hearted Scottish highlander. He earned the nick name the "chief catcher" (Lalhmantau) from the Lushai commoners. He shattered the revolting brotherhood of the Lushais. Shrewd McCabe raised the military status of Fort Aijal. fortified it with more men and ammunition and restored order in the entire North Lushai Hills. In fact he made the distant corners of the Lushai Hills safe for the unarmed representatives of the Government and imperial trade. The fear psychosis among the Lushais went a long way in taming the fierce tribes prone to violence. Thus, the Lushais were tamed considerably by McCabe's gun, which had been the base materials of the evangelists to civilize by their kindness and breadth of heart.

Despite the fact that McCabe as Political Officer was preoccupied with his primary task of maintaining law and order with occasional constraint of camp life outside Aijal the headquarters, quelling the rebellions, he managed time to study the Lushai customary law and their usages. He carefully prepared a draft for the future administration of the North Lushai Hills. Lushai Hills was occupied but not formally annexed before 1895. However, it was clear to McCabe that the formal annexation was only an administrative formality. What was needed a system of governance, set principles for the stable management of the North Lushai Hills. His draft is a classic one and bears the testimony of his constructive genius. This draft report formed the basis of North Lushai administration or the Lushai Hills district administration, B.C. Carey, the Political Officer, Chin Hills of British Burma improved it considerably and finally it received the finishing touch at the hand of Captain Shakespear, the first Superintendent of the Lushai Hills. McCabe's principal recommendations were: supreme authority of the Superintendent, indirect rule through selected loyal chiefs, prevalence of Lushai customary law and no entry of the civilized English law except, however, the law relating to murder etc. McCabe's aim had been very simple but precise.

McCabe, The District Magistrate, Kamrup, Assam

When newly occupied Lushai Hills (Mizoram) had been reeling under the worst kind of militancy the Chief Commissioner of Assam commissioned the service of daredevil R.B. McCabe to put the Aijal administration into order. He accepted the challenge. Despite the optimism in the Assam Secretariat, Quinton, the Chief Commissioner did not expect miracle around the corner. Within three years of his rule in the disconnected distant hills enterprising sharp tongued bureaucrat in the most trying circumstances by his tireless efforts restored order to the satisfaction of the Assam administration. The Foreign Department, Government of India was also relieved of its worries. Quinton, in recognition of the memorable service rendered by McCabe in the most critical period of British administration in Mizo Hills, recommended promotion for the enterprising successful Frontier Officer. McCabe was transferred to Gauhati, as the Deputy Commissioner, Kamrup district, the gateway to Assam and the heart of Brahmaputra valley. Undivided Kamrup district was the largest district with prosperous settled population having high density but free from the insurgent activities. However, the borders of Kamrup touched the frontiers of Bhutan, and independent state. Thus, the Deputy Commissioner, Kamrup was also the Frontier Officer to deal with the Bhutias and the transborder tribes like Garos etc living there in. Moreover, the Assam secretariat considered the advices of McCabe very valuable so, it shifted him to Gauhati, a town very near Shillong, the capital of Assam.

Peasant Revolt in Assam

The Assam Government by a notification in 1892 made a new settlement of revenue in the Brahmaputra valley. The existing rates were increased considerably leading to widespread dissatisfaction among the rural people. The Chief Commissioner paid a visit to the Brahmaputra valley where the rural masses complained to him about the increased rate of land revenue. The towns of Assam like Jorhat and Gauhati were also agog with protests and they criticized the revenue policy of the government. The Chief Commissioner had to reduce the rates. But the reduction failed to satisfy the people and they decided to a no-rent campaign. The local panchayats turned into melas (assemblies). Under the instruction from the secretariat McCabe visited Rangiya, (6 January 1894) a trouble centre and in his camp he met the delegations of the people. He studied their problems and submitted a detail report about the no tax campaign in the Kamrup district.

It is a pleasant surprise to note that the ruthless administrator who was expert in terror tactics to make friends out of foes advised the government to take redressal measures for the pacification of the aggrieved peasantry. He also pointed out the defects of the land revenue settlement in Assam. He narrated the distress of the Assamese ryots exploited by the Marwari traders. However, McCabe outwardly demonstrated his girth as the British officer to the defiant subjects. He arrested several people and when the two thousand strong lathi wielding crowd assembled before the Rangiya police station for the release of the prisoners, McCabe ordered the police to fire. There was, however, no casualty. But the peasant revolt was a success as government failed to collect land revenue from several *tehsils* and *maujas* of Kamrup. Notwithstanding the routine government notices warning the defaulters that their property would be attached and they would be excommunicated, McCabe advised the administration to refrain from taking the extreme measures. In the Sarukhetri *mauja* on 25 January 1894 McCabe faced an angry six hundred strong petititoners who turned violent but they were dispersed by force.

One notable feature of the Krishak Vidroha (Peasant rebellion) of the Kamrup phase is that it did not take bloody turn because of McCabe's skillful handling of the situation and administrative farsight. Unlike his ruthless dealing with the Nagas and Mizos in Naga and Lushai Hills shrewd McCabe applied his policy of persuation to win the people. He was aware that he had been dealing with peace loving exploited Assamese as opposed to the scheming wild tribes prone to violence. Resorting to strong arm tactics was not his nature but the outcome of his policy to meet the exigencies of administrative need. The lack of experience on the part of the District Magistrate, Darang led to the gory end of the agitation a't Patharughat, near Mangaldoi where several people were killed by the police on 24 January. Despite provocation McCabe maintained the political equilibrium.

Assessment of McCabe

McCabe occupies unique place in the history of Nagaland. His role in consolidating the British rule in the Naga Hills is as brilliant as that Captain J. Butler and Grange, the pioneers of Cachar Levy, Captain J.Johnstone and W.M. Kennedy who had to work hard under the backdrop of a hazy policy decision of political control of Ao Naga country to work out a solution to the vexed problem of Naga incursions into the settled districts of Assam. Ironwilled McCabe had little edge over the other officers so far driving home the message to the Nagas that he meant business and for that he was prepared to go any length. Naturally some of his steps smack of horrifying atrocities.

He was appointed the Deputy Commissioner of Naga Hills soon after the inclusion of Ao country into the direct administration of the British Government but the storm of the insurgency did not settle down yet. Murder of the officers were not infrequent (Kennedy, the DC was subsequently murdered) and the freedom loving wild Nagas did not welcome the British rule as such and resorted to every conceivable means to harass the administration. So, MsCabe had not choice but to the firm the his dealings with the delinquents. The stern measures of McCabe had its spin off effects and the terrified tribal chiefs who earlier frequently backtracked taking the advantage of the liberal nature of the officers yielded to military pressure and the peace was restored to the satisfaction of the authorities at Shillong.

The main thrust of McCabe's administration in Mizoram (North Lushai Hills district) was to reap the harvest of the

Chin-Lushai Expedition 1889-90. The uprising of the Eastern Lushais and the Western Lushais were the offshoots of the defects of earlier Lushai policy of the government. The long and short of Major Stewart's policy of Lushai Conciliation had been the surrendering of political interest of the government to further the immediate economic interest of the tea industry in Cachar. That adhoc measure was further extended by John Edgar to prop up the House of Sukpilal taking stock of the situation. However, he was aware that the turbulent sons of Sukpilal would not stand the administration in good stead in future. Necessity compelled Edgar to work out a temporary solution but he could not put a check upon the rapacity of the Western chief Khalkom, who assisted the English in the Lushai Expedition 1871-72, turned a vote face during the Lushai Expedition 1889-90. The fire power of the British forces did short circuit his immediate evil design but he did not bury the hatchet. He and his powerful brother Leinpunga were determined to frustrate the military gains of the Expedition 1889-90 by resorting to under hand methods.

The gory end of Captain Browne the first Political Officer of North Lushai Hills was the result of Khalkom's black deeds according to latter's own admission, thus, under this backdrop of mistrust and violence the successor of Browne had to resort to extreme method of coercion to restore order in the newly acquired North Lushai Hills (Mizoram). The ferocity of McCabe and the lightning speed with which he worked out his action plan often make our blood ceep but in assessing these achievements there is not use of splitting hairs as the most important issues of consolidation of wild and savage area infested with chronic violence was his principal concern. And he was brilliantly successful in his aim. As a successful administrator well-versed in the issues at hand that was his plus point. Without McCabe Mizoram would not have been what it is now. The missionary enterprise could not succeed there to civilize the wild people. Peace is the indispensable preliminary of any socio-cultural development. And McCabe provided Mizoram with that much needed peace. Truth to tell, it was McCabe who laid the foundation of peaceful Mizoram and on that solid foundation Captain J. Shakespear employed his administrative genius to build the new Lushai Hills district. Despite the fuss be the nationalist writers against the lion-hearted sabre rattling Scottish high-lander any historian faithful to his discipline can hardly afford to fight shy himself of the Goliath from England.

R.B. McCabe, however, does not come in comparison with Thomas Herbert Lewin. Lewin is a genius and transcends the limits of comparison with any administrator. His position beyond question is too high. Neither McCabe can be compared with John Edgar the prince among the bureaucrats for the latter's too large encompass of his myriad of activities as diplomat, administrator, economic advisor and Godon's ambassador. Sir John lived in limelight, fat expenses and immeasurable influence at the principle of power. Edgar was as expert in administration of diplomacy as he was quite at home in determining policies of trade and industries. In comparison McCabe's arena was considerably small. But McCabe was an administrator with calibre, of full of vitality, guts and of everlasting hope with a promising future ahead; unfortunately his excellent service career was cut short prematurely by the fate in the middle.

One is tempted to draw parallel between Lieutenant Colonel F.J. Lister and R.B.McCabe. The Officer Commanding Sylhet Light Infantry stood as the symbol of courage and of the sheer will to fight was always at his best under the blazing gun fire with his advancing infantry brigade in the inaccessible mountainous woodland of the North eastern domain of the Indian Empire. His very name evoked a sense of a fear among the mightiest rebels of the Company and a simple message of warning was enough to freeze the blood of the recalcitrant chiefs. The Khasis, the Jaintias, the Nagas and the Mizos all had to surrender before the mighty Titan. Lister although excelled in the operation was equally deft in dodging the files and drafting valuable reports. McCabe, likewise was always at the height of his genius when in the field with the guns and culverins. He, like the legendary dragon, breathed fire in the deadly terrains of Naga Hills and Mizo Hills to strike terror in to the hearts of the proud chiefs. Like Lister's the reports of McCabe are also the most important documents of his time. Lister, however, was a bigger officer enjoying much higher status in the hierarchy of the Company's service being the Agent in Khasi Hills of the Governor General of India having the administrative and military jurisdictions over the whole of southern Assam and a part of eastern Bengal. The wide coverage of area of operations and large varieties of activities of the Agent of Khasi Hills notwithstanding. There had been a striking similarity of the two giants in the approach the prudential use of brute force as administrative convenience with the sole aim of securing the British frontiers. Like expert surgeons resorting to survey for the benefit of the patient those two British officers applied force with the lofty aim of relieving the ills of the revolting communities to ensure peace into that terra incognita for from the pale of the civilization. Both of them were convinced of the prophylactic value of force to the way ward *quam* of the wild tribes under the swaddle of the greedy chiefs who propelled them to the battle field to fight the administration, their only aim being the feathering their own nest. McCabe had no animosity with the Lushai plebeians rather he had sympathy for them and he intended to free them from the overbearing evil influence of the insolent chiefs who in spite of the blowing of their own trumpets had been running out of the time. His magic worked and worked brilliantly as the same Nagas and Mizos who exchanged fire in the hilly raving, the foes of the administration when the dust of the storm settled turned the best friends, the most loyal subjects of the British empire. Herein lies the credit of the administrative efficiency of iron officer McCabe. Undoubtedly, McCabe was one of the tallest administrators of the North Eastern India, However, one is to draw a line some where. Lister's contribution in the history of consolidation is more glorious than McCabe simply because Lister had been the architect of the British policy of the hills in the Northeast. His twenty years of colourful diplomatic service is full with the busy schedule of efforts in crafting that policy. Valiant McCabe followed the footsteps of Lister. If Lister is the master McCabe is the worthy disciple.

That McCabe was an ironwilled, tough administrator was a recognized fact and his assignment in Gauhati was intended to deal an effective blow to the growing peasant rebellion in Lower Assam which generated much heat to worry Shillong but he took away ourbreath when he coolly proposed to the government a second thought into the recently adopted revenue measures in Assam. Not that there had been any mysterious change of heart of the hawk or he lost interest in the efficacy of the use of force in subduing desultory uprising but his clear view had been that the peasant rebellion (*raijmels)* in Assam was somewhat different from the uprisings of the Naga or Mizo chiefs- *the raijmels* being the Assembly of the democratic civilized people having legitimate grievances against an oppressive and unwell legislative measure. The Assamese people had every right to protest democratically against a tax which they considered harmful. Despite the outcry by several intellectuals of giving a false colouring to McCabe's handling the peasant uprising in Kamrup any dispassionate scholar shall give him the clean chit. Even *Hindu Patriot,* the Calcutta newspaper which denounced the increased land revenue measure of the government and expressed sympathies for the peasants refrained from unduly criticizing McCabe's role in quelling the rebellion.

The present rebellion in Assam assumed ugly turn in Darang district because of the Deputy Commissioner's lukewarm attitude and inept handling of the delicate situation but McCabe was ever vigilant to the development in Kamrup and tackled it satisfactorily to the best of his ability. The most turbulent spot was the Rangia thana. He took all the necessary precautions on the receipt of intelligence that trouble might ensue at Rangia. McCabe personally reached Rangia on horse-back on 6 January, 1894. The watchful eye of the DC did not miss to notice the pervading gloom in the countryside during the Assam's most colourful festive season, *Bhogali Bihu.* The *raijmel,* its stormy session did not budge an inch from their demand of withdrawal of increased levy. The police had to round up fifteen leaders. But McCabe did not give up his policy of persuation and desisted himself from riding to hounds. On 10 January 1894 the DC to remove the distrust met the representatives of the people in his camp responded with alacrity to the crowd's incisive queries on spheres as varied as production of foodgrains, its infrastructure and the share of the government investment in providing security, on the peasant's peaceful avocations, and the benefit derived from Pax Britannica, however, McCabe was convinced of the need of reducing the rate of the levy of the poor peasants who had been living on the edge and assured the multitude of raising the issue to the higher authority but as an officer on the spot he did need stand on ceremony and pointed out that he was not within his jurisdictions to waive the levy. McCabe even did not lose his cool being provoked when the mob demanded immediate release of the arrested colleagues. The *thana* officer got the hint from his DC and acted in utmost constraint. A huge mob attacked the *thana* and the *thana* officer resorted to firing but there was no casualty. Because of the omnipresence policy of McCabe's persuasion unlike Patharughat, Darang, the ugly situation at Rangia was not allowed to drift. This judicious administrative manipulation of McCabe throws another spanner into the never ending raijmel debate between the nationalist approach and selfish approach of the rich landlords, i.e. the intentionalist and functionalist. But an impartial historian sees a straight line between McCabe's observations as to the defeat in the tax system and his soft pedaling the law enforcing machinery. It takes away our breath when we see that it was the same McCabe, who in Naga Hills and Mizo Hills was an object of consternation to the foes of administration, had been playing the role of a peaceful mediator. But why? After all, McCabe was the Collector (of revenue) of the Kamrup district. Kamrup was a settled and regulated district in Assam and its administration depended mainly on land revenue. If there was any defect in the revenue policy it was his duty to point it out to the government and at the same time he could not wish away the interest of the cultivators who were in the ultimate analysis the source of revenue. Thus, the *ryots were ceteris paribus* the bulwark of the administration. The enormous bloating of revenue because of the fledgling tea industry in Assam in the nineties of the late century not withstanding land revenue still occupied a preeminent position in the economy of Assam and the wise DC, thus, was unwilling to take any harsh measure against the peasants and did his best to ensure that the situation did not take any turn for the worse. His report discussed briefly the relevant factors responsible for the cause of widespread resentment.[13] McCabe was not a trigger happy hawk but a wise administrator endowed with swift surprise or splendid unselfishness spending his fund of wisdom with grand yet judicious prodigality at the height of *haute administrator*. McCabe's upright report had its long-term effects upon the government which had to admit its faults. Whether peasant rebellion in Assam was actually a peasant revolt having the subaltern class character is entirely a different matter so far the role of McCabe is concerned. The role of middle class in the rising has been stoutly defended by the local historian Ramesh Kalita and disapproved by Manorama Sharma but both of them resorted to McCabes' report as the base material to substantiate their own inferences. It is, thus, useless, in analyzing the role of McCabe, in burning the candle at both ends. Only it can be safely vouchsafed that unbiased report of McCabe in this connexion, is , by all accounts an authentic one and scholars of all colours put reliance on it. This is certainly not a sad commentary on the role of an efficient administrator who believed that only road to excellence was that of the well-being of the ryots. McCabe went down to the shades before the completion of his task; his demise was as sudden as being short.

In the Assam Secretariat at Shillong busy McCabe had always worked hard to prove that he was equally adept in draft-dodging as he was effective in the inaccessible hills and woodlands with his carbines. Secretariat's hurried, haggered and busy middle aged officer McCabe was a new revolutionary role-model beaming with laughter and scowling as well. Indeed, he was unlike a wise own, really a good bank often sharing the cheers of the colleagues and the subordinates. He often made clean breast to his disastrous miscalculations, the squandered opportunities, the wrong turns that made life so picturesque and hairy. He lifts a mirror to the face of Assam's regional patriots, intellectuals and the reflection it carries its one of as sublime picture that is rollicking and logical to the boot.

Death of McCabe

Other that the newspaper reports, the government reports prepared by McCabe are the most authentic records on the topic of peasant rebellion in Assam. This is specially significant when the coming generations having evincing keen interest on the past. Historian's duty is to make an unbiased assessment of McCabe on the basis of the actual facts and the impressive results of his policy. The socialist intellectuals often find fault with the versatile administrator. The Naga and Mizo intelligentsia condemn McCabe for his repressive measures. But history is yet to pronounce its judgement on the iron willed Scottish highlander who did never wilt under pressure or subterfuge. The bureaucrats come and go. They may go with a whimper but arrive they do with a flourish. McCabe was, however, an exception. He flourished at his arrival and in his exist as well. McCabe was an workaholic, he met his end in a house collapse in an earthquake at Shillong (12 June 1897). Was it a nemesis? The severe quake rocked the whole of Assam and British Burma entailing worst disaster but the death of McCabe in such a critical time made Assam Secretariat dumb-founded.

NOTES AND REFERENCES

1. L.W. Shakespear, *History of the Assam Rifles,* p. 161, First Edition 1929.
2. *Ibid,* pp. 161-162.
3. *Ibid,* pp. 166-67.
3a. Animesh Ray, *Mizoram* p. 42, NBT, 1993.
3b. I.F. Extl. A October 1890 No. 142; Chief Secy, Assam to the Secy Foreign Dept. Govt. of India, Dated Shilllong Sept 1891. Also see of *Mizoram Under British Rule,* p. 107.
4. S. Chatterji, *Mizoram Under British Rule,.* p. 107.
5. I.F. Extl. A, January 1891, No. 123, McCabe to Quniton, the Chief Commissioner, Assam.
6. *Ibid.*
7. *Mizoram Under British Rule,* p. 109. Op.cit.
7a. Extl A, January 1891 No. 121-134.
7b. *Ibid.*
8. *Ibid.*
9. *Mizoram Under British Rule,* p. 109-110.
10. *Landmarks of the Freedom Struggle in Assam,* pp. 30-35, Also India, Home, April-Dec. 1894. Assam Riots. Also A. Guha, *Planter Raj to Swaraj,* pp. 32, 33 (Reprint) 1988.
11. *Hindu Partiot,* 5 February 1894.
12. *India Review, Dec. 1888* NAI, Nos. 1-24, Famine Report.
13. India Home, Public 1 (A) No. 2-T 12 January 1894. Assam Riots, McCabe, D C Kamrup to the Commissioner, Assam.

Glossary

Angami	A particular tribe of Nagaland.
Ao	A particular tribe of Nagaland.
Bari	Land suitable for homestead site, so classified for taxation purposes.
Bodo (Bodo-Kachari)	A plains tribe of the Brahmaputra Valley and North Cachar Hills.
Char	A river island or banks seasonally submerged into water.
Chaprasssi	A peon.
Chharra (Cherra)	A Kachari synonym for a small stream.
Chattarchura	The peak named after Chatramanikya of Tripura in the Saraspur ranges on the Sylhet (now Karimganj- Cachar border).
Chaudhury	The highest representative of the Khels in the court of kachari rulers. The highest judicial officer in the Riang hierarchy.
Dao	A dagger.

Daroga	A sub-Inspector of Police.
Doloi	A Superintendent of temple, a headman..
Doong	The Lushai term for a watershed.
Dulien	Language of the Lushai people.
Garo	A tribe mostly living in the garo Hills district, Meghalaya.
Gossain	A spiritual guide in Assam.
Hal	A periodical market in Assam.
Hrangkhawl	A Clan of old Kuki tribes, Tripura.
Jaintia	A Section of the Khasis, living in the Jaintia sub-division of the Khasi and Jaintia Hills district, Meghalaya & Sylhet, Bangladesh.
Jhum	Slopes where hill cultivation is made by slash and burn method.
Jhumia	The inhabitants of the cotton estate *(Kapas Mahals)* in the Chittagong Hills Tracts.
Kachari	A branch of the Bodo tribe.
Karbari	A law officer of the Riangs/A representative of the Lushai chiefs or the Chakma chiefs to the English.
Khas	Revenue collected directly by government.
Khasi (Cosseeyah)	A tribe mainly living in the Khasi and Jaintia Hills, Meghalaya.
Kheda	A special mode of elephant hunting Elephant is captured alive by this method in Assam.
Khel	A union of villages for the revenue collection in old Cachar.

Khel Mukhtar	A revenue collector of Khel in old Cachar.
Kutchary (Cutchary)	The office of the Collector (Deputy Commissioner).
Lal	A Lushai chief; Lushai nobility prefers to add "Lal" to their names.
Lalpitang	A clan of the Howlongs.
Laskar	A village headman of the Kachar of Jayantia tribe.
Lushai	Ruling tribes of the Lushai Hills from 1840-1890. In the Lushai language *Lu* means head and *shei* signifies cut, thus Lushai means head cutter, another philological meaning of the term is long hairs.
Mantri (muntri)	A Lushai ambassador or a minsiter.
Mara	The Lakher tribes, Mizoram.
Mauza	An areal unit of a group of villages, for purpose of land revenue collection.
Maund	A measure of weight equivalent, to a little more than 82.1 lbs.
Mauzadar	A revenue collector on a commission basis, in charge of a Mauza.
Mazumdar	The Law officer dealing with the Kingdom, and also the royal representative in the court, Kachar.
Mazumdar, Bara	The chief law officer dealing with the criminal cases in Kachari Kingdom, (plains).
Mel	An assembly of people in Assam.
Mirasdar	A person owning a superior tenure of land in Cachar.

Mithun	A species of Indian bison.
Mootheelen	The hill ranges in east Mizoram.
Mukhtar	A tax collector in Kachar.
Nazar	A present.
Nazarannah	Tributary gift.
Nazir	The store keeper of the Collectoriat.
Nispwee	The peak in the North Mioram, termed as peak Z by the great Trigonometrical Survey under Captain Fisher.
Pargana	A traditional grouping of villages for revenue purposes, in those parts of Assam, which were once under Mughal rule, and also in British Cachar.
Posa	Personal service or produce payable to the hillmen in Assam.
Pu	Grandfather, now it means mister in Mizoram.
Punjee (poonji)	A village.
Pyke	An Assamese ryot whose duty was to render service to the king at fixed period of the year.
Quom	Community in old social order.
Raij	Public, a local public in Assam.
Raj	The largest unit of revenue collection i.e., union of several khels of the princely Kachari state.
Raja	Chief of the hillmen.
Raj Mukhtar	Kachari raja's revenue collectors.
Rajputra	A Manipuri noble with royal descent.

Ram	Land, Landed jurisdictions of the chief, Mizoram.
Rani	The chieftainess, Manipuri or Mizo or Chakma.
Sardar	A chief.
Sellam hill	The village of the Eastern Lushai chief.
Senapati	The warlord of the Kacharis/ Manipuris.
Syiem	The chief of Khasi tribal state, Meghalaya.
Sokte	A clan of the Kukis.
Sunnad	A proclamation, treaty or a political settlement.
Syloo (Sailo)	A Lushai ruling clan, Mizoram.
Tehsil	Treasury office of the Deputy Commissioner or Superintendent, Assam.
Thana	A Police Station.
Thanglowa	A Lushai clan of the South Lushai hills, and Chittagong Hill Tracts.
Tlang	Lushai synonym for river.
Tong	Lushai synonym for a small river, for example, Tuipui tong, Yambong tong etc.
Vaishnava	Worshippers of Vishnu.
Zadeng	An extinct Lushai clan.
Zamindar	Land lord.
Zowlbook	The Lushai public houses, youth's dormitory.
Zo	The Mizo and other allied tribes.
Zu	Lushai country liquor.

Select Bibliography

(A) PRIMARY SOURCE

I. **Unpublished Documents**

1. National Archives of India, New Delhi: *Foreign Proceedings*, Government of India, 1840-1846. *Land Revenue Records,* Government of India, 1835-1840 (Selected Papers only).
2. State Archives, Government of West Bengal, Calcutta: *Bengal Revenue Proceedings, 1834-1844.*

   Bengal Judicial Proceedings, 1815-1880.
3. Records Office, Assam Secretariat, Shillong:
   (a) Letters issued to the Government of Bengal
   (b) Letters received from the Government of Bengal (Selected Paper Only).

II. **Published**

1. DOCUMENTS AND REPORTS:

Blue Book, Dacca, 1884

Report on Bootan, 1839, Calcutta; also *India Studies, Past and Present,* Calcutta, 1961.

2. ACCOUNTS, MEMOIRS, JOURNALS

Barpujari, H.K.:- 'Facts Behind the Jaintia rebellion, 1862-64', *Journal of India History*, April, 1973.

Buchanan: *Asiatick Researches,* Vol. VI, 1819. Literature, London 1820.

Butler, J.: *A Sketch of Assam,* Calcutta, 1847.

...... *Travels and Adventures in the Province of Assam,* Calcutta, 1855.

Fisher, T: *Memoir of the countries on and near the Eastern Frontier of Sylhet; J.A.S.B.,* Vol.1, 1840.

Intelligence Branch, Army Headquarters, India: *North and North-east Frontier Tribes,* Delhi, 1893 in *Frontier Expeditions.*

M.Cosh, J.N.: *Topography of Assam,* Calcutta, 1837.

..... *Accounts of the Mountain Tribes on the extreme* North-East Frontier of Bengal, *J.A.S.B.* Vol, 1836.

Col. A. "Phayre: History of Arracan", *JAS.* No. 145, 1844.

Robinson, W.: *A Descriptive Account of Assam,* Calcutta, 1841.

.....Notes on the Dophlas and the Peculiarities of their Languages; *J.A.S.B.* XX, 1851.

Thomas Herbert Lewin: *A Fly on the Wheel or How I Helped to Govern India.*

.... *Wild Races.*

Wood, W.H.S.: *Assam Review,* Silchar, 1928-30.

Yule, H.: *Notes on the Khasi Hills and People; J.A.S.B.* VIII, 1844.

Diaries of the Superintendent of the South Lushai Hills District.

The Assam Directory and Tea Areas Hand Book, Calcutta.

The Administration Report, Lushai Hills (North) 1890-98.

The Administration Report, Lushai Hills, (South), 1890-97.

(B) SECONDARY WORKS

Agarwal, A.K.: *North Eastern Economy.*

Aitchinson, C.U. *A Collection of Treaties, Engagements and Sunads,* 14 Vols, 1939.

Alexander McLeish: *The Frontier People of India,* Delhi, 1983.

Allen, B.C. *Assam District Gazetteers,* Shillong, 1905-7, Relevant numbers. *Chittagong District Gazeteers,* Calcutta, 1905.

Banerjee, A.C: *Annexation of Burma,* Calcutta, 1944.

...... *The Eastern Frontier of British India,* Calcutta, 1946.

..... *Indian Constitutional Documents,* Calcutta.

...... *A History of India,* Calcutta, First Edition 1972.

Bareh, Hamlet: *The History and Culture of the Khasi People,* Calcutta, 1967.

...... *Dictionary of North East,* New Delhi.

Barkataki, Satyendranath: *Tribes of Assam,* Delhi, 1959.

Barooah, N.K. *David Scott in North East India,* New Delhi, 1970.

Barua, B.K.: *Cultural History of Assam,* Gauhati, 1970.

Barpujari, H.K.: *Problem of the Hill Tribes of North East India,* Vols I and II, Guwahati, 1974.

...... Separation of Barak Valley, *The Assam Tribune,* Gauhati 11 August, 1986.

...... *Assam in the Days of Company,* New Delhi, 1963.

Baruah, S.L.: *Status of Women in Assam,* Delhi.

Bhattacharjee, J.B.: *Cachar Under British Rule,* New Delhi, 1974.

Bhuyan, S.K.: *Anglo Assamese Relations,* 2nd Edition, Guwahati, 1974.

...... *Kachari Buranji,* Gauhati, 1961.

...... Stray Notes on David Scott, *The Assam Review,* Silchar, May, 1928.

...... *Studies in the History of Assam,* Delhi.

...... *Ahom Buranji,* Gauhati, 2nd Edition.

Bhaveja, J.D.: *The Land Where the Bamboo Flowers.*

Butler, Major: *Travels and Adventures in Assam.*

Carey and Tuck: *Chin Hills District Gazeteers,* Vol.2, Rangoon 1896.

Cambridge History of India, Vol. V-VI.

Chakravorty, B.C.: *Problem of the Hills Tribes of Assam,* Calcutta, 1962.

Chatterjee, Suhas: *Mioram Under British Rule,* New Delhi, 1985.

...... *Mizoram Encyclopaedia,* Bombay, 1990.

...... *Mizo Chiefs and the Chiefdom,* Delhi, 1994.

...... *A History of Mizo Economy,* Jaipur, 2000.

...... *A Socio-Economic History of South Assam,* Jaipur, 2000.

...... *Indian Civilization nd Culture,* Delhi, 1994.

Choudhary, A.C.: *Sreehatter Itribritta,* 1922.

Choudhary, D.K.: *Political Agents and the Native Raj,* New Delhi.

Choudhary, P.C.: *History of Civilization of the People of Assam,* Cal. 1959.

Cox, Hiram, Captain: *The Burmhan Empire.*

Das, B.: *Socio-Economic Development in Assam,* 1997.

Das, F.A. & I. Barua: *Communities of North-East India,* 1996.

Das, H.P.: *Geography of Assam,* 1970.

Dasgupta, P.: A *Common Perspective for North-east,* Calcutta, 1967.

Datta, K.N.: *A Handbook of Records of the Assam Secretariat,* Shillong, 1972.

Davis, A.W.: *Census of Assam,* 1891.

Debi, L.: *Ahom-Tribal Relations,* Gauhati, 1968.

Dutta, D.: *Cachar District Records,* Silchar, 1969.

...... *Silchar Paurasabhar Ithias,* Silchar, 1982.

...... *Haidamba* (Edited), 1961, 1962.

...... *Silchar Government School, Centenary Souvenir,* 1964, Silchar.

Elwin, V.: *India's North-East Frontier in the Nineteenth century,* Bombay, 1958.

...... *Nagaland,* Shillong, 1961.

...... *The Nagas in the Nineteenth Century,* Bombay, 1969.

Gait, E.A.: *A History of Assam,* Calcutta, 1925.

...... The *Census of Assam,* 1891.

Goswami, P.C.: *Economic Development in Assam,* Bombay, 1963.

Griffiths, P.: *History of Tea Industry in India,* London, 1967.

Guha, Amalendu: *Planter Raj to Swaraj,* New Delhi, 1988.

Hall, D.G.E.: *Dalhousie-Phayre Correspondence,* London 1932.

Hodgson, T.C.: *The Naga Tribes of Manipur.*

Hunter, W.W.: *A Statistical Account of Assam,* vols. I and II, London, 1879.

...... *Account of Rural Bengal,* London, 1872.

...... *History of Indian Empire.*

Hutchinson, R.H.S.: *Chittagong Hill Tracts,* London, 1909.

Hutton, J.H.: *The Angami Nagas,* London, 1921.

...... *Report on Naga Hills,* Delhi, 1986.

..... *The Sema Nagas,* London, 1921.

Johnstone, J. Sir: *My Experience in the Naga Hills and Manipur.*

Kalita, R.C.: *Assam in the Eighteenth Century,* Delhi, 1998.

Kabui, G.: *History of Manipur,* Delhi, 1982.

Lahiri, R.M. *Annexation of Assam,* Calcutta, 1954.

Lekhi, R.K. *Economy of India (North-east),* Delhi, 1996.

Longer, V.: *A History of Indian Army,* Bombay, 1974.

Malviya, H.D.: *Land Reforms in India,* 1954.

McCall, A.G.: *Lushai Chrysallis,* London, 1949.

Mackenzie, A.: *A History of the Relations of the Government with the Hill Tribes of North East of Bengal,* Calcutta, 1884.

MacMahon, General A.R.: *Far Cathay and Farther India.*

Maitra, K.: *Darling of the North east,* Delhi, 1999.

M. Cosh, JF: *Report on the North-East Frontier of India,* 1883, Calcutta.

Mali, D.D.: *Revenue Administration in Assam,* 1998.

Mann, R.S. & K. : *Tribal Cultures and Changes,* Delhi

Mann, E.G.: *Sonthalia and the Sonthals,* Delhi, 1989.

Military Despatches of the Lushai Expeditionary Force 1871-72.

Military Report on Assam: Compiled in the Division of the Chief of the Staff, Intelligence Branch, Shimla, 1908.

Mills, J.P.: *The Ao Nagas,* London, 1926.

Milton S. Sangma: *A History of American Baptist Mission in the North East,* Delhi, 1985.

Nanvati and Anjaria: *Indian Rural Problems.*

Naorem Sanajaoba: *Treaties and Documents:* Manipur, New Delhi.

...... *Manipur: Past and Present,* Vol. 3, Delhi, 1998.

Neufville, J.B.: Geography and Population of Assam, *Asiatic Researches,* Vol. XVI, 1828.

Ney Elias: *History of the Shans,* London, 1913.

Parry, NE.: *The Lakhers,* London,, 1932

...... *Lushai Customs and Ceremonies.*

Pemberton: *Report on the Eastern Frontier of British India,* 1835.

Phyre, *Arthur: Report on the Administration of the Province of Assam, for 1874-75 and 1875-76 and for 1882-83,* Shillong 1877, 1884.

Philppart, John: *East India Military Calendar,* Vols. I and II.

Playne, Somerset: *Bengal, Assam, Bihar and Orissa,* London, 1917.

Pudaite, Rocunga: *The Education of the Hmar People,* Sielmet, U.S.A., 1963.

Ramgopal: *British Rule in India,* 1964.

Rao, Ventaka: *A Century of Tribal Politics in North East India,* Calcutta, 1976.

Reid, Robert: *Years of Changes in Bengal and Assam,* 1867.

Reid, A.S.: *Chin-Lushai Land,* Calcutta, 1893.

Roberts, Lord: *Forty one years in India,* London.

Robinson, W.: *A Descriptive Account of Assam,* Calcutta, 1941.

Roy, Animesh: *Mizoram: Dynamics of Change,* Calcutta, 1982.

Roy, J.: *History of Manipur,* Calcutta, 1988.

Roy Choudhary, N.R.: *Tripura Through the Ages,* Delhi, 1983.

Ryle, J. Horton: Ralph Fitch, *England's Pioneer to India and Burma,* London, 1899.

Saha, S.B. (ed.): *Tribes of North East India,* Agartalla, 1987.

Sangermano, Father: *The Burmese Empire,* London.

Sen, Sipra: *Tribes of Nagaland,* Delhi, 1992.

...... *Tribes and Castes of Manipur,* Delhi, 1992.

...... *Tribes of Meghalaya,* Delhi, 1992.

Shakespear, John: *The Lushai Kuki Clan,* London, 1921.

Shakespear, L.W.: *History of Upper Assam, Upper Burma and North-Eastern Frontier,* London, 1914.

...... *A History of the Assam Rifles,* London, 1929.

Sharma, T.R.: *Location of Industries in India.*

Shastri, N.S.R.: *A Statistical Study of India's Economic Development.*

Shaw, William: *Notes on the Thadau Kukis,* Shillong, 1929.

Singh, V.B.: *Economic History of India,* Delhi, 1965.

Singh, Jhaljit R.K.: *A Short History of Manipur,* Imphal, 1962.

...... Manipur, Imphal, 1999.

Sinha, Kamleshwar: *Meghalaya, Triumph of the Tribal Genius,* New Delhi, 1970.

Smith, W.C.,: *Ao-Naga tribes of Assam,* London, 1925.

Soni, H.R.: *Indian Industry and its Problems,* Bombay, 1933.

Soppit, C.A.: *A Short History of the Kuki Lushai Tribes on the North East Frontier Districts.*

...... *A Short Account of the Kachcha Naga Tribes.*

Su, Bhat: *The Challenge of the North East,* 1972.

Thomas, M.M.: *Tribal Awakening,* Bangalore, 1965.

Travernier, Jean Baptists: *Travels in India,* London, 1889.

Tripura District Gazetteer, Agartala, 1975.

Verma, M.M.: Tribal Development in India, Delhi, 1997.

Vumson: *Zo History,* Aizwal, 1984.

Wallace, D.R.; *Romance of Jute.*

Walter, Hamilton: *East Indian Gazetteer,* London, 1815.

Ward, William Erskine: *Notes on the Assam Land Revenue System,* Shillong, 1897.

William, Digby: *Prosperous British India.*

Wilson, C.R.: *Old Fort William in Bengal,* 2 Vols, London, 1906.

Woodthrope, Major R.G.: *Lushai Expedition,* 1871-72 London, 1873.

Zairema, Rev: *God's Miracle in Mizoram,* Shillong 1978.

Zotinhkhma, Kolny: *A Brief survey of the Mizos in Tripura. All Mizo Post Graduate Students Union Magazine,* Shillong, 1981.

(C) ASSAMESE

Bhattacharjya, B.K.: *Dersha Bacharar Asamia Samskritir Ebhumuki,* Gauhati, 1985.

Bhuyan, S.K. *Anandaram Barua: Jivan Charit,* Gauhati, 1955.

Gagoi, Lokeswar: *Dimacha Samskritir Ruprekha,* Vol.1 and 2, Nagaon, 1985.

Goswami, J: *Jagannath Barua,* Jorhat, 1976.

Goswami, Pratap Chandra: *Jivansmriti aru Kamrupi Samaj,* Gauhati, 1971.

Goswami, Prafulaldatta: *Manik Chandra Barua Aru Tenor Yug,* Gauhati, 1970.

Hazarika, A.C.: *Kamrup Ratnamala,* Gauhati, 1973.

Sharma, Benudhar: *Maniram Dewan,* Gauhati, 1950.

......*Gangagovinda Phkan,* Gauhati.

Talukdar, N: *Kanaklal Barua,* Gauhati, 1970.

JOURNALS & MAGAZINES

Milan, Gauhati. Selected Issues.

Sapthaik Nilachal, Gauhati. Selected Issues.

Smriti Grantha, Sadau Assam Tribal Sangha, Special Issue, Jagi Road, 1984.

(D) BENGALI

Banerjee, Suprasanna: *Tripurar Ithias,* Calcutta, 1985.

Basu, Nagendranath: *Banger Ithihas,* Calcutta.

Choudhary, A.C.: *Srihatter Itibritta,* 1918.

Dhekial Phukan, HOliram: *Assam Buranji,* Calcutta, 1829.

Goswami, Dwijendra Narayan: *Tripuraraj Dhanya Manikya,* Calcutta, 1992.

Guha, U.C.: *Kacharer Itibritta,* 1922.

Nirupama Hagzer: *Dimacha Bhasa O siksha,* Shillong, 1972.

Sen, Dr. S.N.: *Prachin Bangla Patra Sankalan,* C.U. 1942.

Sharadia Barak, Silchar, October, 1999 and October, 2000.

Sharadia Haidamba, 1961, 1962, 1963, Silchar.

Singha, Chaitanya: *Manipurer Ithihas,* Sylhet, 1902.

Sinha K.C.: *Rajmala Wa Tripurar Ithihas,* Agartala, 1997 centeneary Edn.

Thakur, M.C.: *Deshiya Rajya,* Agartala, 1922.

NEWSPAPERS AND JOURNALS

Danik Jugasankha, Silchear, selected Issues only.

Dainik Sonar Cachar, Silchar, Selected Issues only.

Samaik Prasanga, Silchar, Selected Issues only.

(E) SANSKRIT

Kalika Purana, Calcutta, 1384 Bengali Era.

Index